RESISTANCE
— AND —
SURVIVAL

THE JEWISH COMMUNITY IN KAUNAS
1941-1944

Sara Ginaite-Rubinson, 1944

RESISTANCE
— AND —
SURVIVAL

THE JEWISH COMMUNITY IN KAUNAS
1941-1944

Sara Ginaite-Rubinson

mosaic press

Library and Archives Canada Cataloguing in Publication

Ginaite-Rubinson, Sara, 1924-
Resistance and survival : the Jewish community in
Kaunus, 1941-1944 / Sara Ginaite-Rubinson ; translated
by Karla Gruodyte and Darius Ross.

Translated from the Lithuanian.
Includes bibliographical references.
ISBN 978-0-88962-816-8

1. Ginaite-Rubinsone, Sara, 1924- 2. Holocaust, Jewish
(1939-1945)--Lithuania--Kaunas--Personal narratives. 3. World War,
1939-1945--Jewish resistance--Lithuania--Kaunas. 4. Jewish ghettos--
Lithuania--Kaunas. I. Gruodyte, Karla II. Ross, Darius III. Title.

DS135.L53G5613 2005   940.53'18'092   C2005-902782-7

Pubished by Mosaic Press, Oakville, Ontario, Canada, 2011. Distributed in Canada by
Mosaic Press. Distributed in the United States by Midpoint Trade Books. Distributed in the
U.K. by Gazelle Book Services.

Copyright© Sara Ginaite-Rubinson, 2005
second printing, 2011
Designed by Josh Goskey
Printed and Bound in Canada
ISBN 978-0-88962-816-8
www.mosaic-press.com

We acknowledge the financial support of the Government of Canada through the
Canada Book Fund (CBF) for this project / Nous reconnaissons l'aide financière du
gouvernement du Canada par l'entremise du Fonds du livre du Canada (FLC) pour ce
projet.

Canadian   Patrimoine
Heritage   canadien

Canada

And with the support of the Ontario Media Development Corporation.

Mosaic Press in Canada:
1252 Speers Road, Units 1 & 2
Oakville, Ontario
L6L 5N9
Phone/Fax: 905-825-2130
info@mosaic-press.com

Mosaic Press in U.S.A.:
c/o Livingston, 40 Sonwil Dr
Cheektowaga, NY
14225
Phone/Fax: 905-825-2130
info@mosaic-press.com

www.mosaic-press.com

*This book is dedicated to the memory
of my perished parents, my family
and the Jewish victims of Kaunas*

ACKNOWLEDGEMENTS

I express my thanks to my dear daughters, Tania and Ania, and my sister, Alice, who encouraged the English translation of the Lithuanian edition of this book. I am grateful to them for the assistance they provided throughout the process of completing the English version.

I am thankful to Myrna Riback and Philip Loosemore for their useful advice in editing the manuscript.

My appreciations go to all my friends and colleagues in Canada, Israel, and Lithuania who directly and indirectly helped shape the final appearance of the work. A note of thanks to the Memorial Foundation For Jewish Culture for the grant which helped in the translation of this book.

Sara Ginaite-Rubinson,
Torotno, 2005

This is the first volume in
The Esther and Maurice Boyman Series of Holocaust Memoirs
Co published by
The Holocaust Centre of Toronto, UJA Federation

&
Mosaic Press, Publishers

SARA GINAITĖ-
RUBINSONIENĖ
ATMINIMO
KNYGA

Facsimile of original Lithuanian edition, 1999.

CONTENTS

PART FIVE: DESTINIES

FOREWORD

Zivia Lubetkin, a heroic leader of the Jewish fighters during the Warsaw Ghetto uprising – and one of the few to survive by escaping through the sewers – wrote in 1946 after illegally reaching Palestine:

"There were times that we believed that the whole world, including the Jewish world, had forgotten us.... We wanted you to know not only for the sake of history, but for the future as well. Let our people know let the survivors know. Remember the past and learn for the future."

It is this sacred imperative that Sara Ginaite-Rubinson fulfills in this meticulously researched and articulately written history and personnel memoir of her resistance and survival in the Kovno Ghetto and the surrounding forests.

Hundreds of histories and film documentaries, memorial books, and thousands of personal Holocaust memoirs have appeared since the floodgates were released by the trial and execution of Adolph Eichman in Israel in 1960. Many hidden areas of the Holocaust have been illuminated in the years since. These illuminations eventually included the fate of the Jews in Lithuania, 90% of whom perished in World War II. Strangely, however, while different aspects of the fate of Vilna's Jews during those years have been told, the story of the Jews of Kovno (Kaunas) did not receive a concomitant attention, especially in the English-speaking world. Moreover the story of the Kovno Ghetto differs markedly from the stories of most other ghettos.

The present volume largely rectifies this omission. Written by one of the surviving fighters and partisans of the Kovno Ghetto, it records step by step the reduction of a vibrant, ancient community of almost 40,000 to its total destruction through starvation, brutal work conditions, and mass murder much of it at the notorious 9th Fort. While this was happening, a courageous Judenrat (Jewish Council), under the leadership of Elchanan Elkes, worked feverishly to maintain some semblance of normal life and to protect and save as many as possible. Unlike in other ghettos, the leadership of the Judenrat maintained good relationships with the Kovno underground led by the redoubtable Chaim Yellin.

Among Yellin's resistance fighters was the author, Sara Ginaite, still only an adolescent, and her husband, Misha Rubinsonas, one of Yellin's young lieu-- ants, whom she married in the ghetto in November, 1943. Sara Ginaite was born in Kovno in 1924 into a comfortable, prosperous family. Her father, a representative of a foreign manufacturer, died in the ghetto while her mother perished in Stuthoff Concentration Camp. Her older sister was liberated in Stuthoff. After the War Sara completed her interrupted education and eventually became a renowned Professor of Political Economy at University of Vilnius, publishing some ten books.

In prose that sometimes reads like an exciting adventure novel, Sara describes the many hazardous missions she and her husband Misha undertook against the Germans inside and outside the ghetto. These included stealing weapons from under the Germans' noses to smuggling resistance fighters and other Jews out of the Ghetto, as well as combat missions attacking German positions or blowing up trains and munitions magazines. More than 300 fighters were smuggled out of Kovno's Ghetto into the Rudninkai Forest.

Without doubt, *Resistance and Survival* is one of the most important contributions to the field of both Holocaust history and the collections of Holocaust memoirs that are our first line of defense against Holocaust deniers. That it is also an invaluable aid to Holocaust education, especially on the tragic fate of Lithuania's Jewry generally and Kovno's in particular, makes it even more important than most memoirs. The Holocaust Centre of Toronto is proud to be the co-publisher of this significant memoir.

Adam Fuerstenberg
Director, The Holocaust Centre of Toronto
Professor Emeritus, Ryerson University

INTRODUCTION

Prior to World War II, with more than 200,000 Jewish residents (including the city of Vilnius and its outlying regions), Lithuania was home to one of the largest Jewish communities in Europe. With the invasion on June 22, 1941, Lithuania became the first country occupied by Germany in its war against the Soviet Union. By June 23-24, there were no Soviet military units left in the former Lithuanian capital of Kaunas or in its surrounding areas. Immediately, the mass murder of the Jewish population began.

Even though the initial impulse for violence came from the Nazis, armed Lithuanian partisans took advantage of the situation to launch a wave of terror against the Jews, which spread across all of Lithuania. In the three years of Nazi occupation (1941-1944), nine out of ten Jews in Lithuania were dead. Behind each number was the loss of a person whose life was tragically and prematurely ended.

The enormity of the Holocaust has been the subject of extensive research for a long time. However, historians have only recently begun to develop a more comprehensive understanding of the process that led to the destruction of the Eastern Europe's Jewish population and culture. A breakthrough in the study of the Holocaust came at the end of the Cold War, when the archives of Eastern Europe became available for investigation. Also very important as a source of that history, however, are the stream of books and testimonies, written by dedicated Holocaust survivors that have been published in recent years. Their eyewitness accounts are helping to uncover new revelations about the war against the Jews and their personal experiences are being woven into the documentary text of that history. By telling the stories of the lives and deaths of the victims, the survivors preserve a living memory of the events of the Holocaust.

The complexity of the history of the Holocaust, the vast geography of the genocide, and the huge scope of the overall human tragedy is of such proportions that a single study can only encompass a very regional, or local, level at best. Having survived the Holocaust, I am telling only my personal story of the evil, of the people of conscience, and of the Jewish resistance movement in the Kaunas Ghetto. In this book, I am describing survival and resistance, but I am also telling of the virtual annihilation of the Jewish population in Lithuania. This book represents my own views on the events recounted here and my own interpretations of the Holocaust in Lithuania.

In writing this book, I have tried to recall the tragic events of the past and to tell the story of the people who did not survive the catastrophe. In so doing, I try to honor their memory. This book is the saga of peoples who did not succumb to Nazi propaganda efforts to dehumanize the image of the Jews. It is the story of people who lived and died, not according to the Nazi plan, but by resisting that plan during their lives and in their deaths. In this book, I recount the lives of those who were murdered, who fell in battle, and who died soon after their liberation. I attempt both to offer a personal view of the historical events and to relate the story of the life of my family. In telling both, words often fail to convey what we felt: our physical and emotional pain. My words can only reveal the lives and fates of the members of my own family and how they reflect the lives and fates of all the Jews of Kaunas.

The events described in the following pages offer no happy endings, no ultimate illumination, even when I speak of courage, of heroism, and of decency. The Holocaust is pure evil as it was perpetrated by the Nazis and their collaborators, by local organizations, and by the governments of the occupied countries.

I discuss in great detail the events of the first months of the Nazi occupation when almost 75 percent of all Lithuanian Jews were killed and all Jewish communities in the Stetlach were destroyed. The Holocaust, defined as systematic mass murder and total destruction of the Jewish people by Nazi Germany and their collaborators, began on Lithuanian soil. This book points to the active role played, and compliance, of the Lithuanian Provisional Government and its administration of the systematic mass murder of the Jews. It also addresses the decisive role played by the Lithuanian military battalions and police in the process of killing their neighbors. In this respect, Lithuania played a unique role in the history of the Holocaust.

My parents were born and lived in Lithuania. I was born and grew up in Kaunas. From my earliest days, I realized that I belonged to the ethnic Jewish minority. But I could never have imagined that our family, and almost the entire Jewish population, would some day be murdered.

My story offers a glimpse into the daily life of the Jewish people in Lithuania before the German occupation. It gives detailed insights into the life of our family, and the lives of other Jews in the Kaunas Ghetto, that no archive can offer. It recounts the birth of the ghetto underground movement, the Anti-Fascist Fighters Organization, and details its aims, military activity, training, weapons acquisition, and acts of sabotage. In discussing our experiences in that movement, I talk of the efforts the AFO made in finding places to hide children outside the ghetto, in establishing an underground school, and finally, in sending ghetto youth into the forest to join the partisans. I recount the daily life and activities of the guerrilla detachment, Death to the Occupiers, to which we, the escapees form the Kaunas Ghetto, belonged. I describe the living conditions, which were rough and primitive, and a life that, although it was full of dangers, offered a taste of freedom that was sweet. It provided an opportunity to fight armed battles against the enemy that gave meaning to our existence.

Finally, I tell the reader about the last days of the Kaunas Ghetto and the fate of my family there. It was in those last days that the rich cultural, spiritual, and religious traditions of the Lithuanian Jews, the *Litvaks,* who had thrived for many centuries on Lithuanian soil, were destroyed or, at the very least, were damaged beyond repair. All that remains today are a few monuments, mass graves, and a very small Jewish community.

The first edition of this book was published in Lithuania in the Lithuanian language. The new English version has been revised and the events described have been carefully re-examined. Every detail of this book came either from research, from testimony of witnesses, or from my own first-hand experience. I have incorporated in it some new and lesser known facts about life of the Jews of Kaunas, the history of their destruction, and their resistance and struggle for survival during the Holocaust. My purpose in writing this book was not simply to offer the reader a source of information, but to share the story of my life with those who were not there. I hope it can give the reader an opportunity to come a little closer to events and lives that are beyond his or her immediate experience.

This book does not pretend to be the definitive history of the Holocaust and the resistance movement in the Kaunas Ghetto. I only hope that this memoir will help to complete the larger text documenting the history of greatest terror in twentieth century Lithuania.

HISTORICAL PROLOGUE

Jewish culture in Lithuania, the *Litvaks*, with its unique character and strong educational and scholarly traditions, had a significant impact upon the cultural lives of many other nations. The notion of 'Litvak' originated in a territory called Litvakija, which originally included Lithuania, Belarus, a part of Poland, and a part of Russia. Jews who lived in these areas regarded themselves as Litvaks and it was they who created the classical Yiddish dialect. First under Lithuanian control, Litvakija then fell under the Russian regime sometime in the 18th century. However, its center was always the city of Vilnius (Vilno), called the Jerusalem of Lithuania.

Vilnius was the cultural center for all Eastern European Jewry. Even when this unified region ceased to exist, the Jews in Vilnius and in Lithuania kept their educational, social, and spiritual traditions. As Professor Vytautas Landsbergis, the first chairman of the Supreme Council of the post-Soviet independent Lithuania put it,

> "The Jewish culture (The Litvaks) was specifically regional and closely related historically to the ancient Grand Duchy of Lithuania. The culture of the Litvaks, particularly the Lithuanian Jews, was an integral part of historical Lithuanian culture. Its loss is our loss. Those responsible for this loss committed a crime not only against the Jews, but against Lithuania itself."[1]

Jews and Lithuanians had been living side by side from the time of the Grand Duchy of Lithuania. The first Jews arrived at the beginning of the 14th century when a policy of increased immigration was seen as a good way to improve the expansion of the Duchy's trade and commerce. Towards the end of the 14th century (1388), Grand Duke Vytautas granted a broad range of privileges to the Jews. He officially endorsed the existence of the country's Jewish Communities and adopted a charter granting the Jews individual and religious protection, as well as offering them various economic opportunities.

Although the Jews quickly became familiar with the customs and lifestyles of the indigenous population, the overall process of assimilation was very slow. The vast majority of Jews spoke only Yiddish and, along with their own houses of prayer, they established Jewish publishing houses, schools, cultural, education, and social organizations.

Over the centuries, Lithuania became one of the most important centers for Jewish secular and religious learning in Eastern Europe, nurturing great thinkers like the great *Gaon* (Eminence*)*, Elijah Ben Solomon, who lived form 1720 to 1797. He was renowned for his deeply insightful interpretations and teachings of both Talmudic and secular Jewish texts.

In the early 19Th century, with the growing influence of Western European Humanism, Lithuanian Jews became increasingly secularized and began to adopt the culture and civilization of Western Europe. Toward the end of the century, many young Jews joined Russian socialist parties and, in Vilnius, a socialist Jewish workers' union, *The Bund*, was formed. Still, traditional religious practices and learning flourished in the major centers of Vilnius and Kaunas, as well as other cities in Lithuania. Many eminent and world-famous Jewish religious and secular writers, artists, scientists, political figures, and educators were born and lived in Lithuania. Among them were such artists as Chaim Soutine, N. Arbit-Blatas, Isaac Levitan, Pavel Antakolsky, Jacques Lipshitz, and Esther Lurie; one of the first modern Hebrew writers and literary critics, Abraham Mapu; Hebrew poets, A. Lebenzon and Liudwig-Lazar Zamenhof, inventor of the Esperanto language; mathematician, Hermann Minkowski; and many others.

The modern Lithuanian Republic re-established its independence with Vilnius as its capital after WWI (1918). However, in October 1920, Vilnius was captured by Polish legions and remained under Polish rule until October 1939 when the Soviet Union occupied a part of Poland and granted Vilnius back to Lithuania. Between 1920 and 1939, Kaunas became the temporary capital of independent Lithuania and the center of the religious and cultural life of Lithuania's Jewry. In the history of the Lithuanian Jews, the period between 1919 and 1926 is referred to as the "Golden Age". During that period, the

Jews won complete autonomy in regulating their affairs. They elected deputies to the Lithuanian Parliament, had their own ministers in the government of independent Lithuania, and a special minister for Jewish Affairs. However, from 1924, this autonomy started gradually to erode and, in 1927, it was completely abolished.[2] The Jews lost their legal equality, were dismissed from government positions, and were banned from further involvement in state structures. They could no longer work in the courts, the police, the diplomatic corps, nor serve as army officers. In addition to being excluded from political life and from holding government positions, many other restricted rules toward the Jews were adopted. They even lost their right to purchase land.

The greatest source of tension between Lithuanians and Jews became their growing competition in industry, commerce, and the independent professions. The growing role of Lithuanians in trade and commerce, the creation of national enterprises and the establishment of such cooperatives and state companies as *Maistas, Lietuvos cukrus, Pienocentras, Parama, Lietukis*, and others further increased competition with Jewish-run businesses. The Lithuanian Government was often the majority shareholder in Lithuanian-run companies and granted these and other Lithuanian enterprises strong financial support.

The Lithuanian government also greatly limited the number of Jewish students at university and their chances of acquiring post-secondary degrees. As a result, the percentage of Jewish students fell steadily, especially in the faculties of law and medicine. In 1932, there were 1,209 Jewish students at Kaunas University, making up 26.5% of the student population. By 1938, this figure had fallen to 445 or 14.7%[3]. In addition, the anti-Jewish press of the time offered detailed calculations that determined the exact percentage of Jewish doctors, lawyers, university students, factory owners, businessmen, and entrepreneurs living in Lithuania. It is important to bear in mind, however, that the curtailment of Jewish rights was not a single act, but rather a gradual process of discrimination that culminated with the beginning of the Second World War.

Despite discrimination and their treatment as second class citizens, the Jews defended Lithuania's interests, political aims, and international reputation. Serving in national infantry battalions, Lithuania's Jews actively participated in the country's 1918 and 1919 battles for independence. In Kaunas alone, 542 Jews were registered as war veterans, including 182 war invalids and 32 men were decorated for bravery during the armed struggle for Lithuania's independence. From 1918 to 1923, approximately 3000 Jews served in the Lithuanian army, where they bravely fought against the Polish, Russian, and German armies, some of them dying in the battlefield.[4]

Even when they had considerable freedom, it must be stressed that not a single Jewish institution ever made either anti-Lithuanian or pro-Soviet statements. Furthermore, Lithuanian Jewry was not a community of communists. Rather, like all other cultures, it contained, in its overall makeup, individuals of various beliefs. Without any doubt, the Jews were pre-war Lithuania's most loyal ethnic minority and, even during the Polish ultimatum of 1938 and the Klaipeda (Memel) crisis, the Jews supported Lithuania's position.

According to the 1923 Lithuanian census, 153,743 Jews lived in Lithuania (not counting Vilnius), 25,000 of them in Kaunas. By 1932, that number had climbed to 154,321, and the Kaunas Jewish community had grown to over 40,000 people.[5] With 215 Jewish organizations and institutions thriving throughout Lithuania, Kaunas alone had 5 Jewish high schools, a teachers college, the famous Yeshiva Rabbinical Seminary, and several vocational schools (*ORT*). Prior to the 1940 Soviet occupation, the city boasted approximately 30 synagogues, 2 Jewish theatres, 15 Jewish periodicals, 5 daily Jewish newspapers and 3 Jewish libraries: *Jellin's*, the *Mapu*, and the *Balosher*. There was a Jewish hospital, an old age home, an orphanage, daycare centres, and the OZE health association, as well as several sports clubs, and various social welfare and charity organizations.

In Kaunas, as in other Lithuanian cities and towns, although the Jews were free to live in any part of the city , they generally settled in neighborhoods either mostly or exclusively populated by Jews. Many of the religious and less wealthy Jews of Kaunas lived in the suburb in Vilijampole (called *Slabodka* by the Jews). A considerable number of Jews lived in Kaunas' Old Town, where they had their factories, workshops, stores, and other businesses and where most of the Jewish schools, libraries, and cultural centers were located. The wealthiest Jews gradually moved out of the Old Town to the central part of Kaunas.

Lithuania's Jews were not a homogenous ethnic minority from either a social or political perspective. There were blue and white-collar workers, employees at various small companies, small shop owners, and craftsmen. Others were bankers, owners of mid-size and substantial companies, and, therefore, distinctly members of the upper and middle classes. Nor were these Jews undivided in their political views. Most politically active Jews in Lithuania were members of the Zionist movement and as such they belonged to various local political organizations. They participated in international Zionist activities, and sent their children to private Hebrew or orthodox Jewish schools. The Zionist organizations supported the study of Hebrew, trained agricultural specialists, and encouraged Jewish emigration to Palestine. According to Jewish agency figures, of the approximately 20,000 Jews that emigrated from Lithuania between 1919 and 1941, 9241of them immigrated to Palestine.[6]

There were also those in the Jewish community who called themselves Yiddishists. Considering Lithuania to be their homeland, the Yiddishists claimed that Jews should continue to live there, but that they must have complete cultural and religious autonomy as well as equal rights with Lithuanians in all aspects of economic and political life. The Yiddishists felt they had two native languages – Lithuanian and Yiddish. They supported the Yiddish schools, theatre and cultural organizations, and maintained close ties with Yiddishists around the world.

Like other national groups, the Jewish community included communists and members of related organizations. Since the Communist Party was banned in independent Lithuania, communists had formed various legal, but officially non-communist, organizations. These relatively small organizations propagated communist ideas, published articles criticizing the Lithuanian government's internal and foreign policies, and informed their readers about the difficult living conditions of workers and peasants. They also expressed their support for the Soviet Union by providing general assistance to political prisoners and forming cells in factory workers' clubs, high schools, and post-secondary institutions. Of the 1120 Communist Party members living in Lithuania in 1939, 670 were Lithuanians, 346 were Jews, while the rest were made up of Russians, Poles, and Germans.[7] In addition to those, 145 Jews and 142 Lithuanians (or individuals of other nationalities) were serving prison terms for communist activities.[8]

As anti-Semitic sentiments grew in Lithuania in the mid-1930s, there was some rise in anti-Semitic statements in general and the occasional act of vandalism committed against Jewish organizations. Lithuanian historian Professor Saulius Suziedelis holds the view that, although anti-Semitism existed in Lithuania as an internal problem during the inter-war years, independent Lithuania can hardly be considered to have been an anti-Semitic state.

"There is no question," writes Suziedelis, "that, as it did in other parts of Europe, German racist propaganda appealed strongly to certain nationalistic oriented individuals in Lithuania. This can clearly be seen in references made in Lithuanian newspapers to the successful resolution of the 'Jewish question' in the Reich."[9]

On the other hand, Jury Bluvsteinas, a well-known Jewish lawyer and journalist, believes that it is highly inaccurate to say that the Jews enjoyed a happy existence in pre-war Lithuania. Even though their situation was far better than in neighbouring Poland, at the same time, the Jews in Denmark or England had much higher status.[10]

I would have to agree with both of these opinions. Lithuania was not an outspoken anti-Semitic state. Racist ideas were not popular among the Lithuanian political and cultural elite, and the government made no moves to "solve the Jewish problem." In fact, the situation of Jews in Poland and Romania, not to mention Nazi Germany, was considerably worse than in Lithuania. On the other hand, it is safe to say that, in Lithuania, Jews were treated as second class citizens and that they were less integrated than the Jews in Denmark, Finland, and Sweden. It is doubtful whether relations between Lithuanians and Jews might have been less strained had Jews been more familiar with Lithuanian culture, customs, and aspirations or had they been more integrated into Lithuania society during the period of inter-war independence. After all, they had lived side by side for many centuries - but not together.

And yet, despite the increasing tensions between Lithuanians and Jews, ethnic conflicts between them were extremely rare, and vague efforts were made, even at this point, to bring the two peoples together in common dialogue. In order to help Lithuanians better understand the aspirations of the Jewish people the Jews published a Lithuanian-language newspaper called *Apzvalga* (Review). Upon the initiative of Mykolas Birzishka, a Lithuanian pre-war writer and historian, a Lithuanian-Jewish friendship association was founded. A survey of Lithuanian literature was published in Yiddish, while the Lithuanians published collections of Jewish poetry and short stories. But these modest efforts at reconciliation did little to encourage the two nationalities to communicate and interact more successfully, and the tensions continued in Lithuanian-Jewish relations.

Then Hitler invaded Austria, Czechoslovakia, and Klaipeda (Memel), and declared war against Poland. It became increasingly clear that, in the event of a direct confrontation with Nazi Germany or the Soviet Union, the three Baltic countries of Lithuania, Latvia, and Estonia were unlikely to remain neutral. They could be swallowed, at any time, by either power. The majority of Lithuania's Jews felt that, because the Soviet Union was more tolerant towards the Jews and did not pose a direct threat to their existence, it was the lesser of the two evils. In the end, of course, no one asked either the Lithuanians or the Jews what they would prefer and neither had any power to influence the two powerful and aggressive states battling over Eastern Europe.

Occupying Lithuania under the terms of the secret German-Soviet pact, the Red Army marched on Lithuania in June 1940. "Whether you agree or not is irrelevant," Soviet Foreign Minister Vyachislav Molotov told the Lithuanian government, "because the Soviet army is going in tomorrow anyway."[11] In August of that year, Lithuania had become annexed by and integrated into the Soviet Union. During the first months of the Soviet occupation, it appeared to the Jews that the "Golden Age" they had enjoyed until 1927 had been restored. Between July and September 1940, the Soviet leadership in Lithuania abolished the discriminatory laws that had regulated minority rights. All ethnic groups were now equal when applying to institutions of higher learning. Jews were elected to parliament and could be hired to fill positions in state structures.

However, the Jewish influence during the first year of Soviet rule was more superficial than significant. From 1940 to 1941, excluding refugees from other countries, there were approximately 200,000 Jews living in Lithuania (including those in the Vilnius regions) and still, of the 79 deputies elected to parliament, only four were Jews. In 1940, three Jews were appointed to government posts: Minister of Health Care, Leonid Koganas; Minister of Industry, Chaim Alperavichius; and Minister of Food Industry, Elias Bilevichius.

By 1941, five Lithuanian Jews held high positions in the state security apparatus. Non-locals filled the vast majority of posts in that institution, almost 82 %.[12] In the first half of 1940, Lithuania's Communist Party had consisted of only 1690 members and approximately 1000 Communist Youth members. These former underground movements had not had any political influence nor played any significant role in the life of independent Lithuania. With the establishment of the Soviet regime in Lithuania, however, Communist Party membership began to grow rapidly. By the end of 1940, the party had 2486 members, and by the middle of 1941, there were 4625. At that point, while the proportion of Lithuanians and Russians in the party grew, the percentage of Jewish members began to drop. On January 1, 1941, the ethnic make up of the Lithuanian Communist Party consisted of 67% Lithuanians, 16.6% Jews, and 15.5% Russians, Byelorussians, and Ukrainians.[13]

In the summer of 1940, the 13-member bureau of the Lithuanian Communist Party Central Committee was made up of seven Lithuanians, two Latvian-Lithuanians (Fridis Krastinis and Karolis Didziulis-Grosmanis), and four Jews. Following the Fifth Conference of the Lithuanian Communist Party at the beginning of February 1941, the percentage of Jews in the party apparatus had dropped. Of the 47 members of the new Central Committee, 24 were Lithuanians and five were Jews, while the Central Committee bureau consisted of six Lithuanians, four Russians and one Jew.[14]

Policies for Soviet unit groups were based on class, not ethnic principles. Because there was a shortage of such cadres in the Lithuania, many were brought in from other Soviet republics. According to estimates made by Lithuanian historian, Professor Liudas Truska, during the first year of Soviet rule close to 2000 communists were sent to work in Lithuania, approximately 40% of the total membership of the Communist Party of the Lithuanian SSR. By June 1941, as many as 3000 non-local Communist Party personnel were working in Lithuania. [15]

The facts themselves, therefore, confirm the inaccuracy of claims that Jews dominated the state and Communist Party apparatus. Rather, the Central Committee apparatus, state security structures, and other important positions were occupied, not by Jews, but by representatives of other nationalities. Jews did work in Soviet institutions of repression, but so did ethnic Lithuanians, Russians, and Poles. All of them participated in drawing up lists of people slated for arrest and deportation. These lists included individuals of different nationalities and included wealthy and politically prominent Jews. It is clear, therefore, that Jews played only a minor role in the sovietization of Lithuania.

It must also be stressed that during the Soviet period, Lithuanian Jews not only shared their countrymen's fate in the political and social spheres, but also suffered in the repression that the new regime conducted against its citizens. Like other members of the Lithuanian population, they were arrested, deported, and, finally forced to witness the ruthless destruction of their culture. Tragically, some of Lithuania's Jews did not grasp the fact, until it was too late, that the Soviet regime's promise of equality of rights only extended to the equal absence of those rights. Most of the Jewish print media, and educational and cultural institutions, were dissolved under the Soviets. Of the many Jewish newspapers that were being published in 1939, the only ones left by the spring of 1941 were *Der Emes* (The Truth), one youth weekly, *Die Shtralen* (Rays of Light), and one monthly literary magazine. All the others were liquidated and their editors arrested and banished from Lithuania. These included Reuvim Rubinstein, leader of the Lithuanian General Zionist Organization and editor of the long-standing Zionist newspaper, *Yiddishe Shtime* (Jewish Voice); Efraim Grinberg, editor of *Dos Vort* (The Word); and Jacob Goldberg, head of the Union of Jewish Soldiers. He was one of those who had fought for Lithuanian independence in 1918 and 1919.

The functioning of all of the Hebrew high schools and the centres for Jewish religious teaching and the study of the Talmud was severely restricted, including the world famous Telsiai and Slabodka Yeshivas. All of the Jewish Zionist organizations, from the leftist *Bund* to the rightist *Beitar*, were banned. All of the leaders and activist members of these organizations were arrested and deported, and many were shot. Most of the synagogues were closed.

The Jewish Museum of History and Ethnography and the Jewish Scientific Research Institute (YIVO), devoted to the study of current Jewish cultural and national issues, as well as Yiddish language studies, were stripped of their independence At the beginning of 1941, the YIVO was absorbed by the Lithuanian Academy of Science and became the Jewish Cultural Institute, one of the Academy's research institutes. As a form of compensation for the abolition of all the educational and cultural organizations, Jewish cultural workers were allowed to produce a special Jewish radio program.

On September 16, 1940, the Jewish Community Centre in Vilnius was closed down. All of its employees were dismissed and its buildings and inventory were confiscated. The Jewish community lost the Jewish cemetery. The activities of most Jewish cultural, social assistance, and charity organizations were terminated. In effect, the sovietization process had destroyed the culture and way of life of the Lithuanian Jews.

It can be said that, relative to other ethnic groups, the Jews suffered as much as or even more from the ensuing confiscation and nationalization of private property than any other group in Lithuania. Although there were Jews on the commission responsible for the nationalization process, Jewish property owners enjoyed no advantages. They often experienced even greater discrimination, probably because the Jewish commission members were workers eager to gain revenge on their former employers. They confiscated light equipment, any personal belongings they found on the company's grounds, prevented the owners from being present during the confiscation procedures, and evicted them from their former work premises.

Wealthy and active politicians from the period of Lithuania's independence were labeled 'anti-Soviet and nationalistic elements'. They suffered discrimination and sanctions whether they were Lithuanians, Jews, or members of other ethnic minorities. These people had little chance of gaining employment in state companies, were evicted from their homes and apartments, and their children's chances for entering post-secondary institutions were severely limited. Many of them were deported to remote areas of the Soviet Union.

The mass arrests and deportations of Lithuanian citizens began on the night of June 13, 1941. Following an order issued at the end of March 1941 by the People's Commissariat for State Security, the Central Committee of the Lithuanian Communist Party adopted a resolution whose purpose was "the arrest and expulsion of counter-revolutionary and socially dangerous elements from the Lithuanian SSR".[16] In addition, this resolution would apply to so-called "nationalist and counter-revolutionary and socially dangerous elements" such as criminals and prostitutes, as well as former police officials and prison wardens, high-ranking employees of the former state apparatus, and wealthier merchants and property owners. Following Soviet instructions, the list would also include "the immediate families of members of counter-revolutionary organizations who were currently in hiding."[17] In practical terms, Clause 9 of this resolution meant that the families of those 'heads' that had fled the country, were no longer living in Lithuania, or had passed away were also slated for deportation. Additional "instructions for the isolation of anti-Soviet elements in the Jewish sector" stated that such elements were meant to include the leaders and active members of all Zionist organizations, employees and journalists of Zionist newspapers, and others. According to Clause 9 then, if a suspect could not be found, members of his immediate family were to be arrested and deported.

The fate of the Nathan Rachmilevich family is a case in point. Rachmilevich had been a deputy in the Founding Parliament of Lithuania, Deputy Minister of Trade and Industry in 1920, and was later an elected member of the Jewish Affairs Committee. In 1935, he was appointed Lithuania's Consul General in Palestine and never returned to Lithuania. His brother, Solomon Rachmilevich, had studied at the Sorbonne and had become a leading industrialist and member of the board of the Bank of Lithuania. In 1940, he became very ill and died. On the night of July 13, security agents came to Solomon Rachmilevich's apartment hoping to find at least one of the brothers. When they learned that one had been living in Palestine since 1935 and that the other had recently died in Kaunas, the security agents carried out Clause 9 of the resolution and told their families to prepare for deportation. On that night, Rachmilevich's mother, wife, and children were deported to a remote corner of the Soviet Union.

There were many more examples of deportations of individuals of various nationalities that were innocent, even from the standpoint of the Soviet regime. Almost all of the male members of these deported families died in the camps in Siberia. Among them was the father of Herman Perelshtein, founder and long-time conductor of the Azuoliukas Boys and Youth Choir. Lora Freidberg, Herman's wife, was a classmate of mine and a professor at Vilnius University. Her father and grandfather also died in the camps of Siberia.

During 1940 and 1941, both native Lithuanians and people of other nationalities suffered from various forms of Soviet repression carried out by the special state security apparatus officials. These officials, in turn, themselves had no power to stop or otherwise affect the course of events. Of course, no Jews, Russians, or Lithuanians were forced to participate in the process of repression. Regardless of the number of Jews (or Jewish Communists) involved in political, cultural, or economic affairs in 1940 and 1941, there is still insufficient evidence to support claims that Jews either contributed to the loss of Lithuania's independence or organized the arrests and deportations of Lithuanians. Furthermore, the participation of individual Jews in the administration of the Soviet occupying regime can neither explain nor justify the treatment of all Jews during the Nazi occupation of Lithuania. Most specifically, it certainly cannot defend what happened to the Jews from June to August of 1941, the first months of the German occupation.

Part One

Persecution

SHATTERED DREAMS

Lithuania was the birthplace of my parents and of their parents before them. It is also the country in which most of my relatives were murdered during the German occupation between 1941 and 1944. It is not my intention here to wail over the tragedy that befell our family. I would like, instead, to offer a portrait of a family whose members were an integral part of the Lithuanian Jewish community that was destroyed during the Nazi occupation.

My father's family was originally from Jurbarkas, a small port town on the Nemunas River. There, my grandfather, Leiba Ginas, ran the shipping business that his father-in-law had begun. His cargo vessels transported goods along the Nemunas River to and from various parts of the Russian Empire and Germany. Around 1890, Leiba and his wife, Zlata Giniene, moved to Kaunas with their three sons and one daughter. They bought an apartment house on Mapu Street 5 and had two more sons, my father, Juozas, whom everyone in the family called Josif, and his younger brother, Samuel. Although the Ginas family were not particularly religious, they kept all the traditions of the Jewish faith. Every Friday night, they dressed in their finest clothes to welcome the Sabbath, which they observed reverently. They attended synagogue and served only kosher food in their home. As their children grew up and got married, they all lived in flats in my grandparents' house. Two of my father's older brothers immigrated to the United States around 1920, before I was born, and for a while the brothers kept in touch with their relatives in Lithuania. At one point they even sent Samuel a *shipkart* (a ticket) to join them in America. But Samuel, wary of making such a long and mysterious voyage, did not go. Instead, he married Berta and they had two daughters, Zlata and Bronia Ginaite, who both went on to graduate from the Hebrew High School in Kaunas and study at the university in Vilnius.

By the time my father's eldest brother, Chaim Ginas, died, leaving his wife Mina Giniene and their two young children, Joske and

Leibe Ginas, my grandparents had already passed away. Unfortunately, all three died before I was born and so I never knew them. When I was small, my parents, my sister Alice, and I lived in my late grandparents' four-room flat and, for a while, we shared the apartment with our widowed Aunt Mina and her sons. From what I can remember, the apartment was heated by a wood stove and had plumbing, but it wasn't very cozy and was quite cold in winter. Also, while I certainly enjoyed the attention of my older cousins, it was not a comfortable living arrangement for my parents and in the early 1930s, we moved out. By 1939, on the eve of the war, Mina's older son, Joske, was about to get married and the younger one, Leibe, was doing his Lithuanian military service.

My father's sister Chava married a railway worker named Shaya Ginzberg and they had three daughters and a son. Chava died quite young of breast cancer and Shaya never remarried. By the mid-1930s, two of their daughters, Fruma (Fanya) and Ester (Asya) were already married. Fruma married a medical student, Isaac Glikman. When he graduated and finished his residency, the couple and their baby son, Leiba (Liova), moved to the small town of Seredziai where Dr. Glikman was physician to the town and all the surrounding villages. He would travel throughout the countryside in his horse and buggy, tending to the sick, treating the children and elderly, delivering babies, and personally driving serious cases to the hospital. Dr. Glikman worked in Seredziai for more than five years and was highly respected and much loved by his patients. But, he and his family became homesick for their families and the big city, and so returned to Kaunas. By then, Fruma's youngest sister, Basya Ginzberg-Shwartz, had graduated from the Hebrew High School and was studying at the university in Vilnius. Fruma and her family joined her there in 1940. The Ginzbergs' only son Moishe, and his wife Masha, had immigrated to Palestine and their daughter Eva Ginzberg was born in Tel Aviv. In 1939, the family was visiting Lithuania and was forced to remain in Kaunas when the war began.

My mother's family, on the other hand, had always lived in Kaunas and we were very close to them. My grandfather, Gutman Virovichius. He was a very tall, good-looking, and well-read man who liked to listen to music and the news on the radio. As a young man he had worked as a tailor but eventually had opened a delicatessen and wine store. My grandparents lived in an apartment house on Maironio Street which my grandfather had bought before the First World War. They were very religious and the family belonged to a small synagogue on the same street where grandfather went almost every day to pray. He loved his *Shul* where he and his friends would sit, debating Judaism and politics, and chatting about family matters. Every Sabbath, my grandparents would dress in their best clothes and I can still see them as they slowly made their way to the synagogue, holding hands and thoroughly enjoying each other's company.

My grandfather loved to tease his grandchildren. Before going abroad on business trips, he would promise to send us very special presents. We knew very well he was only teasing but when he returned we would always ask for our gifts. "What," he would ask, feigning surprise, "you didn't receive them? I'm sure they're on the way. Be patient." Although we knew the presents would never arrive, we would look up at him in wide-eyed astonishment as though wondering how our precious gifts had gotten lost. Then our dear grandmother would give each of us one or two *litas* and we would run happily off to a movie or to buy ice cream.

During the summers, my grandparents spent their holidays at a resort in Kulautuva on the Nemunas River, where my sister and I often visited them. How exciting the two-hour steamboat trip from Kaunas was for us. Grandfather would meet us at the pier and take us home where grandmother was waiting for us with a delicious dinner. We spent our days picking berries and mushrooms with our grandfather in the ancient pine forest and, in the evenings, he told us stories of God's great wonders and of the history and fate of the Jewish people.

My mother had four brothers and one surviving sister. Most of the Virovichius clan lived in all but two of the flats in the apartment house on Maironio Street. The two remaining apartments were rented to Jewish families. In the basement of the house lived the janitor, Mykolas Kaminskis, and his family. They were the only non-Jews living in the building. My mother's eldest brother, Isaac, his wife Anya, and their two small children lived in a luxurious apartment building at Vytautas Prospect 28, owned by Anya's wealthy relatives, the Hirsh Klis family. My mother's second brother, Salomon Virovichius, his wife Zina, and their daughter Nadya, who was my age, lived in a two-room flat in my grandparents' house. My mother's two younger brothers, Abraham (Abrasha) and Liova Virovichius, both strong Zionists, lived with my grandparents and studied at Kaunas University. Only ten years older than my sister, Liova was everyone's adored uncle. He clearly enjoyed his young nieces' company and entertained us with a constant stream of stories and bought us ice cream and candy. Often, he would take me along when he went to his student fraternity. In 1936, Liova married Basya Heleryte, my favorite high school physical education teacher. All the other girls in school envied me now that our beloved teacher was my aunt. My joy seemed limitless.

In 1935, Abrasha Virovichius immigrated to Palestine and, in early 1936, my grandfather passed away. Liova went regularly to the synagogue to say *Kaddish* (the Jewish prayer for the deceased) for his father and I, wanting to spend more time with him, often went along. But in the late fall of 1936, Liova and Basya also immigrated to Palestine. Officially, Basya traveled as part of the Lithuanian team participating at the Hebrew world sporting tournament, the Maccabi Games, and Liova Virovichius went along as a representative of the delegation. They never returned.

A year or two after Liova left, my grandmother traveled to Palestine to spend some time with her sons and their families. She traveled by train through Germany and Italy, where she boarded a boat sailing to the port of Haifa. My grandmother enjoyed getting to know Palestine and became very fond of Abrasha's young wife, Fanya, whom he had married in Palestine. After spending several months with them, she insisted that the young couple come for a visit to Kaunas so Abrasha could introduce Fanya to his relatives and have a break from the hot Palestinian climate. In the summer of 1939, the young couple arrived in Lithuania, planning to return to Palestine in the fall. The outbreak of war forced them to remain in Lithuania.

Although our family was not orthodox, we upheld all of the main Jewish traditions and celebrated all the holidays at my grandparents' home with the entire Virovichius family. My grandmother, Malka Virovichiene, a small woman who loved to cook and bake, would make all sorts of goodies and let us children play as much as we wanted. During the holidays, my mother, Rebecca, was happy to let my grandmother take over the responsibilities of the household.

The most memorable holiday for me was Passover. I remember the beautifully set table graced by a plate of sweet fruits, honey, bitter herbs, and the somber symbolism of a bone, scraped clean. According to tradition, when my grandfather returned from synagogue, his 'royal seat', padded with cushions, was waiting for him. He would wash his hands, sit down in his special chair, and lean back against the pillows. This marked the beginning of the celebration. He would read the *Haggada*, the Passover stories, and it was my role as the youngest to ask the four questions, each of which began the same way: "What makes this night different from all other nights?" Grandfather would reply that when we were slaves in Egypt, the prophet Moses led us out of slavery into the Promised Land where we became a free people. Every year he would always end by saying that he hoped we would all meet in Jerusalem next year.

Then, the feast's first course of stuffed fish, herring, and chopped liver would be laid out on the snow-white tablecloth. This was followed by broth and various other dishes made from matzo. We drank wine and honey nectar as the candles burned slowly in silver candlesticks. It felt safe and good. After my grandfather's death, our dear grandmother tried to preserve the traditions he had led, but his 'royal chair' remained empty. I continued to ask, "And what makes this night different from all other nights?" and the men seated around the table would answer: "We were slaves, but the prophet Moses led us out of Egypt into God's Promised Land."

Apart form being a religious holiday, Passover is also a celebration of spring and the rebirth of nature. It was usually warm at that time of the year in Kaunas and during the holidays, when almost all of the Jewish-owned businesses were closed, the Jews of Kaunas dressed in their nice clothes and went for leisurely walks. The entire city seemed to be celebrating the liberation of the Jews from Egyptian slavery. As children, and later on as teenagers, we also strolled in large groups along *Laisves Aleja*, the Freedom Avenue, where young people liked to congregate. Often, we would stroll up to *Azuolynas Park* where we spoke of the things that preoccupy all young people. We shared our dreams and disappointments, told each other the details of first love, and confessed our fears of betrayal and hopes for the future.

To this day, Passover celebrations hold a special place in my heart and memory. After the war, I tried to preserve for my own family the traditions I learned and loved at my grandparents' home. But the possibilities for doing so were quite limited under the Soviet regime. Still, I made sure that my children grew up knowing of our people's slavery in Egypt and of their liberation. Instead of bread we ate matzo, stuffed fish, and chopped liver. I am very happy to have lived to see the day when our entire family, small as it is, gathers every year at my youngest daughter Anya Rubinsonaite-Sorkin to celebrate the Passover Seder. My granddaughter, Riva, asks her father, who sits in his 'royal chair': "What makes this night different from all other nights?" And Fima Sorkin answers, "We were slaves. Moses delivered us from Egypt and led us into God's Promised Land. Now we are free. Israel is an independent country and we can meet in Jerusalem whenever we choose."

My parents, Josif Ginas and Rebecca Virovichiute (Giniene), met in Kaunas around 1913, shortly before the First World War, and then my father went to France to study engineering at the University of Grenoble. He returned to Lithuania in 1915 to marry my mother after she graduated from the Polish high school. I had an extremely close relationship with my father and it was to him that I revealed all my secret thoughts and wishes, including my intention to study medicine at Kaunas University. We shared a keen interest in economics and I was fascinated by his business activities. I avidly followed the progress of his negotiations with foreign firms and studied his correspondence with them. Often he confided to me that it was difficult for Jewish firms to obtain government import licenses and sometimes he was forced to cancel contracts.

He took me to the Jewish theater and I was never happier than when he took me to a nearby restaurant, *The Rambynas*, where we always ordered freshly cooked crab. After our meal, we would walk arm in arm down Laisves Aleja. Not yet 50 when the war broke out, he always looked very young and elegant. As we walked along together, he might have been mistaken for my boyfriend. It pleased him that I read the Jewish newspaper and he often talked to me about his youth, his two brothers living in America, and the early deaths of his sister and eldest brother. Every night, without fail, he came to my room to wish me sweet dreams. My older sister was very close to my mother. It had seemed to me that mother loved her better. She pampered Alica, buying her expensive clothes and giving her the most comfortable

7

room in our apartment. Theirs was a strong mutual affection that lasted until my mother's last days in the German concentration camp at Stutthof.

Both of my parents were fluent in Yiddish, French, German, and Russian. While my father also spoke Lithuanian quite well, mother spoke it with a Polish accent, peppering it with Polish and Russian words. Father was the representative of several foreign companies that sold imported raw materials to large factories in Lithuania and he had strong commercial ties to Lithuanian businessmen and textile factory owners. Politically, he belonged to the *Volkspartei*, or People's Party, which was officially registered as the People's Cultural and Educational Association and he subscribed to the newspaper they published, the *Volksblat*. My parents were active supporters of various Jewish cultural institutions and events, like the Jewish theater.

Like most of the other middle class Jewish families living in Lithuanian towns and villages at the time, the Jewish community in Kaunas had an intense and vibrant cultural and social life, and cherished its cultural and educational traditions. There were numerous Jewish organizations, associations, volunteer groups, and unions. We did not socialize much with the Lithuanians and my father's interaction with Lithuanians was limited to practical and business matters

In the mid-1930s, I completed Lithuanian elementary school and studied in a private Catholic high school, *Ateitininkai*, for a year. But I was not comfortable there. I felt like a foreigner among the wealthy Lithuanian students who, along with their parents, were puzzled by the fact that a Jewish girl was enrolled in the Catholic high school. After a rather unsuccessful year there, my parents transferred me to the private, newly established, Kaunas Jewish High School. The school provided a strong foundation in the humanities, Jewish religion and history. Even though every subject was taught in Lithuanian, the language we used only in public places, it offered Latin, German, English, Hebrew, and Yiddish, the mother tongue of most of the Kaunas Jews. Although this school catered to wealthy Jewish children who had boycotted and left the German high school, it did not support any specific political position. Our parents were simply concerned that we learn Lithuanian and English so that we could study abroad and be able to live and work in Lithuania. All my friends and teenage relatives attended one of the Jewish high schools. We spent our free time with each other, going to 'our' skating-rink or participating in sports at 'our' Maccabi club. We attended all sorts of events at 'our' high schools, from amateur theater performances, lectures, and dances to sports tournaments. Only those Jewish teenagers who had attended the Lithuanian public schools or were studying at the university or one of the other post-secondary institutions mingled more with Lithuanians.

In high school, my favorite subjects were mathematics and history. I read a great deal and went to the Jewish library every day. I was particularly fond of poetry and read George Gordon Byron; the Lithuanian poets, Juozas Maironis and Vincas Putinas; and the Russians poets, Michail Lermontov, and especially Alexander Pushkin, whose verse I even attempted to translate into Lithuanian. I knew Lithuanian history and literature, participated in sports, particularly basketball, and loved to attend sporting events, the opera, and other cultural events. I felt secure in my Lithuanian ancestry, knowing that my family had lived there for many centuries, and I felt an integral part of its culture, literature, and way of life. Perhaps my forefathers had not fought for Lithuania's freedom but they had certainly contributed to the growth of its economy, its cultural development, and international standing. All of us, the younger generation of Jewish Lithuanians, or *Litvaks*, sought to be part of the traditions and aspirations of pre-war independent Lithuania. At the same time, by no means did we sacrifice our Jewish identity and consciousness. During those golden days of my youth, I couldn't see a single black cloud in the sky above my life. But as the next few years were to show, there was an invisible, yet impenetrable, wall between Lithuanians and Lithuania's Jews. Our lifestyles, traditions, mentalities, and geopolitical goals were very different from the separate, though parallel, cultural and social existence of our fellow countrymen.

By the eve of the war, anti-Semitic rumblings became louder. Our family used to spend summer holidays at a village on the Nemunas River near Kaunas or at the seaside resort town of Palanga on the Baltic coast. Many of my fellow students also came for their holidays to Palanga. We spent many happy times together there, going to the beach in the mornings. Following the European fashion of the day, we took afternoon tea, with cakes or ice cream, at the youth café where we danced to the latest modern music. By 1938, however, some

Lithuanians openly voiced their displeasure at having to rub shoulders with Jews in this relatively small seaside resort. Echoing this distaste, the Lithuanian daily newspaper, *Lietuvos aidas,* suggested that the seaside should be purged of 'dirty Jews'.[18] Yet, despite this and other anti-Semitic outbursts, Jews nevertheless continued to holiday at Palanga. This was mainly because Jews who went to Palanga generally stayed at Jewish hotels which served kosher food. Our family did not eat kosher food exclusively and we stayed at Lithuanian pensions. However, we never encountered the slightest unease or wariness on the part of the Lithuanian owners who provided us with accommodations. We never felt any hostility on the part of the guests staying at these hotels, but we never socialized with them either and certainly made no friends with the Lithuanians summering beside us.

Still, my parents were becoming increasingly uneasy about the international situation. They doubted whether Lithuania could succeed in remaining neutral, caught as it was between two powerful and aggressive states, Hitler's Germany and the Stalinist Soviet Union. They began to seriously consider emigration. My sister Alice Ginaite, after graduating from the Jewish High School, had gone to study in Belgium and my father had connections with Belgian companies. My parents could both speak French and so it appeared a viable emigration option. In the summer of 1938, my mother and I went to visit my sister in Belgium. We spent some time in Brussels and visited several other cities, spending several weeks at the seaside resort of Ostende. I had learned a little bit of French and spent my time, in fascination, watching the ebb and flow of the tides of the North Sea. But I missed my father, Kaunas, our relatives, and my friends.

Our holiday in Belgium was coming to an end and mother was also getting anxious to return home. Life in Belgium did not appeal to her and she did not like the idea of leaving her mother, brothers and sister, and her friends. So my mother and I returned to Lithuania and, although the political situation was clearly worsening, there was no more talk of emigration to Belgium. Perhaps father was beginning to make serious preparations for immigrating to America. If that was his plan, he had already waited too long.

Before the beginning of the Second World War Germany and the Soviet Union had signed a treaty of non-aggression. This led many Lithuanians to hope that the country would remain neutral and be spared military action and occupation. But, nobody knew about the secret protocols of the Molotov-Ribbentrop Pact in which the two predatory states agreed upon how they would divide their spheres of influence. When the Second World War began in September 1939, the German army invaded and occupied Poland within a matter of days. A section of the secret protocol allowed the Soviet Union to occupy a portion of Poland and the city of Vilnius. At the end of October, the Soviet Union unexpectedly 'granted' Vilnius back to Lithuania and the city was re-established as the country's capital. In exchange, Lithuania was obliged to establish a Soviet military garrison within the city's territory. Lithuanian army units entered Vilnius on October 28, 1939, and a Lithuanian civic administration was established.

At the end of 1939, Vilnius had a population of approximately 240,000 including 57,500 Jews.[19] From October to December 1939, the first Jewish refugees from German-occupied Poland began arriving in Lithuania and by the summer of 1940, there were 11,034 Jewish refugees registered in the country. From their stories we learned about the situation of the Jews in occupied Poland. The German occupying administration had confiscated their property and prohibited Jewish doctors, lawyers, and other independent professionals to work for non-Jews. They were evicted from their apartments and many were arrested without any formal reason or explanation. Those few who fled the country only managed to do so by paying enormous compensations. The Jewish refugees doubted that Lithuania would be able to maintain its neutrality and most of them, including many Vilnius Jews, tried desperately to escape to other foreign countries.

Considerable numbers of Jews were granted transit visas by the Japanese Consul in Kaunas, the Honorable Chiune Sugihara, who, in conjunction with the Dutch trade representative in Kaunas. With their help, many Jews were able to travel on the Trans-Siberian Railway to Vladivostok in the Soviet Union and then to Tokyo and Shanghai. From there they immigrated to the United States, Canada, Australia, or Palestine. A number of Jews from villages in the Vilnius region fled to Belarus and from there to the Soviet Union. In June 1940, after the Soviet Union had been toying with Lithuania, Latvia, and Estonia for nearly a year, the Red Army crossed the Lithuanian border. The Lithuanian President, Antanas Smetona, and his immediate family, fled the country.

Even when we saw Soviet soldiers marching in the streets of Kaunas, father still did not believe that the occupation had begun. He was convinced that the Soviet Union was simply increasing its military presence in order to have greater influence in the Baltic region. He thought that, in the worst case scenario, Lithuania would be given the same status as Mongolia (a satellite of the Soviet Union) and would, at least formally, retain its independence. He bought a copy of the Mongolian constitution, and, after studying it, breathed a sigh of relief. The Soviet occupation did not seem to him to be a tragedy for the Jews of Lithuania or indeed for our family. We knew that the Soviets were the lesser of two evils. Whether we approved or not, the Soviet occupation did not pose a deadly threat to our lives or our existence as a people. My father decided that Lithuania would be able to maintain its independence. He was to be bitterly disappointed.

Shortly after the occupation began, the Soviets implemented massive political, economic, and social changes. Justas Paleckis, a Lithuanian journalist, was appointed as the new President and a provisional government was formed. Elections for the new parliament were a complete farce. In its first session, the parliament, following a scenario developed by Moscow, requested that the Supreme Council of the Soviet Union allow Lithuania to join the USSR and be accorded the rights of a Soviet republic. On August 3 to 5, 1940, Lithuania, Latvia, and Estonia were 'solemnly accepted' into the Soviet Union. Thus, all three Baltic States lost their independence and the process of their social, political, and economic integration into the Soviet Union began. This process proved to be disastrous for our family. The company that father worked for was closed down. Moscow took over all import and export operations. Our savings were devalued according to the set rate for exchanging litas to rubles. For almost half a year, father was unable to find work, since the Soviet regime considered him 'unreliable". He finally found employment as an economist in the Ministry of Technical Supply. His knowledge of Russian became a considerable advantage for him and, at least in financial terms, life became a little easier. At that time, my sister was engaged to Philip Benjaminovichius, whose father Leiba owned a textile manufacturing company. The company was nationalized and Philip was appointed to oversee all affairs connected with the firm's nationalization and take-over. His father was forbidden to set foot on the premises. My sister found work in a construction firm.

Both of my grandparents' houses were nationalized. My grandmother Malka's Virovichiene janitor, Mykolas Kaminskis, chased her out of her own apartment, accusing her of capitalist exploitation, preventing her from taking any furniture or other household objects with her. Promptly, the janitor and his large family moved into my grandmother's apartment. She moved in with daughter Berta and her husband Lazar Jurovitski, while Abrasha Virovichius and his wife Fanya moved in with the Klis family at Vytautas Prospect 28, where there was plenty of room for all of them. The Red Army confiscated the house that we lived in and all of its tenants were evicted. The building was allocated for Soviet officers and their families and we were forced to move into a much smaller apartment, with only two bedrooms, on Bugos Street 13.

In January 1941, Alice married Philip Benjaminovichius and they moved into one of our bedrooms. My parents occupied the other one, while I slept in the living room. With nowhere to rest or find privacy, I became increasingly frustrated. I would leave home very early in the morning and return only after dark. An additional room in our apartment had been allocated to a Russian officer and his family who, fortunately, did not like the room and used it only as a storage place. They agreed to let me use the room and it was where I kept my books and did my homework. This small space of my own made my life a little easier.

Like most of the other Jewish schools, our high school was closed down and we were all transferred to the former Jesuit high school which was renamed the Ninth Kaunas High School. A considerable number of my former school friends, however, left for Vilnius, while others refused to attend the former Jesuit high school. I was in my final year and, although I now had to walk from one end of the city to the other to get to school, I decided to stay. My circle of friends became smaller. With the old teaching programs cut back, a completely new program was established in our school. All social and humanities subjects were changed, new compulsory subjects were introduced. Latin and foreign languages was eliminated, as were Yiddish and religion. Instead of these subjects we were forced to study the history and geography of the Soviet Union and the Russian language.

The new historical perspective presented to us, with its glorification of the Russian nation, its belittlement of other nationalities, and its justification of aggressive Czarist policies, seemed ludicrous to us all. I would return home from school tired and irritated, with little desire to go anywhere. I was bored by school events, which were usually chaperoned by specially appointed outsiders whose responsibility it was to ensure that Moscow's instructions were being followed.

At the beginning of the 1940/41 school year, a Young Communists' League, the *Komsomol*, was established at our high school. One of its committee members was a long time classmate of mine, Zalman "Monik" Holzberg. He tried to convince me to join the League but I tried to talk my way out of it. I told him that I did not belong to any political groups and was indifferent to Communist ideas. However, under the current political circumstances, it became obvious that I would have to join. I had little chance of being admitted to university because I was not the child of a working class family and I did not have the 'proper' background. It became clear that joining the Young Communists' League could help to remove those obstacles for me, so I became a member in early 1941. Never a particularly active member, I limited my activities to attending monthly meetings and helping to edit the organization's newsletter. In addition, I was becoming better acquainted with Lithuanians. I studied and made friends with some Komsomol members like Vytautas Kaminskas, Mechis Zumeris, and Elizaveta Boreikaite. I also befriended a very bright student by the name of Viktoras Butkus who, once the ghetto was established, came looking for me and wanted to help me.

In the winter of 1941, father became very ill. He was diagnosed with stomach cancer, a fact that was kept secret from me. He underwent an operation in the spring, but from May onwards he was bedridden. I spent the spring studying for exams while father's health worsened and darkness settled over our home.

Our final high school exam was scheduled to take place on June 14 or 15. As she did every day, mother wished me good luck that morning as I left for school. When I arrived at school, I was startled to find that not all of my classmates were there to take the exam. Nobody seemed to know what had happened. I took the exam and, afterwards, our homeroom teacher congratulated us on having completed our high school studies and invited us to attend the graduation ceremony the following week to receive our diplomas. I did actually receive my diploma, but not until four years later.

It wasn't until I returned home that I learned a large numbers of people had been arrested during the night. They had been taken to the train station, crammed into trains, and deported to far northern and eastern regions of the Soviet Union. Suddenly it became frighteningly clear why some of my classmates had been absent from the exam. The Hirsh Klis family, in whose building my uncle Abrasha's Virovichius family lived, was among those deported. He described to us how uniformed men had entered the apartment in the middle of the night and searched all the Klis' rooms, ordering them to quickly get ready. Then they had been piled into a truck that took them to the station. Their rooms had been sealed and Abrasha had been ordered not to touch anything.

Unbelievable things were taking place. The reasons for the deportations of innocent people and their families were incomprehensible. Fearfully, we wondered whether the deportations were isolated incidents. Did they mark the end of the repression or only the beginning? In addition, there was increased military activity in the country but it was unclear whether the Soviets were preparing for regular maneuvers or for something more serious. By June 1941, the German army had taken over almost half of Europe. Our future hung in the balance.

FACE TO FACE WITH DEATH

Without formally declaring war, Germany attacked the Soviet Union on Saturday night, June 21, 1941. From early the next morning, it was clear that Germany would invade Lithuania within days. Our situation seemed hopeless. We tried to telephone my father's relatives but no one answered their phones and we could only surmise that they were trying to leave Kaunas. It wasn't until later that we learned that only the Ginzberg family had made it to the Soviet Union. Samuel Ginas and his wife Berta Giniene returned to Kaunas after several unsuccessful attempts to reach Vilnius, where their daughters, Zlata and Bronya Ginaite, were studying. At the beginning of July, Zlata Ginaite was murdered at Paneriai (Ponar), a forest just outside the boundaries of the city of Vilnius. From the first day of the German-Soviet war to the last day of the Nazi occupation, Paneriai functioned as a mass extermination site of the Jews. Aunt Mina, her son Joske with his bride, also tried to flee to the East, but they did not succeed and all three perished somewhere in Lithuania on their way to the Soviet Union. Her younger son Leibe Ginas was murdered at Paneriai.

My mother and her family discussed our options. We had no relatives or friends in Russia. My father and grandmother were both very ill, and my uncle Abrasha and his wife, Fanya, had a newborn baby. It would have been impossible to attempt to flee or travel anywhere with them. The Benjaminovichius, my sister's husband's family, had already experienced Soviet repression. Naively, Leiba Benjaminovichius, his wife Roza and daughter Rita thought the Germans would prove no worse. The families remained in Kaunas. On the eve of the German-Soviet war, no one could ever have imagined what a tragic fate was about to befall our family and all the Jews of Lithuania.

On June 22 and 23, it seemed that all of Kaunas was in motion. People were trying to leave the city any way they could, many of them walking to the train station carrying small bundles. On June 23, we noticed that a man, dressed in civilian clothes but wearing a white armband and carrying a rifle, had been posted not far from our house on Bugos Street. Although he did not yet dare enter the house, he was clearly observing us. When I tried to go out to the store, he intercepted me, forced me to give him my watch, and told me to go back home. Later that day, my sister managed to sneak out to buy some bread, milk, and other basic necessities. There were no German soldiers on the street, but the so-called 'White Armbander' were everywhere. Now the city was at the mercy of these armed anti-Soviet partisan units.

On June 24, after speaking to her brothers by telephone, my mother suggested that I move in with my uncles at Vytautas Prospect 28, thinking I would be safer there. Their house was surrounded by a metal fence and locked gates, and the janitor was known to be sympathetic toward our family and the Jews in general. Janitors played a surprisingly important role during those days and the janitor at Vytauto Prospect 28 was determined to protect the Jewish owners and their Jewish tenants. So, instead of going to pick up my high school diploma as I had planned to do that day, I found myself going to join our relatives in a search for shelter that would be safer than my own home.

I reached their house quite easily, taking side streets and going through the cemetery on Vytautas Prospect. The street was quiet and there was no sign of either armed men or German soldiers. However, at around six the next morning, five White Armbanders forced their way into the building. They broke into our apartment, accompanied by Grandmother Malka's former janitor, Mykolas Kaminskis. He ushered the armed partisans into the apartment, proclaiming solemnly, "Here is where all of the Jewish communists are hiding"[20]. We tried in vain to explain that we were not communists and that the Soviets had deported our close relatives whose rooms were still sealed, just a week earlier. Unmoved, the White Armbanders arrested all five Jewish men living in the building, including my mother's three brothers, Salomon, Isaac, and Abrasha. Our pleas for compassion proved fruitless as the men were led out into the yard and taken farther from the house, to the edge of Vytautas Park. I ran out the other door to the fence and looked out to where the White Armbanders were taking their victims and could see them being led towards the park. Standing in the yard, immobilized by fear, I watched in horror as the five men, my three uncles among them, were shot.

A little while later, I saw a horse-drawn carriage pull up to the site of the shootings and watched as the driver tossed four of the corpses into one carriage and carefully lifted the fifth onto a different carriage. We learned later that Jews had been ordered to drive around the city in the early morning to collect the corpses and transport them to the cemetery. The second carriage served as an ambulance for the wounded. So it was that my only surviving uncle, Isaac Virovichius, was taken to the Jewish hospital only to die there a few hours later. When we received the telephone call from the hospital, a Doctor Moses Brauns told us that Isaac Virovichius had described how the partisans, accompanied by Grandmother's janitor, Kaminskis, had murdered the men behind the house at Vytauto Street 28. Broken-hearted, my grandmother Malka Virovichiene died the very next day. Not one of their family members was present when my grandmother and three of her sons were buried. To this day, we do not know the location of their final resting-places.

After I returned home to Bugos Street, I was in such a traumatized state that I had no desire to live. I didn't know whether to commit suicide so that I would never have to witness such horrors again or whether I should struggle to survive, so that I could one day tell the world what I had seen and experienced. I felt as though all Lithuanians despised me and wanted me dead. When I went to the shop to buy milk, I felt the hateful looks of the customers and the store-owner who refused to serve me. Not a single neighbour ever came to ask if we needed anything. I became terrified even of strangers in the street, particularly the partisans, most of whom were probably from Kaunas, just as I was. When I learned, later on, that the Russian language teacher from our school was a White Armbander who, with rifle in hand, apprehended and killed Jews, I knew my fears were well founded. It had become just as dangerous to stay at home as it was to go out into the street.

Two days after I returned home, two partisans entered our home and arrested my sister's husband, Philip. According to the archival record of his arrest,[21] the White Armbanders were searching a suspicious house, Bugos Street 13, in Kaunas when they found a Jewish student by the name of Filip Benjaminovichius (Philip) hiding there. They considered the house suspect because it housed the only Jewish family living on that street in a gentile neighbourhood. After being abducted by the partisans, Philip was taken to their headquarters at Vytautas Street 57 and then driven to the Seventh Fort, a Czarist-era fortress located on the outskirts of Kaunas. During the period of Lithuania's independence, the Fort had been transformed into a military warehouse but its heavy equipment, iron gates, underground barracks, and observation towers were kept in tact. Now it was the site for the mass exterminations of Jews.

My sister Alice had followed the partisans and discovered where Philip was being held. Frantically, she began telephoning her Lithuanian co-workers, asking them for help. Fortunately, one of them was a close acquaintance of Colonel Jurgis Bobelis, the Commandant of Kaunas. Alice's friend promised to try to help her and the next day he called back to tell her that he had arranged an appointment for her with Colonel Bobelis on June 30th. Over the next few days, Alice went to the Seventh Fort. Along with a group of other Jewish women, who had gathered at the iron gates desperately hoping to help their husbands, brothers, and sons, Alice tried to convince the guards to allow her to leave some food for her husband. With gunshots ringing through the air, the guards routinely refused their pleas.

On June 30, as arranged, she presented herself at the Colonel's office. Blond, elegant, and young, Alice was often mistaken for a German. Her Aryan appearance and ability to speak German gave her the advantage of being able to walk the streets of Kaunas freely. Now, Colonel Bobelis received her courteously and seemed pleased by her appearance. Relaxed, he conversed easily with her, not seeming to want to hurry their meeting. He had known Mother's brother, Salomon, quite well, it turned out. Whether sincerely or not, he expressed his condolences for Salamon's death, promised Alice he would try to help her, and suggested that she return to see him in a few days.

On a hot summer day at the beginning of July, my sister went to see Colonel Bobelis again. As friendly as he had been at their first meeting, he repeatedly quipped that it was a pity she was Jewish. Suddenly the telephone rang and interrupted their conversation. He picked up the receiver, shouted the order, "Bring him in!" and hung up. Slowly, the door opened and Philip walked in. He was alive, but barely recognizable. Philip was being released for having fought for

Lithuania's independence in 1918-1919. Over 2000 Jews had fought in the Lithuanian Army during the 1918-1919 war of independence. But Philip was born in 1918 and could not possibly have done so. With no clear explanation for this benevolent act of rescue, Bobelis wished them good luck and told my sister to feel free to visit him more often.[22]

We will never know whether Bobelis was motivated by a moment of compassion or by simple romantic interest. Although he was all-powerful in determining the fate of Jews during that period, it is well known that he often failed to keep his promises and many were murdered for whom similar pleas were made.

Philip's story of horror began with his arrival at the Seventh Fort's sunken courtyard, a kind of ravine encircled by embankments. With countless numbers of men lying all around him, he was ordered to lie down in the pit, not to move, and to remain silent. By way of greeting, and without moving his head, the man beside Philip whispered that any images of hell he could have conjured up would have been a relief compared to what he had experienced here. Philip soon learned for himself how true that was.

In the summer heat, the detained men were not given anything to drink, even though there was an artesian well close by. They were given bread only every second day. The guards tormented the men continually, shooting at anyone who crawled toward the water or dared to raise his head or attempted to help his neighbour. When bread and water were finally brought, those who were sent to fetch it were shot at. But, even though those prisoners who didn't die immediately writhed and tossed in pain, no one was allowed to go near them. Those who did attempt to help the wounded were shot without warning. The living, the wounded, and the corpses all lay together in the courtyard. In the evenings, a truck would arrive. A dozen or so men would be picked to throw the corpses and half-dead men in the truck, go to a bushy slope nearby, dig a ditch, and empty the bodies into it. The subsequent rattle of machine-gun fire would indicate that the ditch-diggers too had been shot into the ditch. New victims were herded into the Fort from the streets of Kaunas in an almost continual stream. Some were crammed into the pit while others were driven directly over the hill at the side of the building and straight into the mass graves.

It is difficult to believe that, in the twentieth century, humans could conceive of such things. The brutality and ability to torment and kill fellow beings is almost unimaginable. Animals are not as cruel. They do not kill for pleasure.

Delirious from thirst, Philip could think only of water. He had little hope of staying alive and prayed for a swift death to end the hellish torture. As he later recounted, the guards would occasionally shout out someone's name. The person called would get up and edge toward the gates, waiting for a shot. As he was led away, neither he nor the other prisoners had any inkling of the fate that awaited him.

Philip's fourth day at the Fort, a Sunday, passed quietly. They were brought bread and allowed to drink some water and spent an uneventful night. However, as the new guards began their shift on Monday, the ritual of torture began again. People were shot, new victims brought in, and no one was allowed to move or speak. A bullet aimed at the man lying next to Philip almost hit him.

The sky was overcast that Monday morning, and the new day promised nothing better than the previous ones. Suddenly, Philip heard his name being called. He was so astonished that he could not move. The guard shouted his name again, demanding that he go toward the gates. It was only when he was called a third time that Philip finally raised himself and began to walk to the office of the Fort. After the secretary determined his identify, Philip was taken to the city and to the Commandant's office. There he was given some water and told to sit down and wait. Too weak to speak, Philip just sat, as the secretary made a phone call. Then Philip was ordered to enter the Commandant's office. When he walked into the room and saw his wife in conversation with the colonel, Philip almost fainted. Even after he returned home, as relieved as he was, he still had difficulty grasping where he was and where he had been. It took a few days for him to recover sufficiently to be able to tell his family about the inconceivable brutality he had experienced at the Fort.

On July 7, the Seventh Fort ceased to be used as a site for the execution of Jews. On July 6, all the women and children were led out of the underground barracks, and about 70 men who had fought for Lithuanian independence in 1918-1919 were released from the pit in the courtyard. All of those who remained in the Fort, over 2000 people, were executed on July 6. The shooting went on all day and all night [23] On July 7, there was not a single prisoner left in the Fort and all the victims had been buried on the slope nearby. Altogether, between 5000 and 7000 Kaunas Jews were murdered at the Seventh Fort during the first two weeks of the war.

In the Central Archives of Lithuania there is a document that contains the minutes of a meeting of the Cabinet of the Lithuanian Provisional Government (LPG). The meeting was held on the morning of June 30, 1941, and at that meeting, most likely without any request from the Germans, the Lithuanian government proposed the establishment of a 'Jewish Concentration Camp'. The proposal was accepted, a document was issued, and it was signed by the acting Prime Minister, Juozas Ambrazevichius (Ambrazaitis-Brazaitis). In reality, that Concentration Camp was the mass murder site of the Seventh Fort. The document stated that Antanas Shvilpa, the Vice-Minister of Communal Affairs of the LPG and Colonel Jurgis Bobelis, the Military Commandant of Kaunas, were to look after the matter. [24]

From the end of June until July 6, 1941, Jews from Kaunas were hunted down, arrested, and brought to the Seventh Fort. The arresting, the guarding, and the killing of the Jews was executed by the White Armbander partisans and later by the members of the Lithuanian military battalions. These battalions were formed upon the request of the German Military Commandant, General von Pohl, in order to reorganize the entire partisan groups into regular auxiliary police units. On June 28, 1941, Bobelis established a Lithuanian National Labour Defense Battalion, known as *Tautos Darbo Apsaugos* or *TDA Batalionas*. Colonel Bobelis had been put in charge of the TDA and appointed Andrius Butkunas as commander of this battalion. Later on, from July 24, 1941, Kazys Shimkus took over command of the battalion.

The First and Third military squads (*kuopos*) of the TDA Battalion were directly involved in the arrest, torture, and shooting of Jews, not only in Kaunas and Vilnius, but in all of Lithuania, Minsk, and other cities of Belarus. The commanders and the high ranking officers of those squads were as follows: Juozas Barzda, Bronius Norkus, Jonas Ralys, Jonas Stankaitis, Stasys Sutkaitis, Juozas Obelinis, Stepas Paulauskas, and Bronius Kirkila, who committed suicide after the mass murder. Many more officers in the Lithuanian military battalions participated in the killings of their neighbours, the Jews. [25]

MIRRORING THE EVIL

Driven By Special Interests

The history of the Holocaust – the state sponsored attempt to annihilate totally European Jews by Nazi Germany and its collaborators – is an extremely complex subject. It involves the study of political and social issues and raises countless economic, religious, and ethical questions. Holocaust historiography examines the behavior of the victims, their living and working conditions in the ghettos and concentration camps, and their struggle to resist their oppressors. Holocaust historians also scrutinize the behavioral incentive of individuals who rescued Jews, as well as the motivation of those who conceived, organized, and conducted the massacres. Surely the Holocaust, which is without precedent in history, both in terms of the depths of its horror and the heights of its heroism, challenged the very foundation of civilization. Studying the Holocaust, therefore, is valuable in understanding the human capacity for evil and for good. It is for this reason that the history of the Holocaust will always be a sensitive subject that arouses strong reactions, but it will always hold universal meaning.

Without a doubt, the Holocaust could not have happened without the involvement of the individuals who carried it out. Regardless of the laws adopted by Nazi German leaders, the massacres would not have taken place without the cooperation of real individuals who agreed to act as collaborators and to perpetrate the mass arrests and shootings of thousands upon thousands of innocent men, women, and children. Documents and the testimonies of witnesses indicate that these criminals were not robots, or blind executioners, carrying out the orders of their superiors. Most of them joined the police and other forces willingly. Survivors and witnesses have corroborated the enormous cruelty of these killers. Their contempt and viciousness, and the eagerness with which they brutalized and tortured their victims, frequently superceded the orders, and even the license, they had been given.

Enticed by promises of various privileges by the Germans, these people were easily recruited to volunteer police battalions and other military units established in occupied Soviet republics, including Lithuania. The new recruits were assured that they would be immune from persecution, even if they had served in the Red Army or collaborated with Soviet institutions of repression. Others were motivated by the promised exemption from military service and hard labour. Personal power was a strong factor too, as were an eagerness to settle personal accounts and the thirst for revenge. In Lithuania, collaboration with the Nazis was based also on the desire to establish the country's political sovereignty at any price. Lithuania's political authorities greeted the Nazis enthusiastically. The Provisional Government (PG) in Lithuania went so far as to proclaim that the young Lithuanian state fully supported Nazi policy and was ready, with great enthusiasm, to take part, along with all of Europe, in putting these new principles into practice. They eagerly demonstrated their faithfulness to the Nazi regime, its ideology, and its actions. They offered their help and support to the occupiers.

Economic factors, such as the possibility of material reward, also contributed to their readiness to kill Jews. Regulations were put in place regarding the privatization of Lithuanian property. Signed by Vytautas Landsbergis-Zemkalnis, a member of the PG and Minister of Municipal Affairs. These regulations stated that, in cases where several owners were seeking to retrieve nationalized homes or land, and "if one or a portion are Jews... the [other] owners [could] take over control of their former co-owners' property."[26] On July 4, 1941, the PG declared that all property nationalized by the Soviets was to be returned to the original owners, but that Jewish property would remain the property of the Lithuanian government.[27] The conditions were thus made perfect for the greedy and self-willed to plunder their victims' property and possessions. Many Lithuanians took part in dividing up both the properties taken from Jews by the government and the property of their murdered Jewish neighbours. The murderers stole jewelry, household items, furniture, furs, clothing, and books, in short, whatever they could lay their hands on. They occupied Jewish homes and pilfered their land, orchards, gardens, and farm animals.

Up until August 5, 1941, the last day of its mandate, the PG issued similar statutes and directives regarding the property and status of Jews.

Another economic factor contributing to the massacre of Jews was the desire to erase personal debts owing to Jewish neighbours and to eliminate the competition traditionally presented by Jewish businesses. The murderers believed that, with the Jews out of the way, they could more easily increase their influence in industry, trade, construction, and other areas. The Lithuanian press of the period wrote a great deal about this.

Definitely, an important root of the massacres was a deeply ingrained anti-Semitism. Lithuanian and Jewish economic interests were already opposed before the war and became increasingly antagonistic during Lithuania's inter-war period of independence. At that time economic anti-Semitism grew sharply. Jews were the primary objects of criticism by the Lithuanian Merchants' Union and its publication, *Verslas* (Commerce), which accused Jews of trying to achieve world domination. Arguing for a limitation on the economic influence of Jews, the weekly publication heightened fascist and nationalist feelings, ultimately encouraging anti-Jewish actions. Drawing on Nazi German terminology, the newspaper introduced Lithuanian readers to the stereotype of the 'Jew exploiter', the 'Jew speculator', and the 'Jew usurper'. These extreme nationalist and racist ideas inspired the Lithuanian Nazi Party, known as *Gelezinis Vilkas* (Iron Wolves), and various pro-German, ultra-nationalist intellectuals and political figures. Among these were the Lithuanian philosopher, Antanas Maceina, who later became the ideologue of the LAF; Kazys Shkirpa, Lithuania's Ambassador to Germany; Bronius Raila, Antanas Valiukenas, and others.

On November 17, 1940, former Lithuanian Ambassador Shkirpa initiated the establishment of the Lithuanian Activists Front (LAF) and its military wing, the National Labour Defense (TDA), which was comprised of activist military troops. Seeking to expand its illegal activities in Lithuania, the LAF established secret cross-border communications and sent in agents and illegal armed groups charged with spreading anti-Semitic propaganda. These actions contributed significantly to Germany's military intelligence efforts. At that point, Germany's special service departments (its foreign affairs, military, and security departments) were not opposed to the LAF's plan to form Lithuania's Provisional Government and did not interfere with its makeup. While at war with the Soviet Union, which was occupying Lithuania, it was even in Germany's interests, particularly at the beginning, to have armed volunteer detachments, which could both liquidate 'unreliable elements' and protect the German army from surprise military attacks.

Having received approval from Germany's special services, Shkirpa drew up a list of members for the PG. But when the Germans occupied Kaunas, Shkirpa was not permitted to return to Lithuania and LAF headquarters were ordered to change the makeup of the government[28]. Juozas Ambrazevichius-Ambrazaitis (Brazaitis) was named Prime Minister and the new Deputy Chairman of the LAF. Leonas Prapuolenis was appointed Chairman of the LAF. On the morning of June 23, 1941, Prapuolenis made a speech on Kaunas radio. In the name of the LAF headquarters, he proclaimed Lithuania's independence and read the names of the Lithuanian Provisional Government.[29]

Laying the Foundations

Anti-Jewish propaganda laid the ideological foundation for the hatred of Jews and later for attempts to justify the Holocaust in Lithuania. Nazi Germany's anti-Jewish propaganda infiltrated Lithuania even before the beginning of the war. By the eve of the war (winter to spring 1941) this propaganda had intensified, reaching Lithuania through well-organized underground channels. The former Lithuanian Embassy in Germany played an important role in this process.

All of the documentation related to LAF headquarters and the Lithuanian Provisional Government (its program, memorandum, decrees, orders, and instructions), particularly those published through its media channels, reveal a great hatred for the Jews. The LAF's program, entitled, *What the Activists Are Fighting For*, accused the Jews of actively contributing to the downfall of the Lithuanian State in 1940. It also attacked the very nature of the Jewish people, asserting that the essential ideology of Communism was descended from the Jews.[30]

In the spring of 1941, the LAF had prepared a document on the Jewish question, in which it declared that Lithuania must completely, and for all times, be liberated from the Jews. With this document, the LAF effectively pronounced the verdict on the fate of Lithuania's Jews:

> The crucial day of reckoning has finally come for the Jews. Lithuania must be liberated not only from Asiatic Bolshevik slavery but also from the historic Jewish yoke...On behalf of the Lithuanian people, the Lithuanian Activist Front solemnly declares: The ancient rights of sanctuary granted to the Jews in Lithuania by [Grand Duke] Vytautas the Great are abolished completely and for all times. All Jews are hereby and without restriction ordered to leave Lithuania...Solely Lithuanians will rebuild the new Lithuanian State – by their energy, love and wisdom. All Jews are forever excluded from Lithuania. Should any Jew dare to expect refuge in the new Lithuania, let him know that an irrevocable sentence has been passed upon his people – that not a single Jew will be accorded Lithuanian citizenship or have any means of sustenance in the reborn Lithuania.
>
> Punishment for all of the offenses and evils committed by Jews in the past will constitute the right and firm foundation upon which the creative and happy future of our Aryan nation will be laid.[31]

This leaflet was issued by the LAF in Berlin on June 22, 1941, the day that Germany invaded Lithuania. From that point on, Lithuanian Jews were deprived of all civil rights and found them beyond the jurisdiction of the law. On June 24, 1941, in the first issue of the LAF and PG sponsored newspaper, *I Laisve* (Towards Freedom), edited by Jonas Virbickas, an article appeared openly supporting the emergence of Hitler's Nazis and issuing anti-Jewish incitements. Before the newspaper went to print, Juozas Ambrazevichius-Brazaitis, the Prime Minister of the PG, personally checked every article. After reading the newspaper, he suggested a slight change in the name of the paper but approved all the anti-Semitic articles. It is important to note that the first issue of *I Laisve* appeared prior to the German military occupation of Kaunas.

In addition to mounting general anti-Semitic attacks, the LAF's anti-Jewish propaganda wing went to considerable trouble to exaggerate the role played by Jews during the Soviet occupation. It claimed that the Jews had 'dug the grave' of Lithuania's independence and had played a crucial role in the integration of Lithuania into the Soviet Union. Proclamations published by the LAF claimed that "Russian Communism and its eternal servant, the Jew, are one and the same enemy". It also claimed that Jews consistently comprised 80-90% of the real agents of Russian Bolshevism and the Lithuanian Communist Party, the 'grave diggers' of Lithuania. Another proclamation encouraged Lithuanians to seek revenge against, and settle accounts with, Jews. It claimed that "the Jews, the Russians, and the colonial Poles are fungi growing on our nation that must be cut off."[32] In another article from the first editorial of *I laisve,* readers were told that

> ...the Bolsheviks and their accomplices are fleeing the country. Communism was the perfect means for the Jews to exploit and dominate others, because Bolshevism and the Jews are inseparable.[33]

The LAF's harsh declarations were understood perfectly by those to whom they were directed and the import of these words contributed to changing minds.

The identification of Jews with Communism was a very effective psychological tool for inspiring both nationalist and anti-Semitic sentiment. The Lithuanian press of the time including *I laisve* (Toward Freedom); *Nauja gadyne* (A New Era); *Naujoji Lietuva* (The New Lithuania); and *Tevyne* (Homeland) openly provoked the genocide of Jews and encouraged seeking revenge on them for all of their 'past and future offenses'.

I have no doubt that the Holocaust constitutes an unprecedented case in human history. It exceeded other genocides not only in its 'competence' and numbers but also in the uniqueness of its very essence and the very nature of the crimes against humanity committed by the German Nazis and their collaborators. Never before or since has a civilized European state, allegedly founded on Christian morality and ruled by an elected leader and a legal government, decided, and openly declared, that certain groups of people (Jews, Gypsies, and homosexuals) must be exterminated. Unique, too, were the places where these killings took place: the concentration camp at Auschwitz and its smaller brothers and sisters: the Seventh and Ninth Forts in Kaunas; Paneriai in Vilnius; Rumbula and Salaspils in Latvia; Vaivara and Klooga in Estonia; Babi Yar in the Ukraine.

INTERPRETATION

What kind of interpretation can be offered for this shocking page of history, particularly the history of twentieth century Lithuania? While there are important studies about the Lithuanian Jewish community during the pre-war years, there is a significant lack of historical analysis of Lithuanian-Jewish relations during the period between 1940 and 1944. Similarly, the issue of the Jewish catastrophe has not been dealt with extensively in the literature of the post-war Lithuanian Diaspora. The memoirs of most Lithuanian émigrés, some of whom participated in the administration, describe only the Lithuanians' suffering under the Soviet regime. They recount the country's struggle for freedom and independence, and the Lithuanian people's ensuing disappointment and despair. Generally, the Lithuanian émigré press has not said a single word about the anti-Jewish LAF proclamations and has not made any comments about Article 16 of the LAF program. In May 1946, the émigré press in Germany issued a memorandum regarding Lithuanian-Jewish relations. It stated that the Germans were to blame for the killing of the Jews and that Lithuanians had nothing to say about it or to do with it. It claimed that it was only in the first days of the war that a small number of Lithuanians took revenge on the Jews and that the PG did its best to help the Jews.[34]

In the 1950s, the Lithuanian émigré press responded to accusations by Holocaust survivors that Lithuanians had actively participated in the murders of Jews. These responses to the survivors' accusations, however, promoted the concept of 'Double Genocide' or the 'Parallel' idea. This thesis attempted to exonerate the Lithuanians by claiming that they had suffered at the hands of the Jews no less that the Jews had suffered at the hands of the Lithuanians. It claimed that the participation of Lithuanians in the killing of Jews was nothing more than retaliation for the participation of Jews in the sovietization of Lithuania, their dominant role in the State Security Forces, and their active role in the destruction of the Lithuanian people. The émigré press defended the 'Parallel' idea, which linked the Jewish Holocaust and the Lithuanian Genocide. Moreover, the concept of the 'Double Genocide' was widely accepted by both Lithuanian communities, at home and abroad. It continues to be expressed fairly often today in its publications.[35]

Angered by one such article, Professor Grazina Slaveniene, who lives in the United States, wrote:

> I read a very disturbing article under the headline, *The Kaunas Events Seen Through Jewish Eyes.* Are Jewish eyes needed to consider the monstrosity of the massacre of the Jews? Are Lithuanian eyes unable to see it? I have wanted to write this article for a long time, because articles published in the Toronto Lithuanian émigré newspaper, *Tevishkes Ziburiai* [Lights of the Homeland], in the name of Lithuanian-Jewish dialogue, are cause for serious reflection. We reproach the Jews for being unforgiving, but are we ourselves forgiving? We accuse the Jews of having been active under the Bolsheviks, but can that possibly justify the barbaric torture of innocent people? We have so closely intertwined our own tragedy with that of the Jews that we are no longer able to separate one from the other and continue to practice a politics of 'settling accounts'. We deny that which can no longer be denied and attempt to justify that which can no longer be justified.[36]

Since World War II, various books about the massacre of the Jews in Lithuania have been published in Lithuania, as they have been in Germany, Israel, the United States, and other countries. Most of these texts consist of memoirs written by Lithuanian Jewish survivors. During the post-war Soviet period in Lithuania, a series of books were published dealing with the German occupation, the atrocities committed by the Nazis and their collaborators, war criminals, and the mass extermination sites that were operating in Lithuania. Containing authentic documents related to the mass murders, the most important of these publications are the two-volume collection, *Mass Murders in Lithuania*; a collections of articles entitled, *The Nazi Occupation of Lithuana; Documents Accuse;* and several books about the fortresses of death and the collaboration of Lithuanian 'nationalist' volunteers with the Germans.

During the first years of Lithuania's independence (1991-1995), many articles were published in Lithuania discussing the catastrophe of Lithuanian Jewry. However, it must be stressed that, in these articles, Lithuanian journalists analyzed the Holocaust in Lithuania and writers drawing on concepts previously developed by the Lithuanian expatriate press. The articles defended the thesis of the 'Double Genocide' and portrayed the Jews as Bolsheviks, Soviet collaborators, and active participants in the genocide of ethnic Lithuanians.

In the aftermath of Lithuanian President Algirdas Brazauskas' visit to Israel in 1995, the stream of articles pushing the 'Parallel Concept' grew stronger in both Lithuania and in the expatriate press. Speaking to the Israeli Parliament, Brazauskas said, "I ask your forgiveness for those Lithuanians who mercilessly murdered, shot, deported, and robbed Jews..."[37]

However, Brazauskas also said that the entire Lithuanian nation could not be accused of these historical crimes and that the search for collective responsibility only leads to more misfortune. In a speech upon his return to Lithuania, Brazauskas said,[38]

> As President of the Republic of Lithuania and as its citizen, I had the right and responsibility to apologize to the Jewish people for the injuries it suffered during the Second World War. This visit to Israel was very difficult, but it was also very necessary.
>
> I expressed those words of repentance, first of all in my capacity as President, and on behalf of all those people who understand and support me.

Despite the strong opposition to Brazauskas' repentance, the circle of historians studying the massacre of the Jewish people in Lithuania has grown during recent years and their approach has gradually begun to change. To a significant degree, this growing study has resulted from the declassification of confidential documents and files, and the new accessibility of archival documents in Eastern Europe and the former Soviet republics. Still, the old anti-Semitic image of the Jews continues to be perpetuated in two recently released books, *Lithuania Against Soviet and Nazi Aggression,* by Adolfas Damushis, a former member of the PG and *The Uprising and the Provisional Government,* by the Lithuanian historian, Algimantas Liekis. Both authors ignore the true facts about the actions of the LAF and the PG against the Jews and the contributions of both of these organizations to the mass murder of the Jews by the Nazis. There remains, therefore, a wide gap in the different interpretations of the Holocaust within Lithuania.

Certain accepted ideas on the subject can now be reassessed and a more objective explanation of these tragic pages in Lithuania's history can be proposed. Encouragingly, a more realistic viewpoint regarding the Holocaust and Lithuanian-Jewish relations is being expressed by a younger generation of émigré researchers and writers. These writers reject revenge as the main motive for the massacre of the Jews. They also discard the 'Parallel' idea and the image of Jews created in Nazi propaganda. Particularly significant are the writings of Zenonas Rekashius, Jonas Shmukshtys, Saulius Suziedelis, Tomas Venclova and others. In Lithuania itself, the following writers and historians are developing this new viewpoint: Antanas Balsys, Valentinas Brandishauskas, Arunas Bubnys, Alfonsas Eidintas, Leonas Tapinas, Liudas Truska, and others. In addition, many Holocaust survivors who are historians, researchers, and publicists agreed in principal, despite their differing opinions, with this new trend in thinking about the history of the Holocaust in Lithuania.

> In this new context, the historian Liudas Truska writes: "Like that of the Lithuanian as Jew-killer, the image of the Jew as the grave-digger of Lithuania's independence, as Communist, or KGB agent is completely unfounded. "[39]

Although this new trend of thinking, represented mostly by liberal-minded intellectuals and historians, is slowly influencing the social consciousness, it has not yet become dominant in Lithuania. Historians Valentinas Brandishauskas and Saulius Suziedelis point out that the role of Lithuanians in the massacre of the Jews was greater than many Lithuanian expatriate writers are willing to admit. Suziedelis still believes, however, that local Lithuanians did not play the principle role in determining the tragic fate of the country's Jews.[40]

THE BEGINNING OF THE HOLOCAUST

The positions expressed today in these and other academic publications and discussions increasingly reveal important areas of agreement between historians holding otherwise different opinions and interpretations. This is particularly true regarding the beginnings of the massacre of the Jews in Lithuania. On the eve of the war, we Lithuanian Jews sensed that under the German occupation we would be treated similarly to the way the Jews were already being treated in Poland under the Germans. Not one of us, however, could have imagined that the Jews would be massacred from the very first days of the occupation, even before the German civil administration was formed.

The massacre of the Jews, as well as other groups of people in the occupied territory of the Soviet Union, was organized by the German Security Police and the Security Department's (SD) operative groups. These groups, Einsatzgruppen (EG), which was formed in the spring of 1941 and then subdivided into smaller groups and military detachments, consisted of approximately 3000 officers and soldiers. Their formal mandate was to ensure the safety of advancing German military divisions, to fight partisans, commissars and communists agents, provocateurs, and other anti-Nazi elements. They were also mandated to conduct a 'cleansing' of undesirable local elements. One of the strategic groups, the EG-A, operated in the Baltic region and was headed by Franz Walter Stahlecker (until 1942, when it was taken over by Horst Jost). Following an order by Stahlecker, 'cleansing operations' in Lithuania were to be conducted by German Strategic Security Police detachments, Einsatzkommando 2, and 3. By October 1941, there was only one Security Police detachment, Einsatzkommando 3 (EK-3), headed by Karl Jaeger and E. Ehrlinger and comprising about 110 to 120 troops left in Lithuania. [41]

On the eve of the war with the Soviet Union, a German Security Police detachment, headed by SS Major Joachim Boeme, was dispatched from Tilsit, Germany. On June 24, 1941, this detachment crossed the German-Lithuanian border and invaded the border town of Gargzhdai. At the same time, German police divisions from the Lithuanian city of Klaipeda (or Memel as it was called after being annexed by Germany in March 1939) also entered Gargzhdai.

Searching for suspected Communists, the Gestapo ordered all Jewish men in Gargzhdai to gather in the Town Square. The men were all arrested and led to a nearby field where they were shot. Altogether, 201 people were killed that day in Gargzdai (200 Jewish men and one Russian woman, the wife of a high-ranking Soviet officer).[42] The 'cleansing operations' continued into June 26, 28, and 29 and took place in the Lithuanian border towns of Kretinga, Palanga, and Darbenai. Seven hundred Jewish men were shot dead over four days.[43]

In 1958, a trial of war criminals took place in the German town of Ulme. The organizers and perpetrators of the above-mentioned massacres sat on the defendants' bench. The trial revealed that the security police detachment, EK-2 had received secret orders from Berlin to begin 'cleansing operations' along a twenty five-kilometer stretch of the Lithuanian-German border.

During the months of June and July 1941, over 5500 people were killed in the designated area and included all the Jews of those towns – all men, women, and children.[44]

Simultaneous with the organized massacres of Jews along the German-Lithuanian border, a campaign of terror against Jews began across Lithuania. Germans themselves did not conduct these arrests and killings. Initially, the local White Armbander (the partisans) also perpetrated them. In those days in Lithuania, there were some 10,000 -15,000 partisans. In Kaunas alone, there were about 6000 White Armbanders. Not all Lithuanian partisans were the killers, but almost all the Jews killed were murdered by the White Armbanders.

The first anti-Jewish pogrom took place in Kaunas on June 26. Never had such a brutal blood bath on this large a scale taken place in Lithuania. The pogrom was organized in accordance with Stahlecker's orders but the massacre was orchestrated and implemented by Algirdas Klimaitis, the leader of one of the local partisan groups. Leading his unit, Klimaitis invaded the mainly Jewish suburb of Vilijampole (Slabodka) in Kaunas. The partisans moved from house to house, from one apartment to another, killing every Jew they encountered and, within two days, Klimaitis' partisans had killed approximately 1500 Jews. They destroyed several synagogues, burning some, and burned down 60 homes. Among the murdered were dozens of students in the famous Jewish religious seminary, the Slabodka Yeshiva. A former student of the Yeshiva, Rabbi Ephraim Oshry, who survived the massacre, writes of the pogrom:

> One of the most terrible instances of savage butchery was the death of the venerable Rabbi of Slabodka, Zalman Osovsky... The invaders bound the Rabbi, hand and foot, and sawed off his head, upon his open prayer book...Their brutality did not end there, for afterwards, they murdered his brilliant young son, Rabbi Yudel Osovsky, and then shot Rabbi Zalman's wife.[45]

Afterwards, when Klimaitis reported the events of the pogrom to Generals Stasys Pundzevichius and Mykolas Reklaitis, they were displeased with this turn of events and asked Klimaitis to resign and leave Kaunas.

A second pogrom took place in Kaunas on June 26 or 27. This pogrom was neither planned nor inspired by the Germans but was organized by a group of Lithuanian White Armbanders – the partisans. About 50 Jews, abducted either from the streets of the city or from their homes, were herded into the yard of the Lithuanian National Corporation – *Lietukis* garage at Vytautas Prospect 43. They were beaten with iron crowbars. Using rubber hoses intended for washing cars, their torturers sprayed water into their mouths until their intestines burst. Among the victims were a Rabbi, a man and his seven-year-old son, and the father of the well known Lithuanian lawyer and political scientist, Alexander Shtromas. Descriptions of that pogrom makes it clear there was one Hell that Dante failed to enumerate in *The Inferno*, and only because that particular one had not been conceived of when he was writing.

The horrific events that took place at the *Lietukis* garage have been described by Henrikas Zemelis, a member of the editorial board of the Lithuanian émigré monthly publication, *Akiraciai,* and a former Lithuanian partisan. Walking down Vytautas Prospect that day, he noticed that a crowd of people had gathered. When he drew near, he saw that,

> ...five or six men were beating their victims with metal rods. There was blood everywhere...One of the executioners

would revive the victims with a water hose so that the massacre could continue…I was struck dumb by this scene, and could not imagine how the desire for revenge could lead to such a massacre.[46]

Zemelis immediately went to the partisans' headquarters to report the incident, but doubted that any attempt was made to help the victims or restrain their torturers.

Julius Vanilevichius and Leonardas Survila also described the slaughter.[47] One of the German soldiers, V. Gunsilijus, photographed the event. These photographs have survived.[48] Copies of the photographs of the massacre at the garage yard are housed in various museums around the world dedicated to preserving the memory of the Jewish victims and commemorating the heroism of Jews during the Holocaust. During his 1994 visit to Israel, Lithuanian Prime Minister, Adolfas Slezhevicius, expressed how difficult it was for him to walk through Yad Vashem and look at the enlarged, wall-sized photographs of what happened at this Lithuanian garage on June 26, 1941.[49]

From August 15, 1941 on, all former Lithuanian military units were reorganized into five Lithuanian auxiliary police battalions. From the very beginning, some of these units were under the jurisdiction of the Einsatzkommando-3 (EK-3) and its chief, Karl Jaeger, who remained in this position until the fall of 1943. By August 1942, there were twenty Lithuanian police battalions, comprised of 8388 soldiers, operating in Lithuania.[50]

At the beginning of July 1941, a combined German-Lithuanian mobile unit, the *Roll Commando* (the Flying Squad), was formed. Their special function was killing Jews[51]. The Obersturmfuerer, SS First Lieutenant, Joachim Hamann, commanded eight to ten men from EK-3 and a special Lithuanian unit led by Bronius Norkus. Over the next several months, this Flying Squad executed approximately 70,000 Jews. Basically, they killed all the Jews living in small Lithuanian cities – stetlach and villages. The units were also sent to conduct massacres in Belarus and other neighbouring countries. As Saulius Suziedelis writes,

A day or two prior to the *aktzion*, the appropriate local Lithuanian and German authorities were ordered to 'round up' the Jews of the region... There is evidence that in certain districts and especially places where large scale *aktzions* were planned, like Marijampole and Rokiskis, orders were given to co-opt 'locals' into the ranks of the executioners... Desensitized by alcohol, these murderers forced the condemned men, women, and children to lie down in ditches and shot them one after another. This is the savage way in which the majority of Lithuania's innocent Jewish citizens, and with them their unique centuries-old culture, met their death.[52]

The manner in which these killings and executions were organized was described in detail in reports that the leaders, Stahlecker of EG-A, and Jaeger of EK-3, regularly sent to German Security Police in Berlin. Both Stahlecker's and Jaeger's reports included statistical information about how many Jews, as well as how many people of other nationalities and groups, were shot in Lithuania between July 4 and December 1, 1941. In addition to the number of people killed, the reports included details of location, time, and nationality. The reports also provided specific figures as to the numbers of men, women and children who were murdered. The reports evaluated the work of the Lithuanian police battalions, the organizational success, and problems related to the first pogroms, and provided approximate figures regarding the number of Lithuanian Jews killed between June 23, and July 4, 1941. It is estimated that 4000 Jews were listed killed in pogroms prior to EK-3's arrival in Lithuania.

Stahlecker's reports explain the process of recruiting local civilians to assist police detachments in killing Jews. Stating how important it was to include the locals in so-called spontaneous anti-Semitic cleansing operations, he described how Lithuanian activists and nationalists took the initiative to organize partisan detachments and actively fight against Bolshevism. Stahlecker pointed out that the Lithuanians were pro-German and eager to assist German soldiers and police officers, especially cooperative in identifying Jews and Communists, arresting such individuals, and reporting them to German police units. [53]

Stahlecker confirmed that local inhabitants in the Baltic States promptly and extensively collaborated in implementing the massacres.

37

In Lithuania, those participating in the shootings were on a ratio of one German to eight Lithuanians. He does mention, however, that attempts to organize pogroms in Latvia were unsuccessful. In that country, the locals killed "only several thousand Jews". All in all, Stahlecker did not consider pogroms an effective military technique, and believed that the strategy should be abandoned in favour of a more organized system of shooting Jews. Still, the report indicated that,

> The attitude of the Lithuanian population is friendly toward the Germans so far. They help the German soldiers, police officials, and other organizations already functioning in the area as much as possible. Their cooperation consists mainly in looking for and turning in Lithuanian Communists, unattached Red Army soldiers, and Jews.[54]

The report states that, during the first days of the occupation, 7800 Jews had been liquidated in Kaunas.[55]

In his report, Karl Jaeger, of EK-3, listed the figures for the Jews still alive as follows: in Shiauliai (Shavli), about 4500; in Kaunas (Kovno), about 15,000; in Vilnius (Vilno), about 15,000. These statistics were not quite accurate. At the end of 1941, there were several smaller ghettos still in existence in addition to those he mentioned. He also pointed out that,

> It was possible to achieve the goal of cleansing Lithuania of Jews only thanks to the setting up of the mobile squad formed with select men and headed by Joachim Hamann, who understood my goals perfectly and was able to enlist the support of the Lithuanian partisans and the respective civil offices... In each town and region it was necessary to gather all the Jews in one place, find a location for the shooting, and dig an appropriately large ditch. On average, the distance from the gathering places to the ditches was four to five kilometers. The Jews were driven to the execution sites in groups of 500. The partisans were able to conduct up to five such operations per week.[56]

Ending his report, Jaeger stresses that,

> The operations in Kaunas, where we had a sufficient num-
> ber of trained partisans, can be considered exemplary as
> a parade shooting, especially in comparison to the enor-
> mous difficulties we faced elsewhere...All of my unit com-
> manders and my commando men participated actively in
> the large Kaunas operations. Only one Habitual Crimi-
> nals Registry official was excused from taking part in these
> actions because of illness.[57]

Jaeger notes that, from July 2 to the end of August, 6033 Jews were
killed at the Sixth and Seventh Forts of Kaunas[58]. From September
on, the executions of Jews in Kaunas were moved from the Seventh
Fort to the Ninth Fort. Not only Jews, but also other victims, were
murdered at the execution site of the Ninth Fort, as well as Jews from
other Western Europe countries[59]. On November 25, and 29, 1941,
4934 Jews from Germany, including 327 children, were shot there.
About 3000 Jews from Czechoslovakia, Germany, and Austria[60] were
also 're-located' to the Ninth Fort and murdered there on December
11, 1941. Altogether, over 10,000 Jews from Western Europe were
killed at the Ninth Fort, among them 5500 children.[67]

According to Stahlecker's report, 81,171 Jews were killed in
Lithuania between June 24 and October 15, 1941.By December 1,
1941, 131,494 Jews had been executed and 4000 killed by Lithuanians in pogroms. An astonishing total of 135,494 Jews, or 75-80%
of the pre-war Lithuanian Jewish population, had been killed in less
than, six months[62] These reports, testimonies of witnesses, and other
documents indicate that the mass murder of the Jew began in Lithuania on June 24, 1941.

THE AFTERMATH

To date, Holocaust history researchers have not come across any documents indicating that Germany had raised the issue of the destruction
of the Jews prior to the end of 1941. As late as 1941, Adolf Hitler had
no single plan for the annihilation of the Jews and considered forced

emigration to be the best means of solving the 'Jewish question' in Germany and Central Europe. In his analysis of the situation of the Jews in Europe between 1938 and 1945, historian Gerald Reitlinger has come to the conclusion that, before the end of 1941, Germany had no master plan for the total extermination of the Jews. Nor is there any evidence of group executions of Jews in German-occupied territories prior to mid-1941. Although Jews were persecuted and forcibly moved into ghettos in German-occupied Poland, there are no known or documented incidents of mass killings of Jews in that country before the Soviet-German war at the end of June 1941[63]. A German historian Goetz Aly stated that mass murder of Jews began in 1942. It was the time during which the decision to exterminate the Jews were taken. Yehuda Bauer in his book *Rethinking the Holocaust* writes that Aly's conlusions are instructive and based on impressive documentation.[64]

The first group killings of Jews took place in the Lithuanian city of Gargzhdai which were followed several days later by massacres in Kretinga and Palanga. This 'innovative' Lithuanian experiment of mass killings of Jews apparently met with approval and satisfaction at the headquarters of the German Security Police in Berlin. It is most likely that suggestions were made to continue the process in Latvia, Estonia, Belarus, and the Ukraine, whose territories were occupied after Lithuania.

Following the 'successful' massacres of Jews from June to December 1941, a conference of Nazi leaders was held on January 20, 1942 in Berlin, am Grossen Wannsee, during which a plan for the total extermination of European Jewry, the so-called 'Final Solution of the Jewish Question', was officially adopted. According to the protocol, approximately 11,000,000 Jews would be involved in the Final Solution of the European Jewish Question. Among others, in Lithuania, 34,000 Jews would be slated for extermination and in Latvia, 3500. Estonia was already free of Jews[65].

The success of the experiment in Lithuania was related to two extremely important factors. First, local partisan and armed civilian units formed prior to the German occupation readily agreed to be recruited into the German Security Police and to participate in the killings. On his 1991 visit to Lithuania, the prominent historian and political scientist at the Kennedy School of Government, Harvard University, Michael Ignatieff, met with witnesses of those horrific events and with several Vilnius University professors. He wrote that the murderers were not a handful of sadists and criminals that helped the Nazis kill Jews in occupied Lithuania, but thousands of Lithuanians[43]. Of course, the essence of the matter does not rest in numbers, either of those killed or of those who conducted the killings. What is important, rather, is the fact that about two-thirds of the Jews killed in Lithuania died at the hands of local partisans or members of the Lithuanian police battalions. In other words, the collaboration of local inhabitants gave a clear signal to the occupying forces that there were sufficient numbers of people willing to help them accomplish the task of 'cleansing' Lithuania of Jews.[66]

Since the German invasion of Lithuania progressed very quickly, there were a very limited number of Jews who were able to escape to the East. Many of those who did attempt to flee for the Germans, or the local partisans, intercepted their lives. Inspired by Lithuanian Activist Front propaganda and eager to contribute to their protectors' plans to purge Lithuania of undesirable elements, the partisans arrested and pronounced these people as 'agents, provocateurs, and communists'. Most of them were shot on the spot.

The passivity of the Catholic Church was another important factor that contributed to the Nazis' success in organizing the massacre of Lithuania's Jews. The official church in Lithuania did little, if anything, to condemn the killing of Jews and was indifferent to the tragedy of their Jewish neighbours. Though some individual members of the clergy spoke out, and even sheltered Jewish people, in general not a single Lithuanian institution either openly condemned or protested what was happening.

The LAF-controlled mass media, which continuously instigated and inspired public hatred of the Jews, also aided in the massacre. Directly or indirectly, they pushed their people to participate in mass murder. One cannot but fully agree with Lithuanian Parliamentary Deputy, Vytautas Plechkaitis, in his view that,

> The Provisional Government must bear full responsibility for everything that took place in Lithuanian prior to the Nazis' complete occupation of the country, [including]...the

41

pogroms initiated against the Jews, their murders, and the confiscation of their property. [67]

Clearly, neither the Provisional Government, nor the local administrations under its jurisdiction, opposed the arrests and killing of Jews that began well before the establishment of the German civilian administration. The documents prove that the PG was continually informed about the massacres and that many appeals were made to them to stop the killings. Significant numbers of Lithuanians called upon the PG, and other government institutions, to restrain the murderers. Shocked by the brutal annihilation of entire Jewish families during those tragic days and seeking support from powerful individuals, Colonel Dr. B. Matulionis and the Reverend Father Leonardas Morkunas appealed to Archbishop Juozas Skvireckas.

It is also worth mentioning that the Minister of Communal Affairs, the architect, Vytautas Landsbergis-Zemkalnis, stressed during a government meeting that he had witnessed an incident of Jews being beaten in Vytautas Prospect. Holding his head in his hands, the minister was visibly angered as he spoke. Other officials participating in the meeting also urged the Minister of the Interior, Jonas Shlepetis, to put an end to these beatings.. Shlepetis replied dryly that it was impossible to do so at the time. [68]

The prominent members of the Jewish community continuously appealed to various Kaunas government institutions. Rabbi Shmuel Sniegas, Chief Rabbi of the Independent Lithuanian Army, and many others, asked these institutions to restrain and bring the activities of the partisans under control. During those days, the Jews of Kaunas elected a delegation which sought to set up a meeting with the Provisional Government of Lithuania. The government, however, refused to see them. General Stasys Rashtikis did agree to meet with them, but after some discussion, the General explained that he, personally, could do nothing for the Jews. The delegation was also told that, due to the confusion sweeping the country, the government was unable to stop the attacks.

It is evident that it was not just a question of the government's inability to stop the killings. The PG had consciously adopted an anti-Semitic policy. Moreover, the policy consisted, not only of obeying the occupying forces, but of pleasing and abetting the occupiers as much as possible. During the months of June and July 1941, not one member of Lithuanian Provisional Government attempted to stop the murder of Jews. Men, women, and children; old people, ex-communists, and rabbis; wealthy businessmen and beggars; former parliamentarians and prisoners of the Soviet regime – all were executed simply because they were Jews.

It is safe to say, therefore, that the Lithuanian Provisional Government, its administration, and the LAF and its military battalions fully collaborated with the Nazi regime, participated in the mass killings, and contributed to the implementation of the 'Final solution' for Lithuanian Jews.

On August 4, 1941, the General Commissar of the occupational administration, von Adrian Renteln declared that, with the introduction of the civilian administration, the work of the Lithuanian Provisional Government was over. But several members of the PG were offered positions as advisors to Renteln. The next day, within a few hours of when the PG gave up power, German administration confiscated its offices, furniture and typewriter.

On September 22, the Germans prohibited further activity of the LAF and confiscated all of the organization's property.

Meanwhile, on July 7, 1941, the Germans informed the members of the Committee of the Jewish Community in Kaunas that a ghetto was to be established in the suburb of Kaunas known as Vilijampole (Slabodka). On July 10, the Military Commandant of Kaunas, Jurgis Bobelis, ordered all Jews of Kaunas to move into the designated area in Vilijampole. On July 12, legislation was passed forcing the relocation of the Jews of Kaunas into the Ghetto in the suburb of Kaunas – Vilijampole.

The relocation of the Jews into the designated ghetto area marked the end of the first phase of the Jewish catastrophe and the beginning of total destruction of the Jews of Lithuania.

"One could say," noted Arunas Bubnys, "that Lithuania was the first country occupied by the Nazis in which, from the very beginning, the policy of physically annihilating the Jews was carried out." [69] One must, therefore, agree with the opinion of some Lithuanian historians that Lithuania was unique in the way in which it treated its Lithuanian Jewish citizens.

Part Two

Return to the Dark Ages

MOVING INTO THE GHETTO

The concept of 'ghetto' originated in the Middle Ages, but in the German-occupied territories, ghettos referred to designated parts of cities in which all of the Jews of that town and its surrounding regions were forced to live. Foreign Jews, as well as children of mixed marriages, were also moved into the ghetto. These areas were generally surrounded by barbed wire fences and guarded by special police battalions. Ghetto inhabitants lived in huts or small houses and families were usually allowed to remain together but all Jews were prohibited from leaving or entering the ghetto without permission or without an armed escort. The Jewish population, regardless of age and sex, was obliged to wear, inside and outside the ghetto, a yellow Star of David on their left chest and on their back as they were deliberately and systematically isolated from the outside world. In addition to all these humiliations, ghetto dwellers were forced to perform unpaid, heavy slave labour at various work places established by the Germans.

Apart from these traits, which were common to all ghettos in the German-occupied territories, each ghetto was marked by its own specific administrative and living conditions, its degree of isolation, and its own particular methods of survival and imprisonment. Each ghetto was a world of its own, an irrational and incomprehensible world. The Kaunas Ghetto, which existed for more than three year, from August 15, 1941 until its liquidation on July 12, 1944, was one of many ghettos it in Nazi-occupied countries. It was one of many, but at the same time, it was different from the others.

In July 1941, the Nazis ordered the appointment of a Council of Elders of the Kaunas Jewish Community (*Aeltestenrat der Juedischen Ghetto Gemeinde Kauen*) and a chairman who was disparagingly referred to as the Eldest Jew (*Oberjude*). A highly respected Kaunas physician, Elchanan Elkes, was elected as chairman. The Germans sought to establish a Jewish administration, drawing its members from within the Jewish community itself, who would help them in achieving their goals. The Committee would be responsible for the immediate and precise execution of all German orders, including moving the Jews into the ghetto. Later, the Committee would be in charge of managing the internal affairs of the ghetto and enforcing German decrees within its territory. The Committee was ordered to organize the relocation of the Kaunas Jews to the ghetto, to work out the transport routes and schedules, and to oversee housing and other related matters. The Germans decreed that the territory of the ghetto be marked by a barbed wire fence, and that the fence be erected by the Jews themselves.

The ghetto, established in the Kaunas suburb of Vilijampole (Slabodka), was a small area of two kilometers in length by one kilometer in width. Prior to the German occupation, the Vilijampole-Slabodka district was home to about 6000 Jews and was the poorest and most underdeveloped area of the city, with no sewage and water supply system. All the Jews in Kaunas, approximately 30,000 people, were ordered to move into a territory previously populated by 7000 to 8000 people. Their living space would consist of about 2.5 square meters per person.

From the end of July 1941, all matters pertaining to Kaunas' Jewish population were handled by authorities of the German special forces. The Germans in charge were as follows. Commander Karl Jaeger, Einsatzkommando 3 and his deputy, SS Captain Heinrich Schtitz, head of SD Fourth Section (Gestapo). The key figure in deciding the fate of the Jews in Kaunas Ghetto was SA Colonel Hans Cramer, the Governor of Kaunas City and Commandant of Kaunas Ghetto. His deputy was SA Captain Fritz Jordan, Chief German Administrator of Jewish Affairs in the Ghetto. Master Sergeant Helmut Rauca was head of the Jewish Affairs Department of the Gestapo. Special Lithuanian police battalions and other military units were appointed to guard the ghetto and were involved in the mass killings at the Seventh, Ninth, and other Forts. Besides these, Lithuanian auxiliary police were in charge of identifying, rounding up, and arresting Jews who were in hiding around the city and then handing these Jews over to the German security forces. The German Security Police were assisted by Latvian, Estonian, and Ukrainian police battalions. Some ordinary

Lithuanian citizens were ready to assist the police in their operations against partisans, spies, Jews, and other enemies of the Third Reich.

The ghetto itself was divided into two separate areas which were linked by a medieval-style wooden footbridge. These two distinct sections could be isolated from one another by simply blocking the bridge, thus allowing the Germans to control the inmates, preventing a large group of ghetto prisoners from gathering in one place or organizing a revolt. It also facilitated the deportation of their victims. The larger part of the ghetto was called the Big Ghetto; the smaller one, the Small Ghetto. Running under the wooden bridge, Paneriu Street was outside the ghetto boundary and was the dividing line of the two parts of the ghetto. Within the Big Ghetto was the old Jewish quarter of Slabodka which extended to the Christian cemetery. A small corridor along the fenced cemetery joined the old quarter of Slabodka to the main part of the ghetto. Krikschiukaichio and Varniu Streets were the two major roads in the ghetto. At one end of Krikschiukaichio Street was the new Jewish ghetto cemetery. The other end of the street ran very close to the bridge spanning the Neris River which connected Kaunas and Vilijampole.

There were two main entrances to the ghetto, with one at the beginning of Krischiukaichiu Street and the other at Varniu Street. These entrances led, in one direction, to the city and, in the other, to the Ninth Fort. The ghetto and its gates were guarded by a Lithuanian police battalion led by Jonas Stelmokas and consisted of about 100 policemen. This battalion was responsible both for guarding the ghetto and executing Jews at the Ninth Fort.

In preparation for the relocation of the Jews to the ghetto, the newly appointed Kaunas Military Commandant, Stasys Kviecinskas, issued a decree specifying which clothing and other personal belongings would be permitted into the ghetto. The boundaries of the ghetto were drawn up by the Minister of the Lithuanian Provisional Government, Landsbergis-Zemkalnis, and the document establishing the ghetto was signed by the Kaunas Commandant Kviecinskas. On August 15, 1941, the ghetto was completely sealed off.

Following the Nazi decree, the Jewish Committee established in the ghetto a Jewish police force. They were responsible for maintaining internal order and carrying out German commands. All of these police officers were required to be young, physically strong, and have had some military training. Three police departments operated in the ghetto, each of which had its police chief, deputy police chiefs, and its senior and rank-and-file officers. Each of the approximately 200 officers was issued a blue cap and a special arm band denoting his rank. The Jewish police had the authority to arrest and take into custody ghetto inmates who were found breaking the rules.

There is no question that the Jewish police officers struggled to find a balance between their forced service to the Nazis and their readiness to help and support the Kaunas ghetto community. Jewish police officers occasionally used force, especially while guarding the gates, and there were isolated instances in which they were forced to help the Germans arrest and deport people. On the other hand, a considerable numbers of Jewish policemen were involved in, and supported, the underground resistance movement in the ghetto. They warned underground activists of impending dangers, *Akzions,* and deportations. Some ghetto policemen helped the underground smuggle fighters and weapons through the gates. Throughout the entire history of the Kaunas Ghetto, there was not one major incident of a Jewish policeman informing on the ghetto underground and resistance activists. The vast majority of these officers refused to reveal underground hiding places to the Germans or to search for ghetto inmates hiding from the Nazis.

Despite the unprecedented circumstances in which they found themselves, the Jewish Committee, its administrative apparatus, and the Jewish police force functioned as all bureaucracies do. Members of the Committee, the administration's employees, and the foremen of the ghetto work brigades and workshops comprised the ghetto community's elite. Their employees and relatives enjoyed various privileges. Some of the high level administrators felt like all-powerful rulers and often treated people who came to see them rudely and arrogantly.

While the Jewish Committee did everything possible to preserve life in the ghetto, this was often done at the expense of certain groups within the community. The Committee had to sacrifice the lives of some people in the hope of saving others and, indeed, the ghetto community as a whole. They were commanded to draw up lists of those ghetto residents who were to be deported and to organize the handing over of the victims to the Nazis. Coerced by their oppressors, the Committee was often forced to make very difficult and painful decisions. Who would be condemned to deportation? Who would be allowed to live a little longer? There is no question that members of the Jewish administration cooperated with the Nazis in the questions of property, of delivering people up to slave labour, and of deportation. On the other hand, both the members of the Jewish Committee and the ghetto police did everything in their power to help the ghetto community survive.

Our family's relocation to the ghetto was organized by my sister, her husband, and my mother's brother-in-law, Lazer Jurovitski. While preparations were being made, Mother and I tended my father, who was dying, and packed our belongings. Mother dried bread, cooked jams, and occasionally went out to the market. Inexhaustible, she was preparing supplies for the long winter ahead. My father, by this point, was indifferent to all the preparations. Earthly matters no longer concerned him for he sensed that he would not survive the winter. Full of sorrow, it saddened him that he had not died earlier so that he would not have to lie helpless and watch his family's suffering and possible demise. He did not believe the Germans' placating words and doubted that any of us would survive the occupation. It had been futile, he felt, to have lived for fifty years only to witness these ghastly days.

Our turn to move to the ghetto came at the beginning of August. Along with thousands of Kaunas Jews, we were to join the caravans of carriages that pushed along those roads designated for the move into the ghetto. My parents and I would be exchanging our apartment on Bugos Street for one room and a kitchen in Vilijampole and we were bringing with us two beds, a sofa, a table and chairs, some household items, clothing, and food reserves. Our new residence was not far from the Jewish Committee's headquarters and the Varniu Street gates.

My sister Alice and her husband were also moving into the Big Ghetto, with Philip's parents, not far away from our rooms. The rest of our relatives were being settled in the Small Ghetto.

While my parents remained on Bugos Street, I made the trip to Vilijampole on my own with a rented, horse-drawn cart piled high with our possessions. It took me eight hours to make the five kilometer trip from Kaunas to the ghetto. When I arrived at the house, I was exhausted and disheartened. I found a small but tidy one-family house which had neither plumbing nor running water. There were two kitchens and two entrances and the other rooms and the larger kitchen were already occupied by two Jewish families who would be our new neighbours. In the backyard there was a well and a small outdoor wooden structure containing two toilets.

I entered the house and consoled myself with the thought that there was, at least, electricity. But when I saw that our room was quite bright and spacious, I felt somehow better. I began hanging our clothes on the walls, stored things under the bed and the sofa, and deposited our cupboard and table in the kitchen. It felt good to know that all of our belongings would fit into our new home. By the time I returned to Kaunas, it was early evening.

We spent a few more nights in our old apartment and, on our last evening there, we all took baths. I lay in the water for a long time thinking how wonderful it was to have a bath with hot running water, and wondered when and where I would have my next proper bath. Or, I pondered, would I even live to see such a day.

We had received permission to transport my father to the ghetto by an easier route. On August 12, 1941, we made our way fairly quickly until we reached the bridge over the Neris River. There, we had to wait in line and it took several hours before we were finally in our new home. When my mother walked into the room, she burst into tears. Alice brought in water and made some tea. She covered the windows and turned on the light. This was to be our new life. Or was it really life? It would be more accurate to say that our real life had come to an end and we were entering the unknown.

As my father grew weaker and his pain grew greater, he slept most of the time. When he was awake, he would continuously repeat, "Why must I suffer such a fate? Why am I condemned to drink the poison to the very last drop?" Every day, a doctor we knew came to give him an injection of sedatives. On the night of August 24, his pain became unbearable and he did not sleep at all. In the morning, the doctor rushed back and gave him another injection to calm him down. When my father fell asleep, I took the opportunity to get some fresh air and ran over to my sister's. When I returned home a short time later, my father was lying in the bed covered with a white sheet and Mother sat quietly weeping. Not yet fifty, my father Josif Ginas was no longer with us.

My mother, as if in a trance, told us the story of how he died. He had opened his eyes and was about to say something. Just at that moment, a strong gust of wind blew open the window and, rushing to close it, she had missed what he was saying. When she returned to his bedside, he was no longer breathing. The neighbours called the doctor who covered my father with the white sheet and issued a death certificate. For the next twenty-four hours, my father remained with us, laying on the bed, covered with the sheet. Then we buried him, in keeping with all the Jewish rituals, at the new Jewish cemetery close to the banks of the Neris River. His grave was in a first row and it was marked 'No.3'. In the row behind him, there were 10 children buried. We sat *Shiva* (in mourning) for him for a full week, according to the traditions of the Jewish faith and every evening, ten or more men gathered in our room to say the *Kaddish*, the Jewish prayer of mourning, and to pray for my father's soul.

Now my mother and I were left alone. That brought us close together, though. I started to feel, not only was I a part of her, but that she had become a part of me. I desperately wanted her to survive this horrible time and to see happier days. I wanted to bestow all my love to her and devote myself to her protection. But it was not to be. I was unable to save her and she later died at the Stutthof Concentration Camp in Germany. I do not even know where her grave is. Many years after the war, I transferred my father's remains from Kaunas to the Vilnius Jewish Cemetery and erected a symbolic gravestone for my mother next to him.

The German war machine required a cheap work force and the Nazis turned the ghetto into a slave labour camp. All ghetto inmates from 16 to 60 years of age were forced to perform compulsory labour. Boys were required to begin at 14 to15 years of age. The Jewish labour office was in charge of assigning the slave labour, finding the number of workers required by the Germans, allocating them to various sites, ensuring that they report to the gates and the conveyances that would take them to their workplaces. Many of the inmates worked in military factories, maintenance and repair shops, and other German establishments and companies. They worked as locksmiths, electricians, fire-stokers, repair persons, cleaners, builders, and ditch diggers. It was very difficult to obtain better work, closer to the city, where it was warmer and where slightly better meals were provided. Only highly qualified specialists or inmates who had connections to the Jewish Committee had a better chance. If someone wanted to change their work or to join a newly formed brigade, they had to apply to the Jewish labour office. The better workplaces were generally reserved for family and friends of the ghetto elite. Those without a permanent job were ordered to appear each morning at the gates to be sent wherever there was a shortage of labourers. Every employable ghetto resident carried an employment card issued by the Jewish Committee that contained all of his or her personal information.

About 7000 workers reported each morning at the Krischiu-kaichiu Street gates, where they waited for their armed escorts. After being counted, they were herded quickly through the narrow opening in the gate. Some were driven by truck to the work sites while others were made to walk in formation along the streets of Kaunas to their workplaces. In the evenings, they returned to the gates, carrying their bundles. Exhausted from the heavy labour, and hungry, they wait their turn for inspection before being let back into the ghetto.

Overnight, I too was transformed from a middle class Jewish student to a slave labourer. My first job under the German occupation was at the airfield. My brother-in-law, Philip, who had refused to work for the Jewish Committee, was already working there, while Alice worked in the laundry and my mother stayed at home. The first shift for the airfield met at the ghetto gate at seven o'clock in the morning for the almost seven kilometer walk to the labour site. Working outside was difficult and we only received one bowl of soup a day. At the end of the day, tired and hungry, we walked back to the ghetto.

Food was one of the greatest problems we faced in the ghetto. The food supplies reached the ghetto in various ways. The minimal food rations established by the Germans were delivered to the Jewish Committee which in turn distributed the food among the inmates. The weekly food ration for each individual was meager and hardly met minimal human nutritional needs. It consisted of 700 grams of bread, 112.5 grams of flour, 112.5 grams of meat (often consisting of frozen horsemeat), 20 grams of lard, 50 grams of salt, and coffee or tea substitutes. But, despite the strict rules forbidding the bringing of food into the ghetto, many prisoners risked their lives getting around the rules to smuggle food into the ghetto in numerous illegal ways. One means was by 'trade' through the fence. Although the Lithuanian police officers guarding the gates had the right to shoot anyone going near the fence, without warning, ghetto inhabitants persisted in conducting their mortally dangerous business. The *czamniks* (fence merchants – from the Hebrew word *czam*, meaning barrier) made deals with the policemen guarding the fence. For a hefty bribe, the policemen would turn away from the fence and pretend they didn't know what was going on there. During periods of relative calm, barter through the fence went swiftly and smoothly. However, it was a very risky undertaking. The *czamniks* might be seen by passersby, higher ranking police officers, or inspectors. Those caught trading were immediately arrested, handed over to the Germans, and usually taken to the Ninth Fort for execution. Their families often met the same fate. Trade usually slowed down after such arrests, only to resume again after a short while by other brave young people. Fence trade continued in this way as long as the ghetto existed.

Defying strict prohibitions and risking their lives, ghetto labourers who worked in the city also sought to exchange their meager belongings for food. It was just as dangerous to acquire foodstuffs as it was to smuggle them through the ghetto fence. Every worker returning from work had to undergo a search at the gates which was conducted by either the Lithuanian police or special Nazi personnel. Jewish police officers were also involved. The nature of these inspections varied considerably. Sometimes the workers passed them easily, while at other times, the process was strict and brutal. On rare occasions, high ranking Nazi officers participated in the search. At these critical times, even the smallest quantity of food was confiscated and the guilty worker subjected to humiliating punishment. Yet, despite the risks involved, hundreds of Jewish workers brought food back with them from the city. They concealed it in the false bottoms of toolboxes, attached it to their bodies and hid it in the heels of their shoes. The availability of these illicit food products slowly improved the diet of some of the ghetto inhabitants because, at least those who had money or possessions, were able to purchase food in the ghetto's black market. The Jewish administration also received additional food products, most of which it distributed to the hospital, the orphanage, and the soup kitchen for the poorest people.

From the very first day of in the ghetto, the Nazis imposed brutally strict rules regulating the life and work of the prisoners. The Germans confiscated all our valuables and the ghetto inmates were warned that anyone failing to obey these orders would be shot on the spot. They took our money, gold and silver objects, electrical appliances, furs, and many other goods. On the day of confiscation, some people obeyed the orders and handed in their valuables, some threw their valuables down a well, others still tried to hide them.

Inmates were prohibited from reading newspapers or listening to the radio, from passing on or receiving letters or messages, from speaking on the telephone, or walking the streets of Kaunas without written permission or a guard. The prisoners were strictly forbidden to leave their workplaces unescorted, to interact with non-Jews, Germans, or prisoners-of-war. Jews were not allowed to buy food in the city, to receive gifts, or to bring anything into the ghetto from the outside. As time passed, more and more requirements and humiliating restrictions were imposed. All the while, the terror, the executions, and deportations never abated.

Notwithstanding the horrible reality of existence in the ghetto, there were inmates who naively believed that they would survive if they worked conscientiously and followed the Germans' orders. Despite the terrifying situation, most of the people in the ghetto tried to keep hope alive that they would overcome the terrible times. To the majority, hope meant not waiting idly for that day of deliverance. They sought ways of escaping, of building hiding places, of discussing ways to revolt, to resist, to fight the Nazis and their collaborators, or, at least, to die with dignity.

The Nazis developed a remarkably comprehensive system of deceiving their Jewish victims. At the beginning of July 1941, the Germans assured us that they intended to restore order and to end the terror imposed on the Jews by the Lithuanian partisans. They claimed that, by moving the Jews to the ghetto, they were protecting them from being shot in the Kaunas forts or massacred in the streets and backyards of the city. They said that the Jews would have their own government in the ghetto and that the only requirement would be to work. The Jews went into the ghetto believing there would be safety or, at least, the absence of the violent deaths that they had experienced in the first weeks of German occupation of Kaunas, The people were uncertain. They did not know and could not possibly imagine what the Nazis had planned for them. No one could have conceived that the Germans were capable of slaughtering a whole people. The Germans wrapped their deception in lies and false hope. Leading people to execution, the Nazis suggested that the prisoners be sure to bring sufficient food and warm clothing with them, thus shrouding their victims in a thick cloud of illusion. Misled, frightened, and confused, these innocent people could not believe, until the very last moment, that they were about to be killed.

The logic behind this strategy was not complicated. The Germans simply wanted to avoid even the slightest revolt. They wanted their victims to go to their deaths calmly, quietly, without panic, or disruptions. They did not, however, succeed in achieving this. Very quickly, the Jews came to understand the Nazis' true intentions. The hope to survive never entirely disappears and most of the Jews did not sit idly by, waiting to be slaughtered. Organized and spontaneous revolts, as well as armed uprisings and confrontations, took place in all of the ghettos and even in the concentration camps. The Nazis leading their victims to their deaths in gas chambers or carrying out executions were often attacked, disarmed, injured, or simply killed, even though it was well known that such actions would mean a more brutal death. Men, women, and even children in the Ghettos resisted.

THE TERROR CONTINUES

During the first weeks of life in the ghetto, it actually seemed that the tyranny and chaos of the beginning of the war had ended for the Jews. Despite the imposed slave labour, severe restrictions, and the poor food and housing, it was tempting to believe the Nazi promises of no more massacres or executions. However, that illusion proved to be short-lived and the Nazis' true intentions became evident very quickly.

Soon after the ghetto was sealed, the Germans demanded that the Jewish Committee gather a group of 500 university-educated men to work on an urgent assignment. Allegedly, they were to work at City Hall, sorting archives. The Committee, believing the Nazis' promise that these men would be returned to the ghetto soon, collected 534 lawyers, engineers, teachers, and journalists – in short, the shining stars of the Kaunus Jewish community. It was inconceivable to everyone, including the men's families, that these men were being taken for any other reason than work and that they would not soon be returned. On August 18, 1941, SA Captain, Fritz Jordan, accompanied by Mikas Kaminskas, an employee and translator for the Kaunas municipal government, piled the men into trucks and drove off. Not a single one of the men ever returned.

By mid-September, a strange rumour began to circulate that skilled craftspeople were being issued special permits signed by Captain Jordan himself. The rumour was soon confirmed and the Jewish Committee received 5000 of these 'Jordan Certificates'. It seemed clear that this document was a passport to life and that something out of the ordinary was about to happen. Everyone in the ghetto anxiously waited to see how and when these permits could be used and what would happen to those who didn't have one. Members of the Committee distributed the certificates to their own families, friends, employees, and the craftspeople who were already working for Jordan.

On October 2, Jordan arrived in the ghetto with an escort. He inspected the Small Ghetto: its hospital, its orphanage, and the wooden bridge connecting the two parts of the ghetto. Then he drove off. The next day it was announced that lepers had been discovered in the hospital; that neither the hospital nor the orphanage was upholding sanitary standards and both buildings were immediately disinfected.

The morning of October 4 didn't begin differently from any other. As usual, people rushed to the gates to be assigned to work details, others went to the workshops, and the medical personnel went to the hospital. But around 8 am, a small German police unit and a Lithuanian police battalion arrived in the ghetto. Soldiers armed with machine-guns manned the bridge, blocking it to any except those families holding 'Jordan certificates'. Everyone else was ordered to return home. The remaining soldiers marched toward the hospital. Dr. Moses Brauns, the Jewish director of the hospital, immediately warned the patients of impending danger and encouraged all those who were able, to go home. Meantime, the Germans ordered all the remaining inhabitants of the Small Ghetto to gather at Union Square (*Sajungos*). Again, only those families with certificates were allowed to leave the square and cross the wooden bridge to the Big Ghetto. Those remaining in the square were shoved into canvas-covered trucks and driven to the Ninth Fort. The hospital, now guarded by soldiers, was boarded up so that those inside could not leave. Its wooden walls were soaked with gasoline and the building was set on fire, trapping all the personnel and the hospital's 67 patients inside. The building next to the hospital also caught fire, but nobody attempted to extinguish the flames. All of the prisoners who had been driven away in the trucks were executed at the Ninth Fort that same day. On October 6, those in possession of 'Jordan Certificates' were given a few hours to retrieve their belongings from their homes in the Small Ghetto and were relocated to the Big Ghetto. That was the first *Aktzion*, the so-called 'Small Ghetto Aktzion'. The terror continued...

Although the Small Ghetto ceased to exist on October 6, 1941, the barbed wire and the wooden bridge remained in place. My uncle Lazar, the only member of my family who was issued a 'Jordan Certificate' had been able to cross the bridge with his wife Berta, his sister-in-law, Fanya, and her toddler. My aunt Fanya and her little daughter, Tanya, who was less than a year old, moved into the room I now shared with my mother. Although there were now four of us living in one room, listening to the child babbling cheerfully somehow strengthened our desire to live. We longed for the war to end, longed to see Germany destroyed and retribution meted out to our torturers and murderers. But, even though there seemed to be a lull at the ghetto after the first *Aktzion*, liberation was still a long way off and, as Mother always said, "before the sun will rise, the dew will drown our eyes".

Less then three weeks after the Small Ghetto Aktzion, again a black limousine entered the ghetto. The vehicle drove around the entire ghetto and suddenly stopped at the large Demokratu Square. Nazi officials headed by Gestapo Deputy Chief, Master Sergeant Helmut Rauca looked the square over and drove off. A wave of suspicion instantly spread through the ghetto. Members of the Jewish Committee and their staff couldn't understand why the Gestapo officials had not stopped, either at the Committee headquarters or at any of the other offices. Everyone debated what it could mean and what measures should be taken. The next day, a Gestapo vehicle appeared again. This time it stopped at the Committee building and Helmut Rauca, accompanied by another official, went inside and demanded to see Dr. Elkes. They had a brief conversation. Rauca announced that the war effort required more workers. Moreover, he added, the 'nutrition' of the workers and their living conditions needed to be improved so as to maximize their efficiency. The Gestapo had decided to separate workers and their families from those unfit to work. The latter would be relocated to the Small Ghetto.

Refusing to discuss the issue further, Rauca assured Elkes that there was no threat of death. He demanded that the Committee post an announcement saying that on October 28, 1941, the entire ghetto population, without exception, was to assemble in Demokratu Square at 10 am.

The ghetto inmates were told to gather in family groups according to their work units. Workers were to stand in the first row, members of their families behind them. The foremen of the work units were to stand at the head and be ready to produce work certificates. The approximate positions in the square of the work units were established and Rauca ordered that everyone, regardless of age, sex, or state of health, must be present. The infirm were to be brought in chairs or on stretchers. The doors of houses and apartments were to remain open. Having defined the orders, Rauca and his associate got back into their limousine and left.

Fear and panic now took hold of the Committee and the ghetto population. During his conversation with Rauca, Dr. Elkes had attempted to appeal to the Nazi's conscience. When that didn't work, he promised Rauca gifts, currency in Swiss banks, and many other bribes. But nothing moved Rauca. He replied quietly and in perfect calm that everything had already been decided, that there was no cause for worry, and that this was strictly an administrative measure. Unconvinced by Rauca's seeming civility, Elkes tried to reach Captain Jordan. He spoke to lower-ranking officials but none of his attempts produced any explanations as to the true nature of the operation. By this point, the entire ghetto was shaken and anxious. The panic increased as news reached the ghetto from Lithuanians living near the Ninth Fort that Soviet prisoners-of-war had been digging large ditches at the fort. It was then that the Committee members realized they had no power and that there were no rational solutions.

The Jews had only been in the ghetto for three months and had not had the opportunity to organize themselves. They did not know how to behave or resist under such extreme circumstances. There were no connections yet with the anti-Nazi underground movement or with individuals outside the ghetto who might be willing to help. The ghetto inmates had no weapons or hiding places, no organized, or even individual, resistance strategies. Until the last moment, the Committee tried to talk the Nazis out of what they were sure would be a tragedy.

The Gestapo decree was posted the day before the *Aktzion*. People responded in different ways to the horror. Overcome by a sense of fatality, some inmates made no effort to save themselves. They put their faith in God, that He might help them. Others believed that the sooner they died, the better. The Germans would kill them all eventually anyway, so why continue to suffer and be humiliated by their oppressors. Still others felt compelled to act, to do what they could to prevent the Nazis from herding them like sheep to the slaughter. A few probably managed to escape and find sanctuary with Lithuanian friends in the city. Most, though, tried desperately to figure out how to survive by improving their families' positions, joining a better work brigade, or trying to look younger and healthier. Worried that single people were more likely to be taken, some even tried to attach themselves to families. Others still sought to reduce the number of unemployable individuals in their families.

Our family seemed to have no advantages for the selection. Alice's husband Philip worked at the airfield and his brigade was stationed at the far end of the square. His parents and sister Rita were to join them there. Because Alice, Philip, and Rita were all young and looked good, they hoped for the best. My uncle Lazar, who had a certificate, was not very worried. His wife Berta, his sister-in-law, Zina, and her daughter Nadya would join him at his brigade's station. One man and three women was not the best combination, but they hoped the certificate would make up for that. But what about my mother, Fanya, the baby, Tanya, and me.

I worked at the airfield which did not issue certificates. It was obvious that three women and a child had little chance at the selection. We decided that it was essential for us to find a man that would agree to join us. All of our relatives set about trying to find a single, sincere person.

Late on the night of October 27, a young man around thirty years old came to our room. Dovid Glikman was from a small town and had worked and studied law at Kaunas University before the war. During the first weeks of the occupation, he had lost his entire family and now, in the ghetto, he worked as a rank-and-file ghetto policeman. Dovid felt sure that a single man would be among the first to be taken away and he was reluctant to go to the selection alone. Mother and Fanya spoke with him late into the night and he agreed to take all four of us with him to the police work unit. When he left, Dovid promised to return early the next morning so that we could march to the gathering place together.

It was a terrifying night. We all sensed that the morning of October 28, 1941 would not bring any of us comfort. No one slept. Many people prayed, others wailed, some sat up writing. In the morning, we began to organize ourselves for departure to the unknown. My mother and Fanya dressed in their nice coats and put on some makeup. Fanya dressed Tanya in warm, pretty clothes. After we had gathered some of our valuable possessions together, we sat down to wait, as if we were embarking on any ordinary trip.

Dovid Glikman arrived at five-thirty, clean-shaven, and wearing a blue armband with the number 126 on his sleeve. We all wore our yellow six-pointed star on our backs and chests.

As we had been ordered, we left the door unlocked, and left the house. It was still dark outside, a cold and damp late autumn morning, the ground already frozen. Slowly, we joined the throng of thousands of people walking toward Demokratu Square.

Although almost sixty years have gone by, it is still emotionally very hard for me to describe what happened on that particular day. To write about what I witnessed is to rip open and expose my soul to the reader. I try to imagine what was going through my mother Rebecca's mind. Over the interminable length of the past three months, she had lost three of her brothers, her mother, and her husband. Now she was facing the unknown with her daughters, the two young women she had given birth to and raised, and whom she might lose forever in the next few hours. I can only imagine what my aunts, my sister, and her in-laws were thinking.

And is there any way of rationally explaining what happened on that fateful day? Why were 27,000 innocent people – the elderly and enfeebled, babies, teenagers, teachers and their students, the religious and the secular, the tall and the short, the fat and the skinny, the poor and the rich, men and women – why were they being herded into a square in the early, dark hours of the morning so that a band of murderous strangers could decide whether they were to live or die? Were not the victims and their oppressors all intelligent and reasonable beings? Who were the individuals who were carrying out this unthinkable psychological and physical torture? What inspired them? Did not our torturers also have parents, sisters, brothers, and children? What gave them the right and freedom to murder people who had lived among them but were completely foreign to them? Did any one of the condemned ever disrupt his executioner's life, steal his bread, his donkey, or his wife? Can any of what happened be explained, let alone justified? It is almost impossible for me to describe the thoughts and experiences of the people with whom I walked to the square on that horrible day. I cannot even describe my own thoughts. I can only hope, in the writing of it, to honour the memory of those who died, and to hope that future generations, reading this or other books about these massacres of innocent people, will honour them.

I have no interest in what the murderers were thinking, whether they felt any guilt afterwards, or what they told their wives, children, and grandchildren of that infamous day. I do know, however, that after the war many of them fled to other continents, where they successfully concealed their pasts and passed themselves off as quiet, respectable citizens. Among those who fled was SS Hauptscharfuehrer Helmut Rauca.In 1950 he emigrated to Canada where he was granted citizenship. He lived in Huntsville, Ontario where he ran a tourist hotel. On June, 7 1988 he was arrested as a war criminal and was deported to the Federal Republic of Germany. There he died in jail before going to trial. Some of the perpetrators have paid for their crimes, many others have lived comfortable lives and have reached old age.

What I did know then was that at six o'clock in the morning on October 28, 1941 all of us were walking together most likely to our death. All of us were overcome by sheer terror. When we entered Demokratu Square, we saw that it was entirely surrounded by Lithuanian police, led by Kazys Shimkus. We saw the cannons and expected the unthinkable to happen.

The square was still in darkness when we arrived. A column of Jewish police was positioned near the column of the Jewish Committee. Uncle Lazar's brigade was also nearby. My mother, my aunt, her child and I stood behind our Jewish police officer, Dovid Glikman. Time passed interminably. It was cold, and slowly, the sun began to rise. At precisely eight o'clock, the German security police and Gestapo officials, including Schtitz, Jordan, and Rauca, arrived. They were escorted by German and Lithuanian police. A deathly silence descended on the crowd when Rauca, who was in charge of the entire operation, entered the square. The selection process began.

Rauca personally approached the first column made up of the members of the Jewish Committee. Without counting them or examining the composition of the group, he gestured for them all to move to the left, which was later understood to be the 'good' side. Then he approached our column and, without speaking a word, indicated that we, too, should march to the left. I have to admit that I never saw Rauca. When he approached our column, I closed my eyes and lowered my head. When someone pushed me and we began to run toward the 'good' side, Rauca was already somewhere else, making similar hand gestures, selecting several more columns. At around 10 am, there was already a considerable group of people on the 'good' side and we had been joined by my cousin Nadya and her mother Zina, and uncle Lazar and aunt Berta. Mother began to weep, both in joy at our survival and in agony, worried about my sister's Alice fate. Since our group was unsupervised, we began to move around and talk to each other while our baby slept quietly in her carriage. We already understood that our death sentences had been postponed and prayed that those sent to the 'bad' side would somehow escape death.

Meanwhile, the selection process in the square continued. One by one, the columns passed in front of those who held our fate in their hands. They each stopped long enough to be selected, while Rauca, equally polite to all, calmly and systematically did his work. With a facial gesture or a slight movement of his hand, or simply his finger, Rauca sent people either to the left or the right. Those sent to the right were surrounded by Lithuanian policemen and led away in groups to the Small Ghetto. Meanwhile, Rauca's Lithuanian assistant, Kazys Shimkus, and Heinrich Schtitz counted those who were being transferred. Sometimes, large families with children were sent to the 'good' side, while work-worthy inmates were sent to the 'bad' side. Rauca sought to avoid arousing panic so that the *Aktzion* could be carried out in a smooth and organized manner, without incident or resistance. The autumn day began to grow dark while there were still a few thousand people in the square. Rauca called Jordan over and together they began to hurry the process of selecting the prescribed numbers of victims for death. Time passed. It seemed that the selection would never come to an end.

The cold and the damp began to penetrate our bones as our fear and worry increased about my sister's family, who had not yet joined us. It wasn't until shortly after four o'clock that Alice, Philip, his sister Rita, and their parents Leiba and Roza appeared. Philip had not waited for his brigade's turn and had offered a policeman guarding them a gold watch in exchange for taking them to the 'good' side. Just as his father pulled his watch out of his pocket, Philip noticed that his sister Rita was still in line. With the policeman at his side, he went back to Rita, grabbed her, and handed the officer his gold pen holder. Together, they were rushed off to the side of the living.

The selection was completed shortly after nightfall when Rauca was certain that his quota of some 10,000 people had been met. After ordering the armed Lithuanian police to guard the miserable prisoners in the Small Ghetto, he and his escort quickly left. The rest of us were allowed to return home. Deadly tired, frozen, and crushed, we made our way back to our homes. None of us had the faintest desire or ability to discuss or analyze what had happened. My mother invited Dovid Glikman, our savior, to spend the evening with us. Finally back in our room, we drank warm tea as my mother warmed some dinner for us.

When I awoke the next morning, it was already light. Putting on some warm clothes, I went outside to the outhouse. What I saw will never fade from my memory. In whichever direction I looked, wherever I turned my gaze, I saw a black, slow-moving mass of people that stretched along Paneriu Street, near the Ghetto gates at Varniu Street, and flowed slowly down the hill. Like a procession of shadows with neither a beginning nor an end, the dark throng of people inched along in the direction of the Ninth Fort, surrounded on all sides by armed policemen. I can still feel the eeriness of the scene as I stood there, frozen in disbelief. How could they be real human beings? I have not, to this day, seen a work of art that has come close to capturing what I saw that morning. How could any single artist's understanding, imagination, or emotion express that nightmare vision of a column of 10,000 people marching slowly toward death.

All of those people, 9200 Kaunas Jews in all, were killed at the Ninth Fort on October 29, 1941. Fritz Walter Stahlecker (EG-A) and Karl Jaeger (EK-3) masterminded the murders and ordered the executions. The victims were selected by their assistants Rauca, Schtitz, and Jordan. Kazys Shimkus was in charge of guarding the victims who were pushed to the 'bad' side during the *Aktzion*, of guarding them during the night in the Small Ghetto, and of leading them the next morning to the Ninth Fort. They were murdered by a Lithuanian police battalion led by Jonas Stelmokas. Among the 9200 killed were 2007 men, 2920 women, and 4273 children.

Several days after the *Aktion*, things seemed to calm down and life in the ghetto returned to its gruesome routine. People rushed to work in the mornings and came home tired in the evenings. The workers were fed somewhat better food and those still living were allowed to move into the empty homes of those that had been murdered. The barbed wire that had surrounded the Small Ghetto was removed and the wooden bridge connecting the two sections of the Ghetto was dismantled.

Shortly after the 'Great October Aktzion', some of the Kaunas Jews who had been hiding outside the ghetto with non-Jewish families were forced to move back into the ghetto. As the German occupation became entrenched, any kind of humanitarian resistance, and in particular the hiding of Jews, became an extremely dangerous undertaking and one punishable by death or a long prison sentence. Some Lithuanians actively tried to rescue individual Jews during the first months of the war, up to the late fall of 1941. They hid Jews in their cellars and attics, in barns and other farm buildings near their homes, or in forests. However, with the onset of winter, and especially after snowfalls, this became increasingly risky. Footprints could easily betray hiding places and it was impossible to survive in unheated buildings. As the laws against both Jews and their rescuers became increasingly harsh, it was even dangerous to be seen buying, or cooking, unusual large quantities of food. Both Jews and their supporters lived under the constant threat of arrest and execution. In addition, as the war dragged on, it became apparent that the Jews would need to be hidden, not simply for weeks or months, but, most likely for much longer. And so, by the beginning of 1942, many of the Jews in hiding had no choice but to leave the homes of the good-hearted, righteous people who had tried to help them. Many made a conscious choice to go back to the ghetto where, by the end of 1941, there were only approximately 18,000 people left.

After the Great Action, I decided to take my fate into my own hands. I completely rejected the way the Nazis had decided to arrange my death – by execution at one of the forts. I truly wanted to live, but I was not afraid to die if I could have a weapon in my hands. This was not the solemn pledge of a sixteen-year-old girl's romantic imagination. I was determined to attempt to establish contact with anyone in the underground, with any kind of resistance movement acting in the ghetto. I remembered having met my former classmate, Zalman (Monik) Holzberg. Since he had been an active member of our high school's Young Communist League, I was sure he would have ties with the underground. I soon tracked Monik down and told him what I was looking for. Although at first he did not seem willing to discuss the issue, he agreed to talk to me after the New Year.

On December 31, 1941 what was left of our extended family met in our room. My mother prepared various dishes made of potatoes, carrots, and onions, baked a cake, and laid the table. My sister brought a small piece of ham. Tearfully, remembering the past year, we desperately greeted the coming year of 1942 with a prayer for better times and a hope for good will.

SLAVE LABOUR

I remember the beginning of 1942 as an endless string of incredibly cold days. I had been working at the Aleksotas Airfield from the earliest days of the ghetto and the harsh outdoor work, the brutality of the German supervisor, and the constant hunger were becoming harder to withstand. Extreme cold and hard labour had become inextricably linked in my life, dominating every other aspect of my existence. Every day of the week was identical – an hour and a half walk to the airfield from the ghetto, nine hours of unbearably hard labour, and an hour and a half walk back. But January and February of 1942 were particularly cold, the temperature often reaching -25° to -30° Celsius, and this put a great strain on life in the ghetto. Only the Jewish Committee, the Jewish police, and the ghetto workshops received a limited supply of logs to heat their premises. Because of the shortage of firewood, the ghetto inhabitants began using their furniture and dismantled fences from around the small houses, in fact everything they could find to heat their homes.

Our room at Vygriu Street 48 served as bedroom, dining room, bathroom, and kitchen for my mother, my aunt Fanya and her infant, and myself. At the beginning of the winter, my mother traded my father's clothes for a small cast-iron stove that provided us with heat and allowed us to boil water and cook meals in the room. The stove also made it possible for us to keep the potatoes we had grown in the potato field behind our backyard from freezing and they lasted almost all winter. Although the little stove heated up very quickly and kept the room pleasantly warm as long as it was burning, as soon as the fire went out, our room rapidly grew cold again.

My mother was always the first one up in the morning, waking me only after she lit the stove and prepared a warm breakfast. Forcing myself to get out of bed, I would wash and begin getting dressed. Wanting to put on as many clothes as possible to keep out the cold, I had come up with a multi-layered, 'work uniform'. First I pulled on warm stockings and socks, my father's long woolen underwear, shirt, and sweatpants. Then I topped that with my skirt, a sweater, my mother's coat, a scarf and, finally, my father's winter boots. But during the harshest winter days of 1942, even all this clothing couldn't keep me warm. Once dressed, I ate my breakfast, lingering over a few heavenly sips of cocoa my mother still had from her food reserves. The cocoa reminded me of my childhood. I often thought about how I had turned up my nose before the war when my mother had tried to convince me to drink at least half a cup of the highly nutritious beverage. Now, as happy memories of my childhood and cruel images of our current reality floated before my eyes, I savored every sip.

When I finished my cocoa, I hugged my mother and kissed her good-bye, took the sandwich she always prepared for me and rush out. The dark, cold streets were already full of people moving toward the gates as I walked towards the corner of Ariogalos and Krischiukaichio Streets where our work brigade always gathered. The first to arrive were the permanent airfield slaves, like myself. Later the ghetto police would fill out our ranks with 'criminals' they brought from jail and those they arrested for walking in the street without a special work permit. Before 8 o'clock, the order would come for our brigade of 100 people to move quickly toward the gates. Beginning the trek to the suburb of Aleksotas, we marched in rows of eight on the frozen cobblestone roads while the guards walked on the cleared sidewalk.

Every morning we crossed the Vilijampole Bridge, walked through the Old Town of Kaunas and turned toward the Nemunas River. Just before we crossed the Nemunas Bridge to Aleksotas, our ranks would begin to thin. A few workers who wanted to barter goods for food or do other business in the city would often joined our group surreptitiously. They would remove or cover up their yellow Stars of David as we approached the Nemunas Bridge and prepare to disappear into the crowd at an opportune moment. In the evenings, as we trudged back from the airfield, they would rejoin us, once again wearing their yellow stars and carrying parcels from their errands in town.

This was an extremely dangerous undertaking. Although the guards were bribed by the brigade foreman to keep quiet, they could not be trusted to do so. Those determined to escape had to move extremely quickly and be very careful to avoid being seen either by guards or passersby as they slipped from the column. The guards might be in a bad mood that day or could simply decide to hand over one of these prisoners to the police. But the many passersby were an even greater threat. There was always the possibility that someone would see a Jew escaping and might deliver him back to the guards, take him straight to the police, or directly to the Gestapo. Often, a passerby might even take the initiative and apprehend a Jew who was trading or buying food in the courtyards and other less public places in the city.

Many Lithuanians continued to be prejudiced against the Jews, even though it had become clear, by 1942, that Germany's *Blitzkrieg* against the Soviet Union had not been a success and that the war was going to last much longer than people had first thought. Lithuania's independence had been short-lived and the Lithuanians themselves were suffering considerably under the German occupation. Still, every day, approximately ten Jews, illegally walking the streets of Kaunas, were caught by Lithuanian citizens and handed over to the police. In his book, *Surviving the Holocaust: The Kovna Ghetto Diary*, Abraham Tory quotes a document written by Karl Jaeger, Commander of the Security Police, on March 11,1942. In that document Jaeger states that,

> Upon my order, twenty-four Jews were shot dead because, contrary to the instructions issued regarding Jews, they had engaged in considerable black marketeering with the Lithuanian population, and were not wearing identification marks.[70]

The gentiles of Kaunas, and other Lithuanian towns and villages, could easily recognize their long-time Jewish neighbours. They could identify us by our clothing, our manner of speaking and walking, the colour of our eyes and hair, the length and shape of our noses. Of course they could identify us because for so long we had been their neighbours and classmates, their students and teachers, their doctors and patients. Yet many of them never hesitated to hand Jews over to the police. To this day, I cannot find a rational explanation as to why they treated Jews the way they did.

I, myself, never considered trying to escape our brigade, even though the work and the monotony were relentless. After reaching the airfield and receiving a bowl of warm water to drink, we were sent to our various work stations by the German supervisors. Usually, my job consisted of pushing a wagon filled with building supplies to and from the open areas where the men worked digging ditches, mixing cement, carrying bricks, and loading and unloading building materials. Once the materials were unloaded, I returned to the hangars where the supplies were kept and loaded the wagon up again for the next trip. Inside the metal hangars it was even colder than outdoors and when we had an occasional moment to rest, there was nowhere to warm up.

At one o'clock, there was a short lunch break when all 100 of us would gather beside one of the hangars where huge soup cauldrons were set up. Each worker's bowl was filled with a liquid we called *jushnik* that barely resembling soup. I have no idea why we called it that, except that something about the word's sound described the mock soup perfectly. It contained no meat or fat and only rarely would we find a sweet piece of frozen potato floating on its surface. It's only redeeming quality was that it was warm. Sitting in the cold, I soaked the frozen bread of my sandwich in the *jushnik* and chewed on the bacon, longing for 5 pm when the night shift would arrive.

Finally, frozen, hungry, and exhausted by the heavy labour and the constant demands of the supervisors that we work faster, my fellow slaves and I took our places in the column for the long trek back to the ghetto. It always seemed to me that we walked faster on the way back to the ghetto than we did on the way to work, even though I was usually carrying small pieces of wood back with me that I had collected for our stove.

On our way to and from the airfield, we always passed through the Old Town, near City Hall Square, where my family had lived from 1934 to 1936. It was in that neighbourhood that I went to elementary school and ran with my friends as we played in the courtyard of a red brick church named after the Lithuanian writer and priest, Tumas Vaizgantas. Also nearby was the Jesuit High School from which I graduated in 1941. During that winter of 1942, I passed the church, and other places that I had known since childhood, twice every day. But I did not look up at the well-dressed people we passed. I simply lowered my head and my eyes, wanting nothing but to return to our little room in the ghetto where I could, at least briefly, forget both the present and the past.

By the time we reached the Vilijampole Bridge, it was 6 o'clock and there was usually a huge concentration of returning ghetto inmates waiting to get across. As the crowd on the bridge thinned, we would slowly begin to move forward. Jewish policemen enforced order on the far end of the bridge. The Jewish police were allowed to leave the ghetto area only to regulate the human traffic coming back from the work details on Krischiukaichiu Street. We could usually tell what the situation at the gate was from the behavior of the Jewish policemen. The noisier and more aggressive they were, the better we could expect conditions to be for getting through the gates. On quiet and uneventful days, the Jewish policemen ruled the situation and decided whether an inmate would successfully pass or fail the inspection. During risky circumstances, especially when there were 'guests' from the Gestapo at the gates, the Jewish policemen neither shouted nor pushed, warning inmates of danger with the single word, *fier* (fire). Cautious now of possible trouble at the inspection station and afraid of the Gestapo, some ghetto inmates would then draw back, hiding their parcels in backyards beyond the gates, or throwing their goods to their Lithuanian business associates who might be standing nearby. Those of us, like myself, who carried neither parcels nor bags, rushed the gates. As we passed through the inspection, we could easily see how those who had been caught carrying prohibited goods were beaten and arrested and their 'riches' confiscated.

My mother was always waiting for me when I got home at night and helped me undress. Often, I would fall asleep over my dinner, only to open my eyes again and continue to eat as images of the German supervisor plagued my mind, the shouts of the Lithuanian guards and the Jewish gate police ringing in my ears. I could barely wait to get into bed, draw the blanket up to my chin and fall into the nothingness of sleep. Not the light in the room, the conversations taking place around me, or the baby's chatter stopped me from sleeping. Moments after I lay down, it seemed, my mother would be waking me again. And it would be morning and the gruesome routine started all over again. On and on, day after day. Sunday was the only day we had to rest, to leave home without fear, and spend some time with the few friends that were left in the ghetto. But it was a short respite from the everyday tedium of the slave labour and the Germans' endless demands, their infinite prohibitions and repression.

Indiscriminately, the Nazis would stage house raids. It wasn't surprising then, that the ghetto inhabitants were always looking for ways to protect themselves, at least temporarily. Each house had one or two root cellars that could easily be transformed into bunkers and people started building hideouts and bunkers in their homes. They stored water, food supplies, clothing, and bedding in their shelters and concealed the entrances with pieces of furniture, stoves, and rugs. Our apartment did not have a cellar, but Alice's husband, Philip, built a large shelter in their house for our whole family. It was decided that, as soon as any unexpected danger arose, my mother and I were to go to my sister's bunker. Our neighbours also had a bunker and intended to share it with my aunt Fanya and her daughter Tanya, if the need came up.

Very soon, the need to hide did, indeed, arise. A rumour began circulating through the ghetto that the Germans were demanding 500 strong, childless men and women to be sent to work at Riga Airport in Latvia. The Jewish Committee labour office had drawn up a list of people to be transferred. No one trusted the Germans anymore and none of the inmates wanted to part from their families and find themselves in a concentration camp. Again we were faced with the horror of selection, deciding who would stay and who should go.

In the middle of the night, on February 4, 1942, a German police unit, assisted by the Jewish police, collected 200 people whose names were on the Jewish Committee's list. Those arrested were taken to a small house and in the morning, they were handed over to the Germans. Furious that only 200 prisoners had been collected, Jordan and Schtitz demanded the remaining 300 workers be found immediately. Allowing the original 200 prisoners to return to their homes in the ghetto, they threatened to execute the entire Jewish administration and deport all of the Jewish policemen to Riga if their demands for the 500 prisoners were not met and promised to return to resolve the problem.

The next day, Jordan came back to the Jewish Committee and ordered all the ghetto inmates to assemble in the Demokratu Square. Assisted by Schtitz, he personally selected 300 people and sent them to the train station under heavy guard. Jordan ordered the Jewish Committee to draw up a subsequent list for the remaining labourers. Later that evening, the required number of people were finally rounded up and driven to the Kaunas train station under German and Lithuanian police guard. When the train carrying the 500 people left for Riga, the Germans ordered everyone back to work. Luckily, no one from my family was taken.

Some time after the first Riga *Aktzion*, I managed to find a new workplace. The *Bahnmeisterai* (the train station workshop) consisted of about 40 people. Our men were digging ditches and paving the cobblestone sections for a new road they were laying from the station to the freight depot. My job was to carry heavy stretchers filled with cement to the work site. The soup was a little thicker here and occasionally we received an additional slice of bread, but as it turned out, it would not be better here than at the airfield I had left. Lithuanian workers were repairing wagons nearby, and, at first, it seemed that we might be able to talk to them and barter things for food. But our armed supervisor, whom everyone called Fritz, would not take his eyes off us for a moment. A slight, thin, fair-haired Ukranian, he had a nose shaped like a hawk's beak. He wore a German uniform and spoke German with a Slavic accent, continually shouting *lios! lios!* (faster! faster!). Occasionally, he came up to a prisoner from behind and punched him in the head or the back. From the first day, I could see he hated me. Cursing at me, he would not let me move away from the stretchers to rest for a second. I felt as if he had the desire to crush me under his boots or strangle me with his bare hands.

One day at the end of my first week, my worst fears about him were realized. Without warning, he crept up behind me and punched me in the back. When I turned around, he hit me in the face. I was stunned and, looking straight at him, quietly said, "Traitor" in Russian. Infuriated, he attacked me again, hitting me hard in the face, beating on my head and back with his fists. As I fell to the ground, he pointed his gun at me, the bullet just missing me as he fired at the ground beside me. Other workers rushed toward us and began dragging me back to the workshop. Cursing in German and Ukrainian, he shot into the air, swearing that he would kill me anyway.

I was barely alive by the time my friends helped me back into the ghetto that evening. When the foreman of our brigade visited us that night, he told my mother that we had better find someone to work my shift for the next few days and that he would arrange a work leave for me until the end of April. Then he ordered me never to show myself in his brigade again. Luckily, my mother found someone who agreed to work for me and punch my work card for a few days. In ghetto slang, an inmate who agreed to work another person's shift for a fee was called an 'angel'. My 'angel' worked for me for three days, at the end of which time the foreman crossed my name off his list and found another permanent worker.

I could not get out of bed for a week. I was badly hurt and my head and body ached badly, my limbs barely able to move. But I had even more difficulty recovering from Fritz's insults and the wounds to my dignity. Physically and morally exhausted, I became indifferent to everything. I had no desire for revenge and did not want to fight or to live.

Slowly though, as the spring days became longer and warmer, I began to recover. In April, we celebrated Tanya's first birthday and all our relatives gather in our room for the event. At that time, the ghetto workshops were manufacturing toys for the German soldiers to send home to their families and my sister brought Tanya a rag doll. It would be impossible to describe the child's joy. She wouldn't let the doll out of her sight. Our aunts gave her a dress and a pair of shoes and my mother knitted her a green sweater. My mother had worked hard to prepare for the birthday party. Using turnip, onion, vinegar, and an egg, she made 'chopped herring' and another popular ghetto dish called 'empty fish', cooking a beet, some onions, carrots, and parsley in a saucepan, then adding whole peeled potatoes. Our room filled with the familiar, remembered smell of gefilte fish as we anticipated the great feast. That night we dined on my mother's 'chopped herring' and 'empty fish', and the thick soup Uncle Lazar had brought from work. I tried not to think of what would happen when the end of April came and I had to find work.

When my work leave ran out, I went to the Jewish Committee labour office to get a new placement. By coincidence, I met Mr. Gershovich, the director of my former Jewish high school, at the office. I told him the story of my unfortunate situation, sad even by ghetto standards, and he immediately offered me a job in a new work unit. Mr. Gershovich was an agronomist and he was organizing a garden section at a model farm at Noreikishkiai. He needed twenty-five women and five men to work six days a week. Chatzkel Lemchenas[71], the well-known linguist and editor of many Lithuanian-Russian dictionaries, had been appointed Gershovich's assistant. Jumping at this opportunity, I gave him my identification papers. *Noreikishkes* was written into my work card and the next day I reported to work.

This job seemed like heaven compared to my previous one. Our guard left us to ourselves, spending the entire day at the farm's office. Two very pleasant Dutch men, who had been mobilized by the Germans to work in Lithuania, were in charge of the project. I was posted in the greenhouse, where the younger, 30-year-old Dutchman patiently taught us how to plant cucumber, onion, and carrot seeds, and how to transplant tomato shoots. We were even allowed to wash our hands before the lunch breaks, which lasted an entire hour, and we all ate together at a long table laid with sliced bread, vegetables, and hot potatoes, a cauldron of soup standing on the floor. At the end of each week, we were given permission to take home a basket of fresh vegetables. Before too long, I became an agricultural 'specialist'.

After I finished lunch on my first day of work, I went out to look around. The area around the farm was calm and quiet, with patches of snow still laying on the fields. The smoke rising from the chimneys of nearby cottages reminded me what the warmth of home life could be like. I decided I had enough time to investigate the neighbourhood and return to the farm in time for the afternoon shift. Wrapping myself in a large scarf to cover the yellow star and looking around to make sure that no one was watching, I set off in the direction of the nearest cottage. I knocked gently on the door and entered the house where I found a family eating lunch. They invited me to join them but I politely declined. Without mentioning that I was Jewish, I told them that I was from Kaunas and worked at the Noreikishkiai farm. I asked if they could sell me some food. The woman understood immediately who I was and asked no further questions. She sold me five eggs, a piece of bacon, and some milk in exchange for my scarf. We arranged that I drop by again a few days later and that I bring with me scarves, clothes, and stockings to trade for food. We had become trading partners.

Our exchanges usually took place quickly and the landlady always reminded me to be careful and to make sure no one noticed me. We agreed that if there was ever any danger, she would stand in the field waving laundry. Luckily, no such risk ever arose and I continued to visit her regularly. I became increasingly good at hiding the more valuable food items. Each time I returned to the farm, I quickly took off my new scarf and then calmly entered the greenhouse, where Lemchenas was always anxiously waiting for me. He knew I was risking my life and breathed a sigh of relief every time I returned to the farm.

Trading goods for food was only half the battle. The other half of the daily struggle to survive was to smugle the food into the ghetto. Very soon I became proficient at sneaking through the ghetto gates without passing inspection, bringing back food almost every day. Now we all had enough food and no longer went to bed hungry. Needless to say, this vastly improved our lives. In the spring I planted cucumbers, tomatoes, and other vegetables in the garden plot behind our house and this gave us enough vegetables for the whole summer and fall.

The spring and summer of 1942 passed relatively calmly and without any further deportations or brutality. Even the families of the prisoners who had been sent to Riga were greatly relieved when they began receiving letters from their loved ones. The atmosphere in the ghetto became more relaxed, especially around the gates and the fence. More food was available and the price of black market goods fell. The Germans returned some of the books they had confiscated and allowed the inmates to open a public bath-house and a laundry. The Jewish Committee received a permit to open a vocational training school. The elementary school was reopened and it offered an expanded program of study. The hospitals and orphanages were allowed more supplies and some medicines were made available. The Germans even provided the ghetto with firewood for the upcoming winter, made other improvements, and extended the curfew. The most delightful surprise came when the Germans allowed ghetto residents to bath, during the two months of summer, at the riverbank that ran along the ghetto.

One day, Misha Hofmekleris, a well-known Lithuanian musician, suggested to the Jewish Committee that a symphony orchestra be established in the ghetto. Many talented musicians were imprisoned in the ghetto, among them former soloists from the Lithuanian State Opera and other popular musical performers. They all expressed a desire to join the orchestra. At first, Dr. Elkes didn't like the idea. He was afraid the Germans would interpret the formation of an orchestra as a sign that the Jews were enjoying life in the ghetto too much. But after some discussion, he agreed to ask the Germans for permission to set up a Jewish amateur orchestra within the framework of the Jewish police. It took some time, but after lengthy consideration, the Germans agreed. The first concert took place in a hall at the former Yeshiva in Slobodka. The audience and members of the orchestra all shed tears of emotion and pride during that first concert as the ghetto inmates escaped the harsh reality of their lives, at least briefly, and regained some sense of dignity and humanity.

Cultural and social activities helped to sustain the inmates. Friendships, the primitive libraries made up of the returned books, concerts, lectures and discussions about Jewish literature and socio-political issues inspired young people to come together and gave all the inmates a moral and emotional boost. More than a form of resistance, these activities took on existential meaning for the Kaunas ghetto inhabitants. They confirmed the unbreakable will of the ghetto inhabitants. The people in Kaunas Ghetto struggled, not only to survive, but to resist the Nazis' attempt to dehumanize them.

All in all, we became lulled into the illusion that the Germans were not planning to kill us. It seemed that all we needed to do was keep working and follow orders and we would be allowed to live. Toward the autumn, however, the illusion that the Nazis had decided to leave us alone began to fade. Despite all of their assurances that work and obedience were our lifeline, in October, the Germans ordered the Jewish Committee to collect 400 inmates for another deportation to Riga. Once again the Committee began to draw up a list. This time, they had a somewhat easier task since relatives of those already in Riga had received letters from their loved ones and wished to join them there. Aside from these people, though, the collection and deportation of the people proceeded in a similar way as the first Riga *Aktzion* and, in the end, 369 Jews and their families were transported to Riga for slave labour.

Shortly after the second Riga *Aktzion*, the Kaunas Ghetto was dealt another blow. In November, a young inmate was caught jumping over the fence of the ghetto. Trying to escape from his captors, Mekas had fired several shots from a gun. He was immediately arrested and taken to the Gestapo. Along with him, the Germans also took thirty hostages, among them three members of the Jewish Committee and Mekas' mother and sister. After interrogating and torturing these prisoners, the Germans discovered that the Mekas family had owned a jewelry store in Kaunas before the war. They had been hiding gold in their ghetto apartment and were planning to escape to Poland with forged documents. Although the other hostages were released, Mekas' mother and sister were taken to the Ninth Fort and shot. The Gestapo ordered Mekas be hung.

The horrific execution took place on November 18, 1942. Early that morning, the gallows were set up across from the Jewish administration building in the potato field behind our apartment, barely one hundred feet from our window. An entire detachment of uniformed high-ranking Gestapo officials arrived at the execution site and surrounded the gallows. From our window, we could clearly see their shiny boots, the pistols hanging from their hips, and their self-satisfied faces. No one in the ghetto was allowed to go to work that day and the Gestapo ordered a small 'audience' to gather at the site. Worn out by torture and barely alive, Mekas was brought in at around 10 o'clock in the morning. Unable to walk, he was held up by two Jewish policemen. Although the Germans had forbidden anyone to close their shutters, my mother pulled me away from the window at the moment the execution took place. When it was over, the Germans quickly left the site but Mekas' body was ordered to remain hanging for the next twenty-four hours, guarded by the Jewish police. After that he was buried in the ghetto cemetery. None of us could shut our eyes that night. I was haunted by horrific visions, the memory of the 'Great Aktzion,' and the terrifying reality of how dangerously we balanced between life and death.

Meanwhile, I continued working at Noreikishkes Farm as if nothing had happened. It was still fall when the younger Dutchman asked to see me in his office. We had become friends during my time at the farm and I trusted him. When I entered the room, I could feel that he was deeply concerned and unsure as to how to begin the conversation. He asked about my health and my mother's, and the general mood in the ghetto. I told him that, although the situation had stabilized somewhat since the execution and that people were more relaxed, there was still a great deal of tension in the air. He told me that the Germans had increased their strong presence on the Eastern Front where they had occupied new territories in the southern part of the Soviet Union and that they were close to surrounding Leningrad. He believed the war could go on indefinitely and was very skeptical about the Nazis' policies regarding the Jews. The Dutch man warned me against trusting any of their assurances. He knew about the persecution of the Jews in the occupied countries and hinted that those who were deported to concentration camps would never return.

My Dutch friend then told me that he and his countryman had completed their military service and would soon be returning to Holland. Because there was no work on the farm during the winter, he told me that our brigade would be dispersed. I was stunned by the news. When he saw my expression, he gently embraced me and kissed my face. At first, I could not quite grasp the content of what he was beginning to tell me. He spoke in an emotional voice that did not seem to belong to him, as he held me and whispered in my ear.

"I am determined to save you," he said. "I have made a plan for your escape. Just listen carefully to me."

Too distraught to speak, all I could do was look up at him, thankful for his friendship. With tears in my eyes, I leaned closer to his face and kissed and embraced him, as he began to explain his plan. His mother would send me an invitation to work at her farm in Holland, he explained, addressing it to a false name. He would present that invitation to the appropriate German authorities and obtain a permit for me to travel to Holland to do agricultural work. He assured me that, although it was a long and dangerous journey, he would cover all of my travel expenses and he was sure I would not have any trouble. In Holland, I would live with his mother. After the war, he and I would decide our mutual future. When I regained the ability to speak, I told him that I would have to discuss these developments with my mother and sister and we agree to meet again the following week.

Overwhelmed by his unexpected offer, I returned to the ghetto. Confused, I was not sure whether I was a child of fortune or whether this could be the beginning of new dangers and worries. My mother was also unsure of what to think when I told her and we decided to discuss it with Alice and Philip. After a long discussion in which Philip's parents also participated, we were still no closer to a conclusion. My mother had no real objections to the plan but she wanted me to make the final decision.

When we met again, I asked my Dutch friend if we would be traveling together or if I would have to make the journey on my own.

He said that he had intended for us to travel separately, but that we could certainly consider this other option. I admitted that I had difficulty accepting his plan. I was frightened of leaving my family and traveling alone through Germany, only to end up living with strangers in a foreign country. In the end, I told him that I did not want to put him in potential danger and, most of all, that I felt I must share my family's fate. I told him how very fond I was of him and how incredibly grateful I was for his noble offer. He gave me his address and I promised him that if I felt my life was in real danger, I would try to contact him and try to get to Holland.

There was no question that strong feelings had arisen between us. I wanted to be with him and to lean on someone strong who wanted to save me from humiliation and slavery and from this unbearable existence. We were both torn by conflicting feelings, the joy of the first sparks of a love between us and the fear of embracing a path that was strictly forbidden to us. We knew that any intimacy between us would be dangerous to us both and decided that it would be better to part. He was an extremely decent man and always treated me with the utmost respect. He never suggested that I stay overnight at the farm and worried terribly about my excursions to the village for food. Our friendship lasted until the day he and his countryman left Lithuania. A few years after the liberation of Lithuania, I sent a letter to Holland to which he replied quickly. He was happy to hear that I was alive and well. He told me that he was married and invited me to visit. But, with that letter, our correspondence ended. We lost contact and I misplaced his address somewhere. Besides, the Stalinist era of terror had strengthened and any contact with foreigners was feared and discouraged.

Part Three

Resistance in the Ghetto

THE ANTI-FASCIST FIGHTING ORGANIZATION

One bright spring day in 1942, Monik Holzberg unexpectedly appeared at our apartment door. He was ready to introduce me to some of his friends and had come to pick me up. That Sunday, Zalman (Monik) Holzberg, the 'strong man' of our high school, brought me into the ranks of the ghetto fighters, something for which I am grateful to him to this day. From that moment on, my life in the ghetto changed profoundly. As soon as I realized that I would be engaging in a tangible fight against our murderers, I acquired a renewed sense of belonging and self-esteem. On a personal level, I developed close friendships with like-minded people and, most importantly, met the man with whom I would share my life and whose love and devotion sustained me throughout our entire life together.

On that unforgettable Sunday, Holzberg and I walked along Krischiukaichiu Street, in the direction of the ghetto gates. Passing the Catholic Cemetery located just beyond the ghetto boundaries, we soon found ourselves among the lopsided huts in the narrow, winding streets of the old part of Vilijampole (Slabodka). We approached a hut that stood somewhat removed from the others and were greeting at the door by our host, Liova Sher. He was a tall young man who had completed his military service before the war and was now in charge of teaching the underground fighters how to assemble, clean, load, and shoot a gun. His girlfriend, Leja, was a thin girl who had been a first-year law student and was also there to be inducted into the resistance. One other member of the underground organization was also expected at that day's meeting, the man to whom Leja and I would pledge our oath.

Shortly after we arrived, a tall, dark-haired young man entered the room and introduced himself as Meishke der Langer (*Meishke*, the tall one). He was, in fact, Misha Rubinsonas. My first impression of Misha was that he was just too tall, that his trousers were too short and his arms were too long. He looked surprisingly boyish. During the meeting, Misha described the situation at the Eastern Front to us. He outlined our organization's goals and activities, stressing that it was crucial to maintain strict secrecy and learn how to handle a weapon. Afterwards, Leja Sheriene and I signed the oath which every new member of the AFO was required to sign:

> Recognizing the battle against fascism and all of its mani-
> festations to be a holy duty, I am determined to join the
> ranks of the Red Partisans in active struggle. I promise to
> fight untiringly against the fascist occupiers, to set fire to
> and destroy their headquarters and enterprises, to interfere
> with their transportation, to explode their bridges, to dis-
> mantle their railroads, and to engage in all possible forms
> of sabotage. I promise to fight with all my strength and to
> sacrifice my life, if necessary, until my Homeland is com-
> pletely liberated from the yoke of the occupiers. I promise to
> be a loyal and disciplined fighter, to follow the orders of my
> superiors in the organization with courage, accuracy, and
> without reservations, to unerringly safeguard the secrets and
> conspiratorial plans entrusted me. I fully understand that
> any breech of discipline or strategy by the partisans warrants
> the death penalty.[72]

After that first meeting and the initial military training, Monik rushed off, Leja stayed on with her boyfriend, and Misha, who lived not far from Sher's hut on Ariogalos Street, offered to accompany me as far as the Catholic Cemetery. As we walked, he told me a bit about himself and his family.

Misha had graduated from the Sholom Aleichem Jewish High School and intended to study journalism. At school he had loved Jewish literature, participated in the school's basketball and table tennis teams, and wrote for the school's Jewish press. It seemed that he was a very busy student who had little time for his studies. Nevertheless, Misha graduated high school with excellent grades. Misha's former classmate, Rivka Ravinskyte-Geleriene, describes him in her memoirs:

From what I remember, Misha rarely prepared for his school assignments. Rather, he would glance at one or another classmate's exercise book or the textbook during recess.

When asked by the teacher to go up to the blackboard, this otherwise athletic young man dragged his feet lethargically as he approached the front of the class. When he turned to face us, we knew from his expression that he was hoping we would give him some clues. All he needed was to hear a few key words and Misha could rattle off the contents of the lesson as though he were reading directly from the textbook. He was clearly a very bright boy but one who didn't much care for studying. Or perhaps, being preoccupied with sports, and especially basketball which he adored, he simply didn't have the time.

I can't remember which grade it was, but one year he sat directly behind me in the last row. And did he give me a lot trouble! I had long braids then, and he tugged at them as though they were a horse's reins. It was taboo in our group to complain to the teacher, and also, what girl could possibly mind being teased by such a good-looking classmate? Occasionally though, the teacher would notice him playing with my hair and he would be asked to leave the classroom.

We graduated just before Hitler invaded the Soviet Union and we barely had the chance to celebrate receiving our diplomas. We never got together in the Kaunas Ghetto and after the war I returned from Stutthof Concentration Camp to Kaunas while Misha settled in Vilnius. I thoroughly enjoyed reading his articles in the papers.[73]

When Hitler's army invaded, Misha's graduation certificate was destroyed along with other documents at the Jewish high school. Misha told me that he and one of his classmate tried to escape from the city but were intercepted on the outskirts of Kaunas. They escaped from the police, split up, and Misha returned safely home. Now here we were, ready to fight any way we could.

My primary cell consisted of three people: Leja, myself and Monik, who was the secretary of our trio. Liova Sher was our military instructor. Meetings took place fairly regularly, at least once a week. The agenda usually consisted of the following points: political news and a report about what was going on at the fronts; a discussion of a currently relevant issue; and military training. We had to inform the group about acts of sabotage we had conducted, debate their effectiveness, and discuss means of improvement.

Ideological discussions also took place at the cell meetings. Misha and Monik took pleasure in explaining the superiority of the socialist system, discussing the dynamic nature of communist ideas, and, in general, painting an idealistic picture of Soviet life. Leja and I, on the other hand, remained quite skeptical of the realities of an existence under communism. We were neither enchanted with communist ideology nor the prospect of the Soviet way of life. We criticized the Soviet Union's policies regarding the Jews, its pact with Hitler, the constant repressions and, especially, the deportations to Siberia. We did not particularly enjoy these discussions and felt that theoretical questions were far removed from the pressing concerns we faced in the ghetto. We understood perfectly well, however, that help would only come from the East, that only the Soviet army could liberate us from Nazi oppression and death, and that we would soon be fighting in the forest with Soviet partisans.

From the vantage point of history, it is undeniable that Jewish resistance in the Kaunas Ghetto played an integral part in the story of the Holocaust in Lithuania. The members of the resistance movement defied the Nazis in political, economic, cultural, religious, and countless other ways every single day. As early as August 1941, a month after the Nazi occupation of Lithuania began, many Jews in the Kaunas Ghetto began organizing resistance to German rule. There were a dozen or more small, isolated resistance cells of varying political and ideological conviction operating independently in the Kaunas Ghetto. Those who participated in active resistance risked their lives in everything they did from engaging in the act of prayer to smuggling food, illegal literature, and weapons into the ghetto. They established illegal schools and, especially, saved lives, particularly the lives of children. All in all, the resistance movement provided spiritual and emotional support to people. For the fighters themselves, the underground movement gave them a great sense of belonging and a renewed sense of self-esteem. Organized resistance renewed people's desire to fight for survival and allowed those who had felt like victims to once again know dignity and honour.

During the fall of 1941, underground clusters in the Kaunas Ghetto, motivated by the same ideology and aim, began to establish contact with each other. These smaller groups were fully aware that by joining forces they could better address the problems, like physical and emotional support, adoption of children whose parents had perished, and mere survival that the ghetto inhabitants faced daily. They also knew that the resistance movement could only succeed if it had strong, organizational unity. One governing body could strengthen memberships and foster greater motivation, dedication, and discipline in those risking their lives for the good of all.

One of those groups was led by a young Yiddish writer and poet, Chaim Jellin. He was born in 1912 in the small city of Vilkija, Lithuania. After World War I, his parents moved to Kaunas where he graduated from a Hebrew high school. In Kaunas University, Chaim studied economics and worked in the Lovers of Knowledge Library, where his father was the director. Under the Soviets, he held a senior position in the printing office.

When German troops invaded the Soviet Union, Jellin had tried to flee but was captured by the local police. He was able, however, to escape and returned safely to Kaunas. Once in the ghetto, Chaim contacted those of his closest friends, colleagues, and acquaintances whom he felt held the same political views as he did. He wanted to negotiate with other similar underground groups already operating in the ghetto to create a strong and united resistance organization. One such group had been brought together by Alte Boruchovich-Teper, a textile factory worker. She knew Chaim from the days before the war when she had visited his father's library and now she contacted Chaim and informed him that her group was ready to participate in a united resistance movement. There was also a small youth underground unit, led by Misha Rubinsonas, already functioning in the ghetto. This group included Misha's classmates, his friends and comrades. Misha had contacts with some of the other groups and through them he met

Chaim Jellin. Dimitry (Dima) Gelpernas and Meyer Elinas describe the meeting this way:

> Contact was soon established with a communist youth group made up of former students of the Kaunas Sholom Aleichem High School, P. Karnauskaite, A. Vilenchiukas, M. Shpitalnikas and others. The first meeting with the group's leader, Misha Rubinsonas, took place in a deserted ghetto street. It had been arranged that the person waiting in the street for Rubinsonas would ask, 'What time is it?' He would be expecting the answer, 'a quarter to three.' When he arrived, Rubinsonas noticed a man in the street wearing a short fur coat and a hat with ear-flaps. He was so disconcerted by the highly unusually outfit that he did not dare to approach him. And so, the two men walked around for quite a while until the stranger, who, in fact, was Chaim Jellin, approached Rubinsonas and asked, 'Isn't it a quarter to three?' The contact had been made.[74]

The first general meeting of the new organization, the birth of the underground, took place on December 31, 1941 under the cover of a New Year's Eve party. For security reasons, it was agreed that each member should take a different route to the party and arrive at a different time. At the meeting, many important issues, such as the resistance program and the organization's structure, were discussed. The primary cell in the organization's chain would be made up of three members, led by a secretary. Seven such groups would make up a brigade, which would also have a leader. The new organization was named The Activists' Union, but this name did not stick and was shortly replaced by The Kaunas Ghetto Anti-Fascist Fighting Organization, or AFO. All those who agreed with its aims and regulations were welcomed into the organization and were required to take the oath.

During this first meeting, a five-member committee was elected with Chaim Jellin, who chose the pseudonym, *Vladas,* as secretary. Jellin was the organization's soul, and as leader, he was the principle organizer of all the movement's most important actions against the

Germans. He established the AFO's structure and regulations, defined its aims and wrote its oath of allegiance. At great personal risk, Chaim repeatedly escaped from the ghetto and met the pro-Communist and other resisters in the city. He and other members of the AFO smuggled badly needed weapons into the ghetto, gathered information, and made contact with Soviet partisans in the forest.

The other members elected to the committee were Dima Gelpernas, Alte Boruchovich-Teper, Peisach Gordon, Moishe Sherman, and Meri Lan. Among those who later joined the committee were Chaim Dovid Ratner, Meyer Grinberg, Peisach Shateris, Dovid Markovski, Leja Zimerman, and others. During that first meeting, the AFO committee appointed Misha Rubinsonas as secretary of the communist youth group and put him in charge of the entire youth branch. Zalman (Monik) Holzberg and Elijezer Zilber were to be his assistants in communist youth matters.

Misha was also named a brigade leader responsible for seven primary cells. He frequently participated in committee meetings and had close ties with Jellin, Boruchovich-Teper, and Dima Gelpernas, Chaim's deputy in charge of propaganda and information.

Misha was given a very important additional function. It was his responsibility to draw as many young people as possible into the organization. Smoliakovas, a member of our organization and a friend of Misha's, writes the following about Misha in his memoirs, *Akistata:*

> Today, I'm working for nothing. Mykolas [Misha] asked me to cover for him [at work] for a couple of days because he had some business to take care of. I knew what business he was talking about. Although Misha didn't have a mustache himself, he belonged to the 'mustachioed'.[75]...So, even though it wasn't a military task, I became responsible for our group's first mission. I remembered that conversation many years later, when, on an autumn day, a huge crowd accompanied Mykolas Rubinsonas – a wonderful person and a great friend – to his final resting place in Antakalnio Cemetery. And I finally understood that it wasn't I who had been his 'angel', but rather, that he had been a real angel for me during some of the most difficult times in my life. For it

was he who had always vouched for me, who had shown me the path that I was looking for.[76]

The AFO consisted of two sections. One was the fighting and sabotage section and included all those who were able to participate in damage operations and to perform other assignments outside the ghetto. The other, much larger group, was the assistance wing responsible for providing the organization with various basic supplies and money in order to support needy and sick people with clothes, shoes, food and medicine, and to arrange additional meals for the children. Membership numbers grew steadily and, by summer of 1943, the organization had about 500 members and supporters, mostly young people between the age of fourteen to thirty.

The AFO's primary goal was mainly to establish contact with the underground resistance organizations outside the ghetto. Through them, the AFO wanted to obtain weapons, information, hiding places, covert apartments, and ultimately, to join the partisans in a nearby forest. Chaim Jellin was confident that Jewish armed resisters would be more effective outside the ghetto once they joined up with Soviet partisans in the forest. He strongly believed that the Soviet Union was the primary source for resistance support. An armed uprising was not the organization's top priority, although the possibility was by no means ruled out.

Our secondary goal was to inflict as much damage as possible on the Nazi military apparatus. Once a week, every member of the AFO had to report the acts of sabotage he or she had personally carried out. In keeping with their other mandates, members boosted the morale of ghetto inmates by keeping them informed, as much as possible, of the events as they occurred in territory outside the ghetto. Following the instructions of the AFO, an illegal primary school was set up in the ghetto under the direction of Sonia and Ronia Rozentals. Polia Karnauskaite-Musel, Misha Rubinsonas, Leja Sher and others also helped out at the school, where the children were taught Jewish cultural history and were led in various activities.

We were not, however, the only ones working underground in the ghetto. By early 1942, Zionist underground organizations were also operating in the Kaunas Ghetto. In April of that year, the leaders of the various Zionist groups agreed that, despite their ideological differences, they would coordinate their activities and, as a result, the joint underground Zionist organization was established. They called themselves MATZOK, the name by which the former illegal Zionist hub in Vilijampole had operated during the Soviet occupation. MATZOK brought together the Zionist organization's youth federation, *Irgun Brit Zion*; several leftist Zionist groups, like *Hashomer Hatzair*; the right-wing group, *Beitar*; the religious *Mizrachi* group; and others.

MATZOK sought to further the effects of resistance by engaging its members in cultural, educational, and political activities, striving to save as many ghetto inmates as they could. They built hiding bunkers and maintained ties with Lithuanians in order to find families who would be willing to take in Jews. The *Irgun Brit Zion* managed to publish a Hebrew newsletter in the ghetto called *Nitzotz* (The Spark) that was written by hand and then copied on carbon paper.

Although the AFO and MATZOK had different political ideologies, priorities, and goals, both organizations had military training, arms acquisitions programs, and a network of contacts beyond the territory of the ghetto. Both built bunkers.

The leadership of the AFO understood that an armed rebellion in the ghetto would be suicidal, affording nothing more than an honorable death. They assumed that no help from outside the ghetto boundaries could be expected. An uprising could only be entertained if they knew in all certainty that the Germans actually planned to annihilate the entire ghetto. Although this kind of battle would be very difficult to implement, the AFO had developed plans for its members' mobilization and armed revolt.

It was not surprising then, that in the spring of 1943, contact between the two underground factions was established and a military commission, popularly called 'The Second Front', was formed to coordinate various anti-Nazi activities. Every week, the commission's members discussed the key issues related to the resistance. Often, Chaim Jellin was invited to visit Dr. Elchanan Elkes, the head of the Jewish Committee, at his home. The two men evaluated ways that ghetto fighters could escape to the partisans and how the Jewish administration could help them, including ways of smuggling clothing out of the ghetto workshops and matters of financial assistance. Dr. Elkes repeatedly asked Chaim to avoid taking extreme actions that could in any way harm the entire ghetto. They discussed involving young people from the Zionist factions to join the partisans. As Gelpernas confirms in his article:

> We collaborated most extensively during the mass escape of fighters from the ghetto to join the partisans. The AFO organized the transportation and prepared fighters, while [Zionist] organizations closely linked with the administration helped to raise funds and orchestrate the action.[77]

Although these two underground resistance cores functioned independently, they continued to coordinate their activities against the Nazis. It was obvious that the Nazis killed Jews indiscriminately, without taking into account their victims' social status, political involvement or age. Communists, socialists, zionists, the devout, and atheists were all killed only because they were Jews. All Jews had one common arch enemy – the German occupiers and their collaborators – and all the Jews in Kaunas Ghetto became united in their effort to fight the Nazis. However, because my husband, Misha Rubinsonas, and I were actively involved in the AFO, I will be discussing mainly the resistance of that underground organization.

One of the first and very important missions undertaken by the AFO was that of smuggling a radio receiver into the ghetto in 1942. It was a very dangerous and difficult action that could put hundreds of lives at risk if it were detected by the Germans. Misha Rubinsonas and Dima Gelpernas carried the radio together through the entire ghetto and hid it at Vezheju Street 8, the home of AFO member Tevje Pilovnik. Soon afterwards, the receiver was assembled and began to function. Most of the time, it was manned by Misha or Moisej Kupric, who took notes on the information they picked up. Dima and Misha later compiled this information, elaborating on the details, and edited it into a newsletter. Many young girls, including Polia Karnauskaite-Musel, Sulamita Lermanaite-Gelperniene and Leja Sher, copied out the newsletter by hand and made carbon copies of the text which were then distributed to the cells who later reported on it during their meetings.

By the middle of 1942, however, it became necessary to move the radio receiver to another location. Once again, Dima and Misha wrapped it in rags and transported it to a new hiding place, where it would be guarded by the director of the ghetto pharmacy, Aizik Sreb-nicki, a member of the Zionist underground.

I, myself, made no significant contribution to our organization's activities during the spring of 1942 since my workplace at the Noreik-ishkes Farm was not a suitable sabotage target. But I tried to help with smaller tasks. Almost every weekend, I would bring back a basket of fresh vegetable from the farm, which Monik would then distribute to sick members of our organization or to the children. I also helped Misha translate and copy our newsletter into Lithuanian, conscientiously attended meetings, and tried to master the 'science' of using a gun.

When I stopped working at Noreikishkes Farm at the end of October, Misha promised to introduce me to Chaim Jellin, who, he said, was willing to help me find a position in his brother Meyer's brigade. Meyer had studied in Germany and worked in Klaipeda (Memel) until 1938, when he moved to Kaunas. Under the Soviets, he worked at a construction company and here in the ghetto he was in charge of a brigade of over 100 people who worked on the merchandise dock at the railroad station. On the day I was to meet Jellin, Misha and I went to a two-storey house on Bajoru Street and climbed to the second floor. An older man opened the door and welcomed us in. Chaim received us in a small room that he shared with his father, Leizer, who served tea and promptly left the room. Chaim's brother, Meyer, lived in another room with his wife Dveira (Busia) and their one-year-old daughter, Esther (Esya).

I have to admit that my first impression of Chaim Jellin contrasted sharply with the image I had formed of the legendary AFO leader. He was rather short and had narrow shoulders. His light-colored, exceptionally long and down-turned whiskers seemed unnatural and mysterious to me. If his intention had been for the mustache to camouflage his appearance, it was not working, for the whiskers left a very distinct impression and did not conceal Chaim's pale face and sunken eyes. Still, I was deeply impressed by Chaim's moustache and his appearance in general.

Chaim asked me questions about my family and living conditions in the ghetto. As we talked, he looked me over and smiled.

"I have thought of a nickname for you," he said. "You will be *Sarke di Gele* (Sara the Blond). And you know," he continued, "you two are well suited to each other. He is *Meishke der Langer*, and you will be *Sarke di Gele*." I did not like this name very much, so I asked him sarcastically which he meant, golden or strawberry blond. Looking at me, he continued smiling and added that there is no differences. My new name quickly caught on in our circle of friends.

Our conversation with Chaim continued long into the night. I liked his husky voice and lively manner of speaking. He spoke passionately about our organization's goals and his determination to lead us into the forest to engage in armed battle against the Nazis.

Whispering secretively, Chaim revealed to us that many of our comrades were escaping to the city every day to establish contacts with like-minded people and former colleagues. He himself spent more time in the city than in the ghetto. Although he seemed tired, his every word and movement expressed an inexhaustible energy and great internal strength. He had a facility to convince people that his ideas and plans were realistic and that the struggle was imperative. Finally, long after night had fallen, Chaim suddenly leapt from his chair and disappeared from the room. He returned a few minutes later and introduced me to his brother.

"This is my brother, Meyer Jellin," Chaim said. "He is a construction engineer and head of a work brigade. He is willing to take you on."

"The work there is difficult," Meyer explained, "but we are taken there in trucks. Our men lay tracks and the women carry construction materials. Also, the conditions are not ideal because the work is supervised by a very nasty German, who watches us very carefully. This makes it impossible to leave the territory."

"After the New Year," Chaim added, "Meyer might be able to transfer you to another work section at the former German high school on Vytauto Prospect which has been converted into a military hospital."

I thanked them both and, when Misha and I got up to leave, Chaim stopped us. Taking my hand, he cautioned me.

"Just don't do anything rash. I strictly forbid you to even think of attempting any kind of sabotage." He squeezed my hand in a fatherly way and continued. "But don't worry, with your Lithuanian appearance and language skills, you will be very useful to us. The time will come when we will need you for some very important missions."

Work at the railway repair workshops (EAW or *Eisenbahn Aus-besserungs Werke*) was very different from the Noreikishkes Farm. The women carried construction materials and helped to load the newly repaired wagons with weapons, ammunition, and medicine. The German supervisor was a former boxer who liked to test the strength of his fist by punching the exhausted workers on the back so hard that, afterwards, they had trouble catching their breath. He referred to it as a 'light workout'. Since many members of our organization worked in this brigade, they were able to conduct various acts of sabotage there. They would send wagons in the wrong direction, load them with the wrong cargo, and cause disruption every chance they had. This was not easy because the work area was completely sealed off and civilians were strictly prohibited from entering it. There was no way of leaving it, even briefly.

A short, attractive man worked in the workshop office, processing worker registration and documents regarding completed work. Dima Gelpernas recognized me as soon as I joined the brigade at the ghetto gates. He knew our family well. He had studied with my sister at the German high school, often helping her with math. But it wasn't until later that I learned that Dima was a member of the AFO Committee and Chaim's deputy.

Dima had a slow manner and was not an idealistic philosopher by nature. If Chaim was always full of plans and visions, his deputy had a completely different personality. He always tried to avoid conflict and went over the most minute details of every operation until he was satisfied it would be carried out perfectly. When I was given an assignment, Dima never just said 'goodbye'. Instead, he always advised me, "Just don't rush. Think everything over one last time." I also liked the fact that Dima did not like Misha's or my nickname. Instead, he called me *Sarinka* and called Misha, *Meishele*, sometimes adding *langer* to Misha's name only to distinguish him from all the other *Mei-sheles*. Dima Gelpernas and Chaim Jellin complemented each other perfectly in their roles as leaders of our fighting organization.

By the end of 1942, I had also become well acquainted with Alte Boruchovich-Teper, another member of the AFO committee. She lived with her boyfriend, Dovid Teper, at Linkmenu Street 8, in the old part of the Slabodka not far from the Krischiukaichiu Street gates and their apartment served as our organization's aid and support center. Comrades brought clothes there, better food for the children and the infirm, medicine, and donations of money. Despite our strategy of caution and secrecy, Alte's home was always full of people and her small kitchen was where we sat, discussing and debating, analyzing the events of the past week. Everyone could be sure of getting a bowl of soup or a cup of tea at Alte's. Even though she was only a few years older than I, she played the role of a mother among us.

I often met Misha at Alte's and it soon became clear that a deepening friendship and love was developing between us. It became a habit for him to walk with me on our way home. However, when we would reach the Catholic Cemetery, the so-called 'corridor', Misha would stop abruptly and say,

"Well, here we are. Halfway. Now it's the same distance to your house and mine, so I won't walk with you any farther."

This would make me very angry. "Don't bother!" I would answer heatedly. "And don't wait for me at Alte's next week either, because I won't show up."

Misha would stand there quietly, not moving. I continued to wait, hopefully, but he would hold his ground, silently. Without saying a word, without looking back or saying goodbye, I would run towards home, leaving Misha standing there in the middle of the road. But the following Sunday, I would appear again at Alte's. And Misha would be waiting for me. Once again, we would leave together and, once again, he would walked with me, but only as far as the cemetery.

As 1942 drew to a close, my family was beginning to run out of food supplies. Soon we would forget the taste of butter, eggs, meat, ham, and sugar. But on New Year's Eve, we bade farewell to the past year and greeted the coming one with hope. We were beginning to hear good news from the Eastern Front. The Germans were suffering greater losses, their soldiers were dying, not only from wounds, but from the unbearable cold. It seemed that the German army was beginning to retreat at every Front. Though we had neither champagne nor wine to toast with, we wished each other the strength to endure until the defeat of the Germans and the fall of Hitler and his supporters. As the clock struck midnight, we toasted to our liberation.

READY FOR ARMED RESISTANCE

At the beginning of March 1943, I was transferred from the railway repair workshop to the *Krankensammelstelle* (Military Transit Hospital). Wounded German soldiers were brought there directly by train from the Eastern Front, usually with frozen hands and feet. Patients undergoing treatment and those recuperating were kept in the hospital for three or four days and then either transferred elsewhere for more extensive treatment or sent home on leave. The hospital was set up in the center of the city at the former German High School on Vytautas Prospect 10. It felt strange for me to come to work every day, seeing the familiar Latin inscription, *Non Scholae Set Vitae Discimus* (We learn not for school, but for life), on the facade of the building. It was even more difficult for me to walk into the classrooms where I had spent two years of my life and where my sister Alice had spent almost seven years. Now those classrooms were filled, row upon row, with beds full of wounded Germans.

Misha Rubinsonas led the Jewish brigade at the hospital. The men took care of general repairs of this and two other buildings and the women cleaned the corridors and other parts of the building. When there were no wounded soldiers, we cleaned the wards, changed the linen, and washed floors and windows. However, the German nurses and doctors in the hospital were very different from the brutal Nazi administrators and guards in the ghetto and in the military enterprises where I had worked before. The German sergeant in charge of the hospital pharmacy was quite a nice man and, before long, Misha had established a relationship with him. A deal was worked out in which Misha would provide the sergeant with lists of medical supplies needed in the ghetto. In return for the medicine he supplied, the sergeant would be compensated with good coffee, alcoholic beverages, and other goodies. A portion of the medical supplies obtained went to the ghetto pharmacy, the rest went to the medical personnel of the AFO. Later on, the medical supplies were sent to the partisans in the forest. Misha continued these exchanges until the end of 1943, as long as he worked at the hospital. Then his sister, Sonya Rubinsonaite, took over.

During the winter and spring of 1943, Misha worked tirelessly on the affairs of our organization. He prepared information bulletins and often went into the city to meet with Lithuanian contacts. In Misha's absence, Sonya would substitute for him at the hospital. She got along well with the German in charge of the Jewish brigade and, through him, she managed to negotiate better working conditions and food for us. Because of her efforts, we were allowed to eat our lunch in the kitchen with the Ukrainian kitchen staff, all of whom were former prisoners of war who had agree to fight on the German side. Because the Germans despised them and did not trust them, the Ukrainians were often treated more like prisoners than like allies. We managed to maintain a warm relationship with the Ukrainians. All in all, the work in the hospital was not very hard and we were reasonably well fed.

On days when we cleaned the empty hospital wards, Sonya insisted that we clean all the mattresses and drawers as well. Although the wounded German soldiers had to surrender their firearms to the hospital armory when they came into the hospital, they often hid ammunition under their mattresses or in the drawers. Misha and Sonya were determined to collect as much of this ammunition as possible and transport it to the ghetto by hiding it in the false bottom of a kettle.

One day, while cleaning a ward, I spotted a rifle and a small bag of bullets under a mattress. Excitedly, I wrapped my find in rags and took it into the room where we kept our clothes and bags. I told Sonya about what I had found and that I was determined to smuggle it into the ghetto. The short, Japanese-made rifle easily fit into my bag which I lined with twigs. I dumped some potatoes over the rifle and I was ready to go. My heart was pounding with joy as I got into the truck. It was only when I started walking towards the inspection point at the ghetto gate that I began to feel frightened. Slowing down a little, I stepped back hesitantly to let others go ahead. Not daring to go closer to the gates, I waited as long as I could. Finally, I decided to take the risk and ask Tanchun Aramshtam, the head of the Jewish police at the gate, to help me. In Yiddish, I timidly whispered to him, *"Ich bin zejer treiff"* (I am very unkosher). This let him know that I was carrying something strictly forbidden.

Without checking my bag, he immediately started yelling at me, threatening and pushing me forward through the gate. The German guard, apparently happy to see one Jew pushing and berating another, paid little attention. As soon as I was through the gate, I literally flew to Chaim Jellin's house. He was surprised to see me but he let me catch my breath, understood from my excitement that nothing bad had happened. Without a word, I took the rifle and the bullets out of my container. He was speechless. In the long moment of silence that followed, the leader of our organization didn't know whether to scold me or to praise me. Although he felt he must criticize me a little for disobeying his order, Chaim soon relented.

"You are a reliable comrade," he said. "But you must never bring arms into the ghetto again. We now keep them in town, in a secret apartment. From now on, just alert *Langman* (Misha) when you find something and our people will pick it up from the hospital." We were both overjoyed.

The story of how the Japanese rifle was smuggled into the ghetto was first described in a book by Nechemija Endlin: "Sara Rubinson brought the rifle in parts [in fact, the rifle was not disassembled. S.G.-R.]. At that time, this was the only long weapon in the ghetto and it was used to train our group."[78]

Armed only with this one rifle, our group later escaped from the ghetto to meet up with the partisans in Rudninkai Forest.

Soon after this incident, I detected another rifle hidden under a mattress. I wrapped it in rags and hid it in our little storage room with our belongings. This time, I told Misha about what I had found and arrangements were made for me to pass the gun over the fence to Ida Pilovnik-Vilenchiuk, our organization's arms carrier. The next day, when I went to the fence, I noticed a country girl whom I barely recognized as Ida, standing on the other side of the hospital fence. She was standing with another member of our organization, Zan Shperling. When Ida saw the long parcel I was holding, she refused to take it. "We are right next to the Gestapo building," she exclaimed, fearfully. I tried to calm her down, telling her that the Gestapo building was across the street at some distance away. Besides, I told her, we were always successfully 'conducting our trade' across the fence. We were used to passing goods from the ghetto over the fence to the 'traders' who passed food back over to us.

Finally, Ida agreed to take the rifle. I climbed up on the fence, carefully handing her the bag. She put the package in a large basket and walked slowly away from the fence and the Gestapo building. These two brave members of the AFO carried the basket containing the rifle across the whole city, from Vytauto Prospect to Jonavos Street. There, they handed the rifle over to one of the Kaunas anti-Nazis fighters, Petras Trofimovas, and from him it found its way to the partisans.

Ida was by no means a novice and the transportation of this rifle from Vytauto Prospect to Jonavos Street was neither Ida's first or her last assignment. She once even managed to bring a sub-machine gun which needed repair through the ghetto gates. Along with other Jewish workers, she had came, one morning, to a workshop where the Jewish brigade, led by AFO member, Moishe Musel, was repairing German military trucks. Ida remained at the workshop all morning, enjoyed a hearty lunch prepared by Mrs. Polia Musel, and then began packing the broken sub-machine gun. She filled a bag with sticks and twigs, placed the sub-machine gun in it and covered the bag with half-rotten potatoes. The package was very heavy but the weapon was well hidden. Even the Jewish workers had no idea what was really in the bag. At the end of the work day, the men, who were puzzled by the weight of the bag and the quantity of potatoes, helped Ida heave the bag onto the truck. When the truck approached the ghetto gates, they helped Ida lift the bag out of the truck and put it on her shoulders. Bent under the weight of this bag filled with stinking potatoes, she avoided inspection and entered the ghetto. Her comrades, waiting inside the gate, delivered the bag containing the sub-machine gun to the ghetto workshop where it was repaired by our weapons instructor, Liova Sher.

My chance to become involved in our organization's activities came in the spring of 1943. One morning, Misha told me that Chaim Jellin wanted to meet with us. This time, when we came to see him, I wasn't observing Chaim's sunken eyes and pale face. This time, he watched me carefully, paying attention to the way I looked and to my posture. He looked me over for a while, then he said, "You look like a real Lithuanian girl. A perfect young lady from Kaunas. Are you ready to undertake a really dangerous assignment?"

Without any hesitation, as if replying to a well-rehearsed lesson, I replied, "Any time. Even Today!"

Chaim appointed me liaison between himself and Dima Gelpernas. I would be required to walk the streets of Kaunas without a yellow star, meet designated people who would help me find and establish contact with anti-Nazis and other underground activists. Chaim advised me to renew contact with my former classmates and acquaintances. Every new contact, he said, improved the likelihood that we would reach our objective. At the end of our talk, Chaim became very gentle. He looked at Misha and me and said, just like at our first meeting, "You and *Langman* are so well suited..." When we said goodbyes, I smiled and told him that we already belonged to each other.

My friendship with Misha had been getting stronger. It had not been love at first sight, but we had become closer. He was a loving comrade and a considerate friend. He had also become a welcome guest at our home and was very fond of my mother, whom he greatly admired. Misha had lost his own mother, Chana Rubinsoniene, at the tender age of 13 and his father and sister had not been able to sustain a warm and nurturing atmosphere in their home. He developed a real concern for my mother's welfare, often helping her with the hard, 'manly chores' like chopping wood and bringing water in from the well. Once, when talking about her, he even called her 'Mama' before realizing what he had said. He quickly corrected himself and said, Sara's Mama.

Despite the horrible living conditions, the constant threat of death, and the absence of any privacy, Misha and I had managed to develop a relationship that gradually grew into a true and faithful love. For the first time in his life, Misha felt the warmth, care, and concern of a woman. As for me, I finally had a true friend, a strong person who loved me. We shared the same beliefs, and in a sense, we were dreamers. Even in such circumstances, it turns out, people can be dreamers. We knew that we could be killed, but we did not think about death. We thought and talked only about life, about our future. We lived in dreams and illusions, held strong the belief that we were masters of our destinies. That is what made it possible for us to be so determined, to strive for a goal which seemed utterly impossible at that time, and to do what had to be done.

Once I received my orders from Chaim, I took on the role of a carefree young lady from Kaunas. My mother must have suspected that I had started working for the underground, but I never spoke about it. I started ironing my dresses, skirts, and blouses and putting on a little makeup, just as I used to in the days before the war. I behaved as though I had any ordinary job. But, as soon as our truck stopped at the hospital gate, I would be the first to get off, quickly don a jacket without the yellow star on it and melt into the crowd of people. I knew this part of the city quite well, having lived near Vytauto Prospect just before the war. I began to wander into the suburbs of Kaunas (Aleksotas, Zaliakalnis, and Vilijampole) and to the City Center. I would meet the contact, explain who I was, and pass on information, indicating where and when the contact should pick up a letter, a 'toy' (a weapon), or 'a parcel from mother or an aunt'.

Often, following Chaim and Dima's instructions, I would deliver objects. There was always a German military uniform or an officer's cap which our people had succeeded in stealing from the ghetto workshops and was needed by a well-known underground activist. At other times, I would deliver a rubber stamp made in the ghetto that was to be used to stamp forged documents or certificates, or a linoleum plate for printing proclamations.

I got so used to running around the streets of Kaunas on those warm spring days that I almost felt as though I were living in an ordinary world. Perhaps, in the evening, I would not have to return to a ghetto encircled by barbed wire. Perhaps I would not have to pass through a humiliating inspection or suffer the indignity of being searched. I never thought about the danger or the punishment that might await me for my acts of disobedience to the Nazis. I only thought about carrying out my duty to my people and, of course, I knew that I had to be careful. These were the thoughts in my mind when I knocked on a designated door, uttered the password and, for safety's sake, offered to trade something for food. When I was invited inside, I carried on a conversation, exchanged information, agreed upon a new password, and, after carefully glancing around, walked out into the yard or the street. If I were stopped or arrested when my basket still contained some products from the ghetto, I knew that I would have to explain. I would say that I had knocked on a stranger's door hoping to exchange my clothes for food. Secrecy was a our strictest code of behavior.

At every meeting, though, I expected a miracle to happen. I wanted so badly to meet people who would be able and willing to connect us with the partisans or members of other underground resistance groups. Unfortunately, no such miracle occurred, but as a result of all those meetings, our network of reliable contacts kept expanding. Keeping this in mind, I decided to visit our former housekeeper, Frania Grunskaite. She had raised me and I had loved her dearly. Some time before the war, my father's financial help allowed Frania to buy a kiosk on Mickevichaus Street. Now she sold newspapers, magazines, postcards, stamps, tobacco products, and other sundries there. Frania was surprised and delighted to see me when I showed up at the kiosk. She invited me to visit her sister, Liuda Buziene, who also lived on Mickeviciaus Street, not far from the Nemunas embankment. A few days later, Frania and I dropped in and met, not only Liuda, but her husband, Pranas, and their daughters, Irute and Laimute. I told them about our life in the ghetto, about the cruelty of the Nazis, the endless arrests, the deportations and killings. We discussed how and where we could hide my mother, my aunt and, especially, her two-year-old daughter, Tanya. Frania promised first of all to find a place for the child. In the countryside not far from Kaunas, she had a friend and hoped her friend would be willing to take the child, where she would be safer. She also agreed to accept letters addressed to me at her kiosk. I passed all the information about the kiosk on to Chaim and from then on, Frania Grunskaite's kiosk became a communications point for our organization.

Always on the lookout for new contacts, I took my Uncle Lazar's advice and visited some old acquaintances of his, the family of the architect, Dush-Dushevskis. Lazar knew the architect's Polish-born wife quite well and he was certain that she had contacts with the Polish underground. When I first approached her, she became quite agitated. She warned me that her husband had a high position and that German officials often visited their house, even during the day. Reluctant at first to get involved in conversation, she eventually agreed to provide us with forged Polish refugee certificates if we provided photos of our people.

Later on, we decided to ask her to make forged certificates for my mother, my sister, and Fanya. In return, she took the fur coats that my mother and sister had left with her for safekeeping. But when I received the certificates, they did not look very reliable and we doubted whether, in fact, we could use them. I showed them to Chaim and he thought that an inexperienced policeman might not notice the forgery. Chaim gave me photos of some friends and asked me to obtain the same kind of certificates for them. Mrs. Dush-Dushevski produced the certificates, which cost us our silver and all the other valuables we had left with her for safekeeping. But I don't know if any of our friends ever used these certificates. We discovered later that a Jewish family had been hiding in the Dush-Dushevski house. When the Gestapo discovered the family, they were arrested and executed but, apparently, the Dush-Dushevski did not suffer any consequences.

At my sister's request, I also visited her ophthalmologist, Dr. Elena Kutorgiene. Although I did not know her personally, I knocked on the doctor's door and conveyed my sister's Alice greetings. She did not ask me who my sister was but invited me into her office, examined my eyes, and asked me how she could help. As usual, our conversation began with my tale about the terrible situation in the ghetto. I asked her if she could find a hiding place for my sister. Dr. Kutorgiene suggested that I meet with her son, Viktoras Kutorga, who was also a doctor and worked in Zapyshkis, near Kaunas. From my talk with Viktoras, I understood that he was in touch with some ghetto inmates who were ready to set up a partisan base in a forest near Kachergine.

It turned out that Chaim already knew about this situation but suggested that I maintain contact with them. With the help of Kaunas underground activists like Viktoras Kutorga, the AFO committee was planning to establish contact with small partisan groups who were active in the Kaunas district. Misha's mission was to visit Viktoras and explore the possibilities for the ghetto resisters to join the groups in the Kachergine or Zapyshkis Forests. Misha took the river steamer to Kachergine, then went on foot to Zapyshkis. He surveyed the area to become better acquainted with the location and its reliability. The forest did not seem very dense to him and he felt it was very close to inhabited areas. Viktoras Kutorga suggested that an underground bunker could be built there, which could operate as a partisan support point.

Not long afterwards, a small group of ghetto resisters was sent to build the bunker. Misha and I were to join them later on. But before it was completed, the bunker was discovered by a forest ranger. The man pretended not to notice it and walked on to the village. Later, he returned to the site with the police who surrounded the bunker. Fortunately, the ghetto resisters had managed to escape in time, but the construction of the bunker had to be abandoned, dashing hopes to escape to the forest. This development, however, did not stop Doctor Kutorgiene and her son, Viktoras Kutorga, in their underground activities.

During the winter and spring of 1943, the AFO continued its search for partisans. Many young, courageous members of the AFO were sent to search for partisan bases in various parts of Lithuania. Unfortunately, many of them were killed, arrested, or executed. Not one of them come across any substantial partisan group. It finally became apparent that they could not find partisans because there were no partisan groups operating on Lithuanian soil at the end of 1942 and the beginning of 1943. The partisan movement only began to appear in the fall of 1943.

A few nationalist underground movements were functioning in Lithuania at that time. In March 1943, however, a group of Lithuanian intellectuals were arrested and imprisoned at the Stutthof Concentration Camp in Germany. The Liberal Lithuanian Freedom Fighters' Union (LLKS) was also quite active. It maintained foreign contacts, published an illegal newspaper, *The Freedom Fighter*, and operated a secret radio station. In April-May 1944, the Gestapo arrested a group of LLKS members and also imprisoned them in Germany. [79] The LLKS, like the other nationalist underground organizations, avoided contact with the Jews and did not want any contact with the leadership of the administration of the Kaunas Ghetto, the Zionists, or any anti-Nazi underground groups. They detached themselves completely from the problems of the Jews of Kaunas Ghetto and the ominous possibility of their total destruction.

Abraham Tory writes in his diary that he, personally, along with other members of the Kaunas Ghetto administration, approached their influential Lithuanian friends with whom they had fought for

Lithuania's independence or with whom they had been imprisoned during the first Soviet occupation. However, Tory and his friends did not succeed in obtaining any significant support or cooperation from these people. They were not even able to maintain regular contact with them. [80]

One of the members of our organization, Nechemija Endlin, did manage to establish contact with Pranas Baleniunas, an activist in the Lithuanian national underground movement. Baleniunas promised to consult with his leadership about establishing contact with the Kaunas Ghetto underground. In a subsequent meeting, Baleniunas informed Endlin that General Nagevichius declined to cooperate with Communists, meaning Jewish anti-Nazis. [81]

At the same time, some Lithuanian intellectuals and individual priests were looking for ways and means to help the Jews. In the fall of 1942, a former President of Lithuania, Kazys Grinius, and Professors Mykolas Krupavichius and Jonas Alekna wrote a memorandum to the German Reich Commissar in Lithuania in which they expressed their disapproval of the colonization of the country and the measures applied against Lithuanian Jews. For this act, Krupavichius and Alekna were deported to Germany, while Grinius was exiled to Kazlu Ruda, a small village in Lithuania. [82] In spite of the great efforts and numerous attempts made, neither the ghetto underground organizations nor the leadership of the ghetto administration were successful in establishing ties with the Lithuanian national underground or to secure any assistance from it.

Aside from the AFO's top priority of expanding connections and links with Lithuanians and with the Kaunas underground anti-fascist movement, our second most important goal was to obtain weapons. Our organization desperately needed arms. Chaim and Dima repeatedly urged Misha to find out where the soldiers were keeping their weapons at the hospital. Once, while wandering around the building, Misha by chance noticed a strange little storage shed. The next day, Misha suggested to the German in charge of the Jewish brigade that he tidy up the hospital yard and the storage shed. Pleased with the suggestion, the German promptly brought the key and opened the shed for Misha. The shed was stacked full of weapons.

Stunned at the sight and barely able to hide his joy, Misha could hardly wait to finish cleaning out the shed. When he was finished, the

German locked the door and pocketed the key. Although it seemed unrealistic at first, Misha, Sonya, and I decided to rob the weapons storage shed. Slowly, the idea was developed into a concrete plan. After long deliberations with Chaim and Dima, it was decided that the first thing we had to do was have a key to the shed made in one of the ghetto workshops.

It was a difficult task because, first, we needed to obtain the key and copy its shape. Sonya repeatedly suggested to our German overseer that the yard and shed should be cleaned. Having nothing against the idea, the German would open the shed, put the key in his pocket, and leave her there alone to clean. One day, our break came when he forgot to pocket the key. Sonya quickly made a drawing of it, cut out its contours, and copied its shape. The ghetto locksmiths were then able to make a copy of the key. Once we had the key, Sonya had to be very careful not to arouse any suspicions when she and Misha tried to open the lock. They tried several times but the key did not work and the locksmiths in the ghetto had to keep making adjustments. After many trials, Sonya finally succeeded in unlocking the arms storage shed and then locking it again. The first part of the arms seizure plot had been completed. Now a night schedule had to be scrutinized. Misha suggested to the German overseer that the Jewish brigade work late and clean all the windows of the hospital. The brigade worked late into the night while Misha analyzed the German guards' schedule and itinerary. He made note of their procedures for changing the watch, the times when they took their breaks and other details. A plan for the arms seizure project now had to be prepared and a truck had to be located to haul away the arms.

By the time this operation actually took place, Misha and I were already in the partisan detachment. I only learned the details of this successful operation from Sonya Rubinsonaite when I returned to the ghetto. After Chaim Jellin made arrangements with a truck driver, the operation to seize the ammunitions could go ahead. Three courageous, very young ghetto resisters were assigned to this risky operation: Itzchak Miklishanski, Mendel Moskovich, and Moishe Geguzinski. The three young ghetto resisters escaped from the ghetto, walked through the entire city of Kaunas, from Vilijampole to the Vytauto prospect, without wearing their Yellow Stars. They hid in the cemetery next to the hospital until nightfall. Then they climbed over the fence, opened the arms storage, removed all weapons and, after carefully relocking the shed, hid in the cemetery again. At dawn, the truck pulled up at the cemetery. The young ghetto resisters loaded the bags containing the weapons and jumped into the truck which then made its way to Kestuchio Street where Jellin was waiting. He let the resisters out and the three young men then safely returned the ghetto. Because of the need for secrecy and in the interests of safety, Chaim then switched the truck and the driver. With the new driver Chaim delivered the bags to a secret apartment on Jonavos Street that belonged to a member of the underground Kaunas Communist Party Committee, Petras Trofimovas. This was the first AFO arms annexation operation.

The day after the seizure, when the Jewish brigade came to work, there was great commotion at the hospital. The Gestapo and their search dogs were everywhere. They interrogated the German staff and the new leader of the Jewish work brigade, who, of course, knew nothing about it. But really, the Germans did not suspect the Jews. The Jewish brigade carried on with its work as usual and the Gestapo never found the culprits. A new lock was installed in the shed, which was now constantly under guard.

Unexpectedly, one day in September of 1943, a turning point occurred in our organization's activities. The miracle we dreamed of, a contact with real partisans, occurred. A Lithuanian man approached one of the Jews working in a military car repair garage on Kestuchio Street and inquired about the writer, Chaim Jellin. The suspicious Jewish worker told him that he didn't know such a person but suggested that the man return the next day. He told Moishe Musel, the foreman of the Jewish work brigade, about the incident and Dima Gelpernas and Chaim, who happened to be in the ghetto, were immediately informed.

The next day, Dima went to the workshop to meet the stranger. But before Dima met with him, Moishe Musel spoke to the man. He turned out to be Juozas Tubelis, a member of the anti-Nazi underground of Vilnius. In the small kitchen of the workshop, Juozas Tubelis told Moishe about a Jewish woman in Vilnius, a friend of Chaim's, who wanted to help him. If it were possible to contact Chaim, Tubelis persisted, he could bring a letter from this woman. When Moishe was convinced that this was not trick, he invited Dima to continue the conversation. Dima had a long discussion with Juozas Tubelis and, as they spoke, the two men developed a trust between them. Dima promised to try to locate Chaim and Juozas promised to bring a letter from Vilnius the next day.

Back in the ghetto, Dima and Chaim discussed the situation. Chaim decided to go with Moishe's work brigade and, once at the workshop, they would decide what to do next. Juozas Tubelis was already there when they arrived. He was first approached by Yankel Levi, a member of the AFO and the person Tubelis had contacted the first time he came to the workshop. As they were speaking, Tubelis pulled a small letter out of a cigarette and handed it to Levi. The letter was not addressed to Chaim but to Levi who immediately recognized the code used in the contents. He knew the handwriting and the signature,'G.' The letter was from Levi's close friend, Gese Glezer, who was inviting Chaim to come to a meeting in Vilnius.

Gese Glezer's (code name Albina) trip to Lithuania began in Moscow. She had come to Lithuania as a representative of the Central Committee of the Lithuanian Communist Party and had been flown from Moscow and parachuted to a place in Belarus behind enemy lines. From there she made her way, on foot, to the Rudininkai Forest where the first partisan units were being formed. After spending some time with the partisans, she went to Vilnius. Once she established contacts with the underground movement in Vilnius, she attempted to link up with the Kaunas underground, and, primarily, with prisoners in the Kaunas Ghetto. Before the war, she had known Yankel Levi, as well as many others, including the young Jewish writer, Chaim Jellin. Glezer had sent her reliable friend, Juozas Tubelis, from Vilnius to Kaunas, to find Jellin.

Once Chaim spoke to Juozas, he decided to go to Vilnius immediately. Moishe Musel made arrangements on the spot with a driver who agreed to take the two men. Everything then fell into place. Within a few hours, a loaded truck was due to leave for Vilnius. Moishe persuaded the driver to take a 'worker' and one other person along on the pretext that the parents of the brigade worker were sick in the Vilnius Ghetto and he needed to visit them for a few days. And so, Chaim went to Vilnius in a truck driven by a German soldier to meet a Jewish woman from Moscow, Gese Glezer(Albina). Instead of a few days, Chaim spent more than two weeks with her. Musel writes:

> One nice autumn day, a limping man with a railway work-er's cap appeared at the gate of the workshop and asked for Moishe. It was Chaim and he was back from Vilnius, alive and well, except for a twisted ankle. He put on his yellow star and returned to the ghetto with the workers of the bri-gade.[83]

Chaim told an enthusiastic tale of his trip to Vilnius and to the partisan unit in Rudninkai Forest. He told his close friends and members of the Committee of the life of the partisans in the forest and their armed struggle with the Germans. In the forest, Chaim had met Genrikas Zimanas (code name, Jurgis), commander of the partisan movement there and Secretary of the underground Communist Party Committee of southern Lithuania. As he described his participation in a fighting action, a smile played on Chaim's lips, his eyes sparkled and his face radiated with satisfaction. "Our true place is in the forest." Chaim kept repeating. "In the forest, we will enter a free world. Yes, it is dangerous, but we will be fighting the Nazis, our enemy, and nobody here is afraid of danger."

A few days after Chaim returned, Gese Glezer (Albina) came to Kaunas and entered the ghetto with Chaim Jellin and Moishe Musel from a safe house on Shauliu Street. Paul Margolin, a member of the Jewish administration's labour department, was on duty at the gate and helped to smuggle Albina's pistol in the ghetto. Albina presided at the next AFO meeting and declared that ghetto resisters would not be sent to the Rudninkai Forest but to Augustava Forest in southwestern Lithuania. This forest was about 160 km from Kaunas and the ghetto resisters from Kaunas were to establish a new partisan unit there. Albina informed the members at the meeting that there were already support points, such as bunkers, in place and that code names had already been established for the liaison people. Albina stressed the urgency of the situation because Vilnius Ghetto had already been liquidated and its remaining inmates were being shipped off to various concentration camps. She urged that preparations begin immediately to organize the escape of the ghetto resisters to the forest of Augustava.

Many rank and file members of the organization considered this plan unfeasible. They felt that the ghetto youth should start fighting in Rudninkai Forest, where they could get some initial experience in partisan warfare. Some even refused to take part in the Augustava mission. Musel also saw it as unrealistic and excessively risky, and he had grave doubts that the destination could even be reached. He suggested that the leadership consider other plans for escaping from the ghetto to the partisans. After hearing Moishe's arguments, Chaim suggested that Albina meet separately with Moishe, but she would not even consider his opinion. She categorically refused to change her proposed plan and replied curtly, "Orders are to be followed, not discussed." That was the end of the discussion.

The first group of fighters left for Augustava Forest on October 21 and the last one on October 28, 1943. All of them met with disaster. Of the seventy-one fighters, three died in an exchange of gunfire with the police. Thirty-five were arrested by the Gestapo and, after long interrogations, were taken to the Ninth Fort. Three others found shelter in a farmer's house and the rest returned safely to the ghetto. Only two fighters reached the destination, Nechemija Endlin and Shmulik Mordkovski. They did not find any support bunkers or liaison people, either along the way, or at their final destination. From Endlin and Mordkovski's stories, it became clear that Augustava Forest was ill-suited for the founding of partisan units.

Quite a few mistakes were made during the preparations for the Augustava mission which contributed to the failure of the operation. The fighters were poorly armed, their maps were inaccurate, and their itinerary was not properly worked out. In addition, not a single fighter had any luck in finding the liaison people or underground activists. Perhaps there were no liaison people there at all or maybe they were afraid to reveal their hiding places. But the main reason for the failure was the fact that the forests of Augustava were not well suited for setting up partisan bases. This was something the AFO Committee could not have known. Southwestern Lithuanian was well behind the German front line and there was a substantial concentration of police and military units in the area. The local population was hostile and did not want the partisans there. They were afraid of German vengeance for local support and shelter of partisans. Some farmers would have been ready to hide a few Jews in their homes, but not to have partisans in their neighborhood. However, soon after the failure of the mission to Augustava Forest, permission was received from Zimanas (Jurgis) to send fighters to Rudninkai Forest. They were to join a new partisan detachment to be called, "Death to the Occupiers". Contacts were to be established with guides through underground activists in the village of Murava, not far from Kaunas.

While Albina was still in Kaunas Ghetto, I unexpectedly received a request from Dima Gelpernas to come with him to the home of Chone Kaganas, a member of our organization. When we arrived, Chaim was already waiting for us with a blonde woman whom I didn't know. Chaim introduced her as our comrade, Albina. I was quite surprised by the respect Chaim and Dima showed this woman and I wondered where she had come from. In the course of the conversation, I got the impression that this woman, not Chaim, was the leader of the AFO and it amazed me that her identity had been kept secret for so long.

Forcefully, Albina told me that I should make contact with the young communists – classmates from high school. I told her that I had attended a school for children of prosperous Jewish families before the Soviets took over. Under the Soviets, the school I had attended had been merged with the Jesuit High School and, therefore, there were very few communist youth there. Beside, I told her, I had attended that school for only one year and knew very few people there. I had somewhat closer relationships with Kaminskas, Zumeris, and Boreikaite, who were young communists, but I had heard that Boreikaite had been successful in escaping to the Soviet Union. Kaminskas and Zumeris were around and I told Albina that Monik Holzberg knew them better than I did. Albina suggested that Holzberg and I go immediately to visit them and that, through them, we should link up with the Kaunas Young Communist League. Albina wanted us to become more involved in their activities, she said. She wished me luck and the meeting ended. Seeing me to the door, Dima warned me not to mention this meeting to anybody, not even to Misha. But my curiosity got the better of me. Casually I asked Misha who was the real leader of our organization, Chaim or this mysterious woman. Misha was very surprised at my question and thought that I meant Meri Lan, a member of our committee. Not wanting to argue, I just said that Meri was just one of Chaim's deputies while this 'mystery' woman seemed to be Chaim's superior. That was the end of our conversation.

Soon after this meeting, Monik Holzberg and I started planning a meeting with our former classmates. Moishe Musel promised to drive us there in a truck from the workshop and, at the agreed time, he was waiting for us at the ghetto gate. Monik and I got through the gate without any trouble and climbed into the truck. Moishe was sitting in the front next to the driver and the truck began rolling through the old town of Kaunas. Before we arrived at Zumeris' home, Moishe stopped the truck and told us that he couldn't go any further and that we would have to walk the rest of the way. I got out and the truck drove away. Angry that Moishe had not keep his promise, I began looking around for Monik but he was nowhere to be seen. Monik never showed up.

Alone, I began climbing the path up the hill and found Zumeris' house. As Zumeris and I talked, I told him that the ghetto young people would like to join the activities of the Kaunas underground. We needed arms, I continued, and were looking for new contacts with the anti-Nazi underground. He was quite skeptical about my requests and the proposals I had made. He said that it was very dangerous to live in the city, that young men were being mobilized into the German army, and that people were being rounded up and shipped to Germany for forced labour. Nevertheless, he promised to talk to his friend Kaminskas, who was in hiding himself and lived in a safe house. He agreed to meet with me again and we fixed the day and the time. I suggested that, if possible, Kaminskas should also come to our next meeting. Zumeris insisted that Monik come to the meeting.

When we finished, Zumeris offered to accompany me to the Vilijampole Bridge, for my own safety. He put on a railway worker's uniform and we walked down the path to Jonava Street where the bridge was. There he stopped and said he wouldn't accompany me any further. I told him I was afraid to cross the bridge alone but we finally agreed that we would cross separately. I would go first and he would follow. Halfway across, he kissed me and, after quietly reminding me that we would meet soon again, he turned back. I crossed the last part of the bridge myself, turned into Krischiukaichio Street where I changed into a sweater with a yellow Star of David and joined a brigade returning to the ghetto.

When I reported on my meeting, I learned that I would have to go to see Zumeris alone again. And this time, Moishe Musel would not be able to take me in the truck. I would have to get out of the ghetto by sneaking over the fence. Misha promised that our friends, who were experts at going through the fence and worked with the *czamniks* (fence traders), would help me over the fence. He also told me that nearly all our communications girls were getting out of the ghetto by going over the fence and that this was the way Sulamita Lermanaite-Gelperiene, Ida Shateriene, Sonya Vechteryte, Chana Volbe, and others often went illegally to the city of Kaunas without the mark – the yellow stars on their clothes.

On the appointed day, it took me only a few seconds to get over the fence unnoticed. From there I went to the adjacent Catholic Cemetery to calm down a bit and then went on toward the Vilijampole Bridge. I crossed the bridge calmly and climbed the path again from Jonavos Street to the hill where Zumeris lived. Although Kaminskas couldn't make it either, Zumeris gave me some very important information. He told me that every one of the inhabitants of the village of Murava was an underground activist and maintained contact with the partisans in Rudninkai Forest. This fact would allow us to establish contact with the young communists in the small village. It was only later that we learned that, through Albina, the AFO Committee had already established relations with the Murava underground and partisans. My meetings with Zumeris were only a way of confirming that Murava was a reliable place for meetings with the underground and with partisan guides.

My meeting with Mechys Zumeris was brief and he only agreed to accompany me as far as Jonava Street. We walked down the path, he kissed me again and we parted. I decided that, before I continue, I would stop at a courtyard and have a good look in all directions. Suddenly, I noticed that there was a short man watching me very intently. I quickly stepped into the courtyard and from there, crossed from one yard into another, going further away from Jonava Street and the bridge I needed to cross. After a while, I came back, looked around, and saw that the same man was still standing in the same spot. It seemed to me that he noticed me, so once again I walked away, going from yard to yard. About half an hour later, I came back to the same courtyard, climbed to the second floor and, through the staircase window, I could see that the man was still there, carefully looking around, observing the yard and the bridge. I noticed that he was limping as he was slowly walked back and forth, constantly looking around. Quickly, I calculated the time I would need to run out of the yard before my limping persecutor returned to his observation spot. I believed that I could make it across the street and run up to the bridge before he returned. I ran across the street and was already on the bridge when he noticed me and started after me, limping toward the bridge. I was running faster than he was, but I was afraid to run too fast, afraid of attracting greater attention. Soon he was catching up and the distance between us was getting smaller. Nervously, I looked at the Neris River below me. If I'm unable to escape from him, I thought to myself, I'll jump into the river.

Fortunately, I think he wanted to catch me himself and turn me over to the Gestapo, so he did not ask a passerby to stop me. I managed to turn into Krischiukaichiu Street, took off my jacket and, on the run, pulled on the sweater with the yellow star. I rushed up to the Jewish policeman at the gate of the ghetto, begging him to protect me from the limping man who wanted to rape me. Because it was a Sunday, there were no work brigades returning from work and the area was empty. A German guard came out from his booth, wondering what all the commotion was. I kept repeating that the man wanted to rape me and that I had barely escaped from his clutches. The Jewish policeman was saying something to the limping man but my persecutor didn't speak German and was trying to explain in Lithuanian that I had committed a 'crime'. He was trying to tell the German guard that he was going to capture me and take me to the police. Luckily, the guard didn't understand a word he was saying and let me in through the gate. He ordered the Jewish policeman to lock me up and told the man to get out of the area that was forbidden to strangers. The Jewish policeman took me a few meters into the ghetto and let me go.

I came home terribly upset. I didn't want to talk to or see anyone. I only wanted to cry over my misfortune and my lack of rights. The memory of running across the bridge, of wanting to jump into the river, continued to haunt me. To this day, I can't erase this scene from my memory. I still can't cross a bridge alone, afraid that I'll get the urge to jump into the water.

The relatively calm period in the ghetto that started at the beginning of 1942 was disrupted in the fall of 1943 by a change in command of the Germans in charge of the ghetto. The administration of the affairs of Kaunas Ghetto was taken away from the Gestapo and given to the SS. In the fall of 1943, an order came from Berlin to appoint a new ghetto commandant. The new commandant, SS officer Obersturmbannfuerer Captain Wilhelm Goecke, had been a commandant at a concentration camp before his transfer. In the beginning, to gain the confidence of the inmates, he, like the former commanders, tried to pretend he was a well-meaning man. He relaxed controls at the ghetto gate, allowed the string orchestra to continue performing, personally reviewed the work of Jewish institutions in the ghetto, and even made various concessions. But these concessions barely lasted a month and, soon enough, he showed his true face. He began reorganizing the ghetto and instituting more precise methods of liquidating it. Basically, he was turning the ghetto into a concentration camp.

With Goecke's arrival, came the death and destruction of the Kaunas ghetto. He never used the word 'ghetto', always 'camp'. He changed the name of the ghetto and, by October 1943, it was renamed the Kaunas Concentration Camp (*Konzentrationslager Kauen* or *KL-Kauen*). He had considerable experience in setting up labour camps and was going to break up the ghetto into a number of small camps, take away all possessions from the Jews and send the old and the children to an 'unknown' destination. SS men began patrolling the streets of the ghetto constantly and terrorized the inhabitants. Goecke reduced the ghetto territory and set up small concentration camps next to the places where the Jews worked, in the areas surrounding Kaunas. The prisoners lived in wooden sheds, men separated from women. Following his orders, permits to leave the ghetto without guards were taken away from some members of the Jewish administration and the Jewish Committee. Any permit could only be issued by Goecke. At the end of October, Goecke organized the kind of *Aktzion* that was becoming very familiar, a deportation. He demanded that the Jewish Committee supply 3000 people for work at the Estonian concentration camps of Vaivora and Klooga. The 'Estonian *Aktzion*' began on October 26, 1943.

Misha was instructed to inform our organization's members of the impending danger. Those who didn't have anywhere to hide were to quickly take shelter in the organization's bunkers. Our family already knew of the danger. Mother went to my sister's bunker, while my aunt Fanya and her daughter went to the neighbour's shelter. Misha and I rushed to Chone Kaganas hiding place and found quite a few of our friends, including Chaim's brother, Meyer, and their father, Leizer, already there.

I sat down next to Meyer and we spoke in hushed voices. He was very nervous. His wife Dveira (Busia) and their three-year-old daughter had been taken in by a Lithuanian family but he felt they were not really safe there. They were supposed to return to the ghetto that day. I tried to calm him down, saying that his wife would be able to see that the ghetto was surrounded from a distance and would then surely return to their old hiding place for another day or two.

Chaim came to our hiding place a few times. Like Misha, he was wearing the armband of the Jewish police assistants. He told us that the Germans could not round up enough people to be send to Estonia. Those that were rounded up were being transported to the railway station by trucks. A little later Misha dropped in and told us that the Germans had brought in additional battalions of Lithuanian and Ukrainian police and that the roundup was continuing. They were grabbing whomever they caught and pushing them into the trucks. The Jewish administration could do nothing to help. One after another the trucks were rolling to Aleksotas train station.

The Estonian *Aktzion* ended late in the evening. The streets were deserted, not a German, Ukrainian, or Lithuanian in sight. When the ghetto was dark and quiet, people began running from house to house looking for their next of kin. One out of three ghetto inmates had been deported – shipped off to unbearable work and death.

The next morning, the Germans ordered everybody back to work. There was no need for tears, they said, everybody had to work. Some people perished and that was hard for everyone, but war was war. After a few days, Meyer's wife and little girl returned to the ghetto and some time later, they were given temporarily shelter by a Lithuanian family, Danute and Vladas Zubovas. The Zubovas family also found a safe hiding place for Jellin's daughter in the Chiobishkes orphanage. This family managed to find hiding places for another dozen otherwise doomed Jews. They themselves were hiding the families of Anatoly Rosenblium and Jasha Gurevich.

"Through their humanity," Dveira Jellin wrote later of these families, "they restored our faith in humanity and in a brighter to-morrow."[84] Esther Jellin went on to became a well-known pianist. A girl of unusual talent, she finished the Cziurlionis School of Music in Vilnius and continued her studies at the Moscow Conservatory. After returning to Vilnius, she was a soloist with the State Philharmonic Orchestra for nearly ten years. Esther now lives in Switzerland and is a piano professor and the director of the Heinrich Neihauz Fund that is named after her former teacher.

After the Estonian *Aktzion*, Misha and I discussed the question of our marriage. The Jewish Committee's marriage registration department was still functioning. We were always together and we decided to formalize our life together because we wanted to join the partisans in the forests as husband and wife. My mother supported the idea and even promised to host a modest 'feast' for the occasion. We asked Dima Gelpernas and Dovid Markovski to be our witnesses. It was an early November day, dark and rainy, when we gathered with our families in our little room. But even though it was a gray au-tumn day in the ghetto, the sun hardly peeking out of the clouds, we could not have been sad. We were so young. I was only nineteen and Misha would turn twenty in another month. My mother Rebecca Giniene, Alice and Philip Benjaminovichius, Misha's sister Sonya Ru-binsonaite and his father, Lipe Rubinsonas, along with my uncle and aunts, raised a toast to our future, wishing us better times. Our wed-ding feast was very modest and our quarters very humble but we were together with those closest to us and we were happy. For a few hours we could forget the horrors of our life. Our eyes were lit with the joy of the profound love we felt for one another. Misha's strong arms held me close and his softly spoken words of love flooded my soul with happiness. When the wedding feast ended, we happily rushed off to our own quarters to savour our love, our youth, and the prospect of being together forever.

FROM GHETTO RESISTERS
TO PARTISANS

After the failure of the march to Augustova Forest, we received permission from Zimanas (Jurgis) to send ghetto inmates to join the partisans in Rudninkai Forest. In November 1943, the first small group of nine ghetto resisters got ready to escape. From the ghetto, they had to go to the village of Murava to meet up with their guides. From there, they would march about 150 kilometers on foot, with the guides, to Rudninkai Forest. The nine ghetto fighters made their way to Murava in groups of two. Ida Pilovnik-Vilenchiuk knew the road and carried all the weapons in a basket as she walked together with her boyfriend Aaron Vilenchiuk. At the moment when Aaron took Ida's heavy basket from her, they were stopped by police who asked for their documents. Ida, in perfect Lithuanian, started to explain that she worked as a seamstress and that she was merely out for a walk with a friend.

"Why would one Lithuanian want to arrest another Lithuanian?" she asked, and begged the policemen to let her go. The policemen waved Ida on and told her to hurry home. She grabbed the basket full of weapons from Aaron and walked on ahead. Then she slipped into a small woods and hid. Aaron had much more difficulty explaining himself and pretending he was Lithuanian. He admitted that he was a Jew and said that he was going to the village to barter for food. Of course, his pleas were to no avail. One of the policemen took Aaron to the police station and the other one, having concluded that Ida must also be Jewish, took a bicycle from a passerby and went after her. The furious policeman cycled around the road but was unable to find her; he did dare to go to the forest. Riding the bicycle along the road, the policeman noticed another suspicious young man. He stopped the ghetto resister, Aba Diskant, also on his way to Murava. Aba was arrested and taken to the police station. There Aaron and Aba were beaten, taken to the Gestapo, then transferred to the Ninth Fort.

Ida spent the night in the forest. Attempting to cross a small ice-covered river, she had fallen into the water. Early the next morning, tired after walking for hours and soaked to the bone, she finally reached Murava. There, in a safe house, she changed her clothing, rested a little bit, and delivered the basket of weapons. In the evening, she returned to the ghetto. This first group of resisters met with even more misfortune. Near Murava, one of the guides accidentally injured the group leader, Moishe Upnicki, who was forced to return to the ghetto. Very close to the partisan base, another ghetto fighter Elijahu Olkin was mortally wounded under unexplained circumstances. Of that first group, only four fighters reached the "Death to the Occupiers" Detachment of partisan.

After this unsuccessful mission, the AFO committee accepted Moishe Musels' proposal to transport the fighters to the partisans by truck. Being the foreman of the Jewish brigade at the German military transport repair workshop, Moishe knew non-Jewish drivers who were working there. He managed to establish good relations with some of the more trustworthy Lithuanian drivers who agreed to drive him out of the city. He reached an agreement with one of the drivers, who, for a large compensation, would take a few Jews to a village to barter for food. These people, Moishe told the driver, had to be picked up at the ghetto gate and then brought back to the ghetto. He assured the driver that all the documents needed for leaving the ghetto would be ready. Once the transportation arrangements had been made, the AFO started to prepare another group for escape from the ghetto, this one consisting of about ten people. Misha and I were among them.

I learned about our escape from the ghetto to Rudninkai Forest in early December and immediately told my mother about it. She wept with joy, thinking that this would save me. I, on the other hand, was very confused. I felt that I was betraying my mother, leaving her to an unknown fate. I felt that I was being unfair to my closest family and that I had no moral right to leave them. In my soul, I struggled with two conflicting feelings. One whispered that I must go and fight the enemy, the other one urged me to remain with the family – either to perish with them or survive with them. Misha had similar feelings. He was not so concerned about his sister, Sonya, but felt especially badly about his father, Lipe. Misha's father tried to allay our concerns and supported our determination to leave the ghetto. Both of us were somewhat relieved that both our sisters, Alice and Sonya, were staying behind. At night, my mother wept in my arms as I reassured her that I would return to the ghetto and help her. Partly, I would keep my promise. At the beginning of 1944, I did return to the ghetto with a group of five fighters on an important mission, but unfortunately, I was unable to help my family.

By early December, we had completed our training for the guerrilla war and all the details of the mission had been worked out. Mother prepared a bag with blankets, clothes, and my other belongings. As I looked at the bag, I had the feeling that she was ready to put her heart in it as well and wished she could add her life's experience and her soul. As I took a few old photographs, I kept repeating, "I will come back. I'll find a way to return to the ghetto, if only briefly. We will see each other again." Mother looked at me sadly, probably thinking how childish my illusions were. I left the names and addresses with my family of a few Lithuanian families who were contacts in the city and urged my sister to visit Frania Grunskaite more often, to keep in touch with Dima Gelpernas, and Chaim Jellin.

Finally, the date of departure was set. On the evening of December 12 we were to gather in small groups at the ghetto gate where a truck was supposed to pick us up and take us to 'work'. Chaim and Moishe Musel were to go with us. Everything appeared to be in order. A few trustworthy workers of the Jewish Committee and Jewish police were supposed to wait for us at the gate, to help the group of resisters get out. My family and closest friends gathered in our room. I tried to rush the farewells, because it was so hard for me to part from my mother and sister. Mother saw me to the door and, with an aching heart, I left the home where I had spent the last two and a half years. My father had died in this home. It was from here that we had taken him to his final resting place. Tanya had grown up here. It was here that she had taken her first steps, spoke her first words. It was here that, just three years old, she had hidden in the bunker, knowing that when the Germans were around, she had to keep quiet.

Misha was already waiting for us at the gate. We, the young ghetto resisters, were all dressed alike in overcoats, warm headgear, gloves, scarves, boots, and bags. It was cold and we were waiting for the agreed signal, but it did not come. We didn't know what was happening and why the truck had not arrived. A few hours later we returned home disappointed. The departure was postponed to the next day. Misha went home to his father and sister. I went home too. My mother was happy that she could spend another day with me. The next evening, we went through the same exercise. It was not quite the same sad parting. Only my mother saw me out. We met with our comrades at the gate, nervously waited for the truck. Again it didn't come; again we went home.

On the third day, I parted from my mother more formally. She smiled and wished me a good trip. "See you soon," she said, and went to my sister. Wearing my 'uniform', I went to the gate. We waited, wondering if once again the truck wouldn't come. Suddenly, we heard the signal and rushed to the gate. On that evening, December 14, 1943, the long-awaited truck showed up at the ghetto gate. A man in a German uniform got out of the truck, showed the guard a forged document and demanded workers for some urgent job outside the city. The Jewish policemen quickly rounded up the needed workers. The gate opened, the truck pulled in. Within a few minutes, we were in the truck and it left the ghetto.

Late on that December day, eleven ghetto resisters escaped to the "Death to the Occupiers" partisan detachment in Rudninkai Forest. Among them were: Peisach Gordon, and Meishale Sherman, members of the AFO committee; Misha Rubinsonas, the leader of the youth branch of AFO; Zoja Tintaite-Sherman, the medical nurse; Shmulik Mordkovski; Zunia Shtromas; Leizer Codikovas; Boruch Lopjanski; Aaron Gafanovich; Shleime Abromovich; and I..

The truck began rolling through the dark and deserted streets of Kaunas. Moishe Musel was sitting next to the frightened and as-tonished driver. He had told the driver that the truck would be taking a few workers to barter in the village. Now the driver suspected that he was transporting people, not to the village, but to some uncertain destination. He wanted to stop but Moishe persuaded him to drive on, that there was no other alternative. Moishe was concerned about the driver's reaction to this suspicious and frightening trip. The rest of us, including Chaim Jellin, were sitting in the back of the truck. Chaim was worried about the trip's success and about the guides. I was sitting on my bag and my thoughts were with my loved ones who had remained behind the barbed wire while I was here. Although I felt all alone, I knew that I really wasn't. I felt Misha's strong shoulder and the warmth and love of his arms around me. I was with my husband and my friends.

The truck was heading toward the village of Murava, where it was to pick up the guides. Suddenly, the driver noticed a German patrol and tried to turn back. Moishe calmed him down, telling him that we had all the necessary papers. Suddenly, Chaim asked the driver to stop the truck, got out, and started walking toward the Germans. They were not Germans at all, but our guides from Murava village in German uniforms. When they jumped into the truck, the driver stubbornly refused to go on. Moishe and Chaim tried to convince him to go forward but he wouldn't. Finally, Chaim took off his wrist watch and gave it to the driver. We drove on. The truck rolled on through dangerous places, on the bumpy, frozen winter road. We sat in the back of the truck, the young ghetto resisters, ready to join the armed resistance, ready to fight Nazi oppression.

After a few hours, we successfully reached the Vilnius-Gardinas railway line. Then the truck passed the city of Onishkes and stopped a few kilometers further on. We had covered more than 130 kilometers, the most dangerous part of the journey, but now we had to cross the railway on foot and walk some fifteen kilometers to reach partisan-controlled territory. We got out of the truck and, for a few minutes, Chaim Jellin and Moishe Musel stood together, breathing deeply. They were not only breathing in the fresh air of the winter forest, but the sweet smell of freedom. Both of them had to return to the ghetto, to prepare new resisters to escape from the ghetto and to arrange for drivers and trucks to carry the young ghetto inmates to the Rudninkai Forest. They shook our hands and bid each of us farewell. They got into the truck that then turned around and took them back to the Kaunas Ghetto. We were the first truckload which had escaped from the ghetto to Rudninkai Forest. In less than four months, AFO would organize seven more truckloads of escaped ghetto inmates who would successfully reach the partisans.

After carefully crossing the railway, the guides led us through endless forests and desolate roads, until we reached partisan territory. Once inside their territory, we were stopped by a partisan patrol, which appeared out of nowhere. The guides quietly exchanged passwords and we moved on. It was then that I suddenly realized that I was not dreaming. That I was really free and that I was a partisan. I could barely control my joy and my pride. I had become a soldier, a fighter against our oppressors, our killers, the worst enemies of mankind: the German Nazis.

On December 15, 1943, we reached the base of the "Death to the Occupiers" Detachment which was to be our home for the next seven months. We were far from our families and would be living in the woods without toilets, water, baths, or electricity. Snow had begun falling, the wind was rustling in the trees, and it was white and beautiful all around us. This was the beginning of my life as a partisan.

In Lithuania, the anti-Nazi, pro-Soviet partisan movement began in 1943. It was actually set up in Moscow and was headed by Antanas Snieekus, the Secretary of the Lithuanian Communist Party's Central Committee. At the end of April 1943, a strategic paratrooper group from Moscow, led by Motiejus Shumauskas (code name: Kazimieras) and Genrikas Zimanas (code name: Jurgis), landed in the Kazenai Forest near Lake Narutis, in German-occupied Belarus at the northeastern border with Lithuania. There, the group of about 40 Lithuanian partisans received some first-hand experience in guerrilla warfare. The newly formed military unit then moved inside Lithuanian territory to the Rudninkai Forest.

The Northern and Southern Regional Lithuanian Communist Party Committees grew out of this strategic paratrooper group. The Southern Committee was headed by Zimanas and operated in the areas around Vilnius, Kaunas, and their surrounding districts. Its headquarters was located in Rudninkai Forest, in the Mickevichius Detachment. At that time there where a few small partisan units already functioning in Rudninkai Forest, composed mainly of several hundred escapees from the Vilnius and Shvencioniai Ghettos. In the early summer of 1943, the first large partisan detachment, *Uz Tevyne* (Defenders of the Homeland), was established. Led by a paratrooper, Fiodor Pushakov (code name: *Genys* -The Woodpecker), it was located at the very fringe of partisan-controlled territory, on the western edge of Rudninkai Forest, not far from the village of Inklerishkes. This village was an important transportation crossroads, where roads from Vilnius led to Grodno and Trakai.

123

All of these partisan detachments were equivalent to regular army units where the partisans were subordinate to the unit commanders. But there was no strict military discipline or code of regulations concerning the partisans' duties, their relationship to each other and to the command. Unlike regular army units, partisans were required to fend for themselves and were left on their own to gather everything from the very basics, like food, to weaponry and even explosives. On occasion, a night-time drop would be pre-arranged with Moscow and the partisans would light campfires so that the planes could spot the drop zone. Pilots would drop paratroopers and supplies such as weapons, small food items, propaganda literature, radio transmitters and receivers, batteries, medical supplies, and so on. All of these packages had to be handed over to headquarters and only then would the leaders redistribute the supplies to the units.

As the partisan movement grew in strength, the whole of Rudninkai Forest, along with the surrounding villages, was proclaimed partisan territory and the local residents were informed that, in order to enter the forest, they would require official permission from the partisans. When the Germans learned of this demand, they began reinforcing their military positions in the small cities and towns like Varenai, Jashiunai, Rudishkes, and Vechiorishkes that surrounded the Rudninkai Forest. Ongoing skirmishes between the partisans and German army and Lithuanian police units were taking place in these towns. But, despite their attacks and blockades, the Germans were not successful in pushing the partisans from their strategic positions or from the towns and villages under partisan control. On the contrary, these strategic positions, towns, and villages became extensions of the partisan territory into which neither the police nor the Germans dared to go.

Without a doubt, the partisan movement had become one of the most effective means of combating the German occupiers. The partisans, with the active participation of the escapees from the Vilnius and Kaunas Ghettos, threw effective wrenches into the machinery of the military operations of the German State. They sabotaged German railroad lines, destroyed German communications systems and, of course, engaged in armed skirmishes. A report written at the end of 1943 stated that,

In one month, partisans successfully attacked 27 state-owned farms and appropriated animals, rye, hay, straw, milk and other food products. They destroyed dairies, sawmills, granaries, telephone lines; they burned bridges and blew up sections of railroads in the railway corridors on lines leading to Vilnius, Grodno, Kaunas, Lentvaris, Kaishiadorys, Lyda, Ignalina, Valkininkai.[85]

In fact, at the beginning of 1944, Rudninkai Forest was the most important base of pro-Soviet partisan resistance in Lithuania. The Southern Regional Communist Party Committee had established there three large partisan brigades – Vilnius, Kaunas, and Trakai – that united over 2,000 fighters of the eleven detachments. The first coordinated attack on the occupiers consisted of a declaration of war on the railroads by the Southern Region Headquarters.

A railway corridor was assigned to each unit and it was then up to individual commanders to decide how best to blow up the lines, attack trains carrying troops, sever underground cables, and destroy telephone and telegraph lines. The effectiveness of these techniques is documented in Lithuanian police reports to the army field commanders in Vilnius, the Comissioner General in Kaunas, the Vilnius Regional Commissioner (*Gebietskomisar),* and others.[86]

Another report, written in February 1944 to the Head of Police in Lithuania by a police liaison officer, contains the following summary of the situation:

> Partisan activity has spread throughout all of Lithuania with the exception of the northwestern districts (Mazeikiai, Kretinga). If we do not seriously begin deploying powerful retaliatory measures, the partisans' activity could grow in scale and greatly hurt our activities on the front by affecting transport, communications, production, and the collection of food products. The continuing destruction of railway lines and bridges is extremely dangerous…In the Vilnius district we have noticed not only small units but also formations of 300 to 700 persons. These formations have become so arrogant that they are not only attacking small hamlets and villages but even towns…the

> partisans are systematically disarming outposts and even
> confiscating the uniforms of police officers...[87]

The detachment to which we belonged, *Mirtis okupantams* (Death to the Occupiers), was located about 40-50 kilometers from Vilnius and 150-160 kilometers from Kaunas. It had been formed in October 1943 and was made up of about twenty partisans, led by a paratrooper, Kostas Radionovas. Four of the partisans were local inhabitants: Nifantas Radionovas, Kostas' younger brother; the wife of Kostas' older brother, Jekaterina Radionova; and a nurse named Ania Borisova. All of them were from the village of Murava. There were several other paratroopers and the rest were escaped Soviet prisoners of war (POWs).

The day following December 15, 1943, our 'baptism' into partisan life began. It was not that of active combat but of a somewhat more prosaic nature. We were ordered to build another larger dugout. Many of the partisans were tradesmen and our men immediately took to the work. Some were carpenters, others were metalworkers, and we even had a stove-maker. There was as much building material as we required, enough, in fact, to build a small town and we had little trouble finding tools. It took about a week for us to build a strong and comfortable dugout that, we learned, was to be the men's quarters. We women were to use the older one.

We also became aware, quite quickly, of the social tone of the partisan camp. Dimitry Parfionov (code name: Davydov or simply Dima) was the Commissar. He was a former Red Army officer who had escaped from a German POW camp and he ran all the affairs of the detachment. There was no doubt that he was prejudiced against Jews and because we were from the ghetto, he greeted us coldly. Parfionov did not understand our Yiddish language or songs, nor did he grasp the solid attachments of friendship that bonded us. At first, Parfionov treated me and some of the other Kaunas Ghetto escapees favourably, especially those of us who spoke Russian. The ones who suffered the most discrimination were those who spoke no Russian or those who were potential competitors for his position. In due course, his unfriendliness turned into downright hostility and he started openly murmuring anti-Semitic sentiments to his comrades, especially the other escaped POWs.

He always criticized the new ghetto escapees who joined our unit for not having brought enough weapons with them. He berated their inexperience and their lack of knowledge of the Russian language. But his criticisms were unwarranted. The ghetto partisans were brave fighters who participated in all the combat activities and were totally determined to fight the enemy. They blew up railways and destroyed communication lines and enemy garrisons. They became excellent guides and participated in a large variety of military and non-military activities and operations against the German occupiers. The ghetto partisans even managed to establish friendships with some of the former POWs. Nevertheless, a small group within the detachment remained loyal to Commissar Parfionov and blindly followed his every command. They were directly, or perhaps indirectly, responsible for the killing of several of our very close ghetto partisan friends. Nothing, absolutely nothing, could have prepared us for losing somebody we knew in that way.

Today, it is difficult for me to explain why Parfionov was so hostile to the Jews. Perhaps his anti-Semitic sentiments were shaped during his incarceration by the Nazis. Probably he was affected by all of their propaganda which cited the Jews as the instigators of the Second World War and the organizers behind the Bolshevik revolution. In the mid-1960s, Parfionov sent me a very complimentary letter to which I now regret not having responded. He wrote that, though he was teaching in Moscow, he was also a member of the council of the Moscow War Museum. He went on to say that the museum contained many exhibits relating to the partisan war, including our detachment's typewriter, my own handwritten bulletins and proclamations, entries in our log book, and more. He then invited me to come to Moscow to see the museum exhibits. But my dislike for him was still quite vehement, particularly concerning the events surrounding the death of Meyer Liberman (code name: Misha Karecki), a great fighter and a close, devoted friend. I never answered the Commissar's letter and, though I traveled frequently to Moscow, I never once set foot in that museum.

In our detachment, all the duties of the partisans were divided in two groups. One group belonged to the combat unit which carried out military operations. They mined railways, destroyed communications lines, bridges, electricity transformers, and blew up plants and mills. The non-combat group was involved in activities, which included guarding the territory of our base and the villages that were incorporated in our territory. They also operated the health and sanitary installations, were in charge of food collection and the preparation of meals, among other things. There was also a group of partisans that was designated as military intelligence. Despite the division of duties, though, all partisans frequently fought together. We all participated in attacking German garrisons, police battalions, and national defense units. On the other hand, very often the combat partisans participated in many non-combat operations. They participated in clandestine missions to the villages and cities, drew maps, published leaflets, and participated in seizure of food and weapons. These activities, as well as other non-combat duties, were as dangerous and as important as the military operations.

Part Five

Destinies

FIRST MISSIONS

My first serious assignment involved the gathering of grain. Our detachment's liaison staff informed us that some farmers had transported grain to a mill and were preparing to hand it over to the Germans. A group of our partisans was engaged in the mission ~~to confiscate the~~ grain.

Captain Michail Ceiko, a former POW, was put in charge of the operation, which would involve a long trek. We departed base camp during the day but left partisan-controlled territory only at dusk. Captain Ceiko was the man 'on point', the one with the most experience, and we followed his lead. Occasionally he would halt, scout ahead a few steps in one direction or another, return and, with a soft but firm voice, command us onward. Finally, we arrived at the edge of the woods from which point we could see a few small houses of the village in the distance. Ceiko divided us into smaller groups, appointing a squad commander for each one. He ordered us to confiscate two sacks of grain from each farmer and to leave a certificate of requisition. One group of partisans ordered a village elder to harness a horse-drawn carriage and have it ready. Others were sent to the mill at the top of a hillock to rouse the miller and get him to grind the grain.

I went with two others to the farmhouse assigned to us. When the owner opened the door, I could see his wife get out of bed and his children cower under the blankets, crying. An uncomfortable feeling came over me and I was unable to utter a single word. The partisans rudely demanded the allotment of grain from the farmer, ordered him to be quick about it but promised not to take anything else from him. The farmer hesitated but brought out the two sacks of grain. I calmed down a little and thought that we too must have food to eat. Better for us to take that grain, I told myself, than for it to fall into the hands of the Germans. I sat down and began to write the requisition certificate that said, in effect, that we, the partisans of Rudninkai Forest, had requisitioned 200 kilograms of grain. I signed it Zose (my code name), stamped it as best I could, and handed it to the farmer. The farmer's wife offered us food but we declined, saying we were in a hurry. She looked me over carefully and told me that war was not for women to fight. I didn't wait for a reply as I asked her, "And is the killing of women and children proper work for men?" and left the house.

It was freezing outside as we left the warmth of the farmhouse and all I wanted to do was sleep. The cold reminded me of the frigid hangar at the airport when I was a slave labourer. Just the thought of that time was enough to shake off my lethargy. The mill seemed large and eerie to me. I watched as the grain was milled. It was the first time I had set foot in a mill and the first time I saw how grain is transformed into flour. When the milling was complete and the sacks were loaded onto the cart, the order was given to return. The peasants wished us a safe trip, not because they had any true sympathy for us, but simply because they hoped for the quick and safe return of their horse-driven carriage. A farmer without a horse is not a farmer.

The following morning, we reached the boundary of our territory and after a few hours were back at base camp. My first assignment had gone well. It was successfully completed without casualties or collateral damage and our granary was now full. Once the sacks had been unloaded, the men led the horses to the road, gave them a quick flick of the whip, and the driverless carriage headed back to its village where the owner was no doubt waiting impatiently for its return. After only a few hours of rest, I was back on duty peeling potatoes.

That evening, after I finished typing another proclamation, I had my first experience of night-watch duty inside the base. For the first time, I found myself alone in the woods at night with a gun. Although I had been through some military training, I had no idea what I should do with the gun if anything happened. I felt anxious and alarmed in the forest. But I knew I had to obey my orders and I knew that, although I felt very alone, I was not really by myself. Only a few hundred meters away, my comrades were guarding the second post at the entrance to the camp territory. Nearby, in the dugout, our fellow partisans slept peacefully. The moon shone over my territory as I walked back and forth from one bunker to another. The forest was not asleep and its noises reminded me of a familiar melody. As I listened to this melody, I tried to isolate the noises of the forest from the noises of possible approaching intruders. In the deep, dark woods, only the snow crunching under my feet and the rustling of bare branches as they swayed in the wind disturbed the quiet of the night. Finally, I saw my replacement approaching and, with relief, knew the three hours of my guard duty were over.

My first weeks as a partisan were spent participating in a variety of missions. Aside from regular secretarial duties and household work, there was frequent night-watch duty, and the gathering of food, weapons, and information from nearby inhabitants. During this time, I saw Misha only on rare occasions, usually by the campfire. He was designated to an intelligence unit led by a paratrooper, Bronius Olishauskas (code name: Borisas Lisauskas). Misha's small group of scouts went almost daily to the nearby village of Senoji Macele. One of the inhabitants there was from a fairly wealthy family named Jurgelevich who served as a liaison person for Borisas Lisauskas. Borisas needed intelligence information about the nearby village of Zagarine that was separated from Senoji Macele by only a narrow footbridge. Our "Death to the Occupiers" Detachment was planning to incorporate Zagarine into its territory and it was important to find out what the general nature of life and work was in the village. We needed to know what the inhabitants of the village thought of us and what their relationship was to the Germans. But, entering Zagarine was going to be risky. We would have to cross the footbridge and a small garrison of Germans was positioned just beyond the village. From their watchtower, it would be easy for them to spot us.

One Sunday afternoon, at Borisas' request, Jurgelevich invited several of his neighbours from Zagarine to gather at his house after mass. Misha, hiding in the rafters, quietly listened to the ensuing conversation that quickly turned to the subject of politics. One of the guests said that the Germans had set a trap not far from Senoji Macele and intended to ambush the partisans. The neighbours also complained about the German soldiers from the nearby garrison who regularly came to their village to demand *Schnapps* (vodka) and bacon. The conversation carried on well into the late evening hours and, having consumed large amounts of alcohol, the neighbours decided to spend the night. Once the house was quiet, Misha was able to climb through a window and return to base camp.

That night I was on watch at the second post, near the road leading to our territory, and I anxiously waited for any sign of Misha. Finally, I heard him approaching and saw him come into the camp, quickly heading towards me. Because it was rare for us to be alone, to just hold each other and talk quietly, we treasured our private moments together. Our love had grown and matured since we came to the partisans. We developed great respect for each other, fierce loyalty, and a deep friendship. We shared these strong feelings during our whole life together, until Misha took his final breath. They have remained in my heart to this day, even though more than twenty years have passed since his death.

First thing the next morning, Misha briefed Borisas on the trap that the Germans were preparing and the whole group of scouts set to work discovering where it was. They found it easily enough at the edge of the woods somewhere between Zagarine and Senoji Macele and dismantled the trap's camouflaged signposts on the spot. Borisas was determined to teach the Germans and the police officers a lesson so that they would no longer dare to approach territory under partisan control. He took Misha and one other scout with him and went to see the local forester at his home in Zagarine. The puzzled forester curtly asked what they had come for and Borisas very politely informed him that they needed to call the police station in Rudninkai. Noticing that they were armed, the forester agreed to let them in and pointed to the telephone. Calmly, Borisas called and informed the policeman on duty that he was a partisan and that his group had discovered the trap that had been set for them. He told the bewildered officer to inform his superiors immediately that, if they continued this course of action, the entire police department would be blown up. With a trembling voice, the policeman agreed. At the end of the conversation, Borisas ripped the telephone out of its socket and left the forester's house. All three scouts happily crossed back over the footbridge to the village of Senoji Macele. The terrified forester left Zagarine that following day.

In mid-February 1944, our detachment attacked the German garrison at Zagarine and liberated the town. The partisans put the forester's house to the torch, blew up the water tower, and crippled the train station by dismantling three engine-houses and two platforms. One German soldier was slain and the rest fled. Now the town could be incorporated into our territory.

At the end of December 1943, a new group of Kaunas Ghetto fighters had joined our detachment. We had been overjoyed to see our old friends and to get news about the ghetto, about the underground movement, and about our loved ones. The commanders of "Death to the Occupiers" Detachment, on the other hand, were far from happy at the arrival of the new partisans. Our supplies were almost exhausted and the new arrivals had brought little in the way of arms with them, only one rifle and a few pistols. We were fully aware that pistols were not effective in the forest. What we needed were rifles. At first, Kostas and Parfionov refused to allow them to join our detachment. Their objection was that the camp was not a hideout but a military unit and that it was impossible to accept anyone without a proper weapon. Once tempers cooled, though, Kostas allowed them to stay as long as they agreed to find some weapons for themselves. But, he added, this would be the last group he would admit to the detachment without their own rifles. Adding his angry voice to the discussion, the commissar complained that without guns, the ghetto escapees were nothing but a burden on the other partisans. It became very clear to us that we needed to inform the AFO Committee about the frosty reception to the ghetto resisters and to alert the Committee that new groups be sent at least properly armed with rifles.

I decided to write to Jellin and Gelpernas as quickly as possible. Before I had left the ghetto to join the partisans, I had arranged with our former housekeeper, Frania Grunskaite, that, should I need to, I would send her a letter that she should then hand over to my sister. Alice had also been forewarned that should such a letter arrive, she should give it to Chaim Jellin and Dimitry Gelpernas as quickly as possible. I decided to write two identical letters to two different addresses, for safety's sake. The letter was a length one. I began by euphemistically informing Jellin and Gelpernas that I had successfully reached my assigned post and that I was now 'teaching' (fighting). I told them that the 'small pencils' (pistols) that the 'students' (partisans) had were not suitable and of no use. I asked that Vladas (Chaim) send 'larger pencils' (rifles), without which it was not possible for me to continue working here. I sealed the letters in envelopes, addressing one to Frania Grunskaite and the other to Dr. Elena Kutorgiene. I hoped that at least one of the letters would reach its destination.

When the letters were ready I wanted for an opportunity to send them. The opportunity arose very soon.

Meanwhile, our detachment had been preparing for a very important and dangerous mission in a hostile district, far from our camp, to seize food. An experienced officer, Michail Trushin, a former POW, was to lead this operation. Our group of about thirty partisans also included the recently arrived newcomers from Kaunas Ghetto who had not yet had an opportunity to gain any experience in guerrilla warfare. As we all knew, experience could only be acquired by going on missions and fighting in skirmishes. We left our camp before dawn, after all the rifles and automatic weapons, and even our only submachine gun, had been distributed. When we reached the village of Inklerishkes at daybreak, we stopped for a short rest. There, I handed the two envelopes to Mr. Janchevski, our friend and supporter, and he promised to mail them the next day.

It was a promise he kept. I learned later that Chaim and Dima received the letter through my sister with little difficulty and that they had had little trouble deciphering its contents. Meyer Elinas (Jellin) and Dimitry Gelpernas later wrote in their book that they had received the first news about the fighters' successful arrival in Rudninkai Forest from Sara Ginaite.

> She [Sara] wrote a letter to us that we received through her friend, F. Grunskaite, who handed the letter over to the underground. Using code, she wrote to us about their arrival in that forest and of their initial activities there. A similar letter was sent to the ghetto through Dr. Elena Kutorgiene.[88]

We rested in Inklerishkes until dusk when we left the village, following order to stay on high alert to potential dangers from all directions. We were heading close to the hostile village of Koletanca, known for its support for the Polish White Partisans. These White Partisans (anti-Soviet) lived quasi-legally among their friends and family. They claimed to be members of the underground Armija Krajowa (AK) organization which was led by the Provisional Polish government in exile, headquartered in London, England and also had leaders and cells in Poland and Vilnius. Formally, the White Partisans had been against Germany, but yet they received arms from them and the Germans didn't interfere with their activities. The White Partisans only fought the Germans on very rare occasions. Most of the time, their weapons were aimed at us and they would ambush the partisans of Rudninkai Forest, particularly if we happened to pass through areas or villages under their control.

In order to reach the destination of our operation, we had to go through the edge of the village under their control and cross a narrow footbridge. We did this noiselessly, thinking we had not been spotted. When we reached the designated village, our group leader, Michail Trushin, used all the defensive tactics at his disposal. He positioned guards at both ends of the village and ran to the home of the village elder, ordering him to prepare horse-drawn carriages. Once again, partisans were split into small groups and assigned to houses from which to requisition foodstuffs.

Zunia Shtromas, Boruch Lopjanski, and I knocked on the window of the house assigned to us. The frightened owners lit the sapwood lamp and opened the door. Zunia demanded they bring bread, bacon, and salt. Boruch ordered them to open the door to the cowshed and bring out a cow. The farmer hesitated. Immediately, Boruch opened the door of the cowshed. He led out a cow, tied a rope to its neck and told me to lead it to the carriage. Zunia handed me a bag of salt.

All I wanted was to get out of that house and get away from the plaintive, pleading looks and moans of the owners. Before long, the command was given to gather at the carriages with our booty and the train of carts started back for base camp. I proceeded to the footbridge and, though my cow bucked a little, we both made it across.

One of the newcomers, Peisach Gordon, was one or two carriages behind me. He put his sub-machine gun on a cart as he went behind the carriage to try and cross the footbridge. Suddenly, a volley of machine gun fire hit us like a hurricane. The White Partisans were shooting at us from cover of the cemetery, directing their fire at the footbridge and those partisans who had not yet crossed. It cut Peisach down first. He was followed by Itzik Segal.

Newcomer Masha Endlin, disappeared in the fray. I heard Trushin's command not to cross the bridge, but I was already on the other side of the river and I hit the ground, holding onto the cow. All the cows and horses began to run in a frenzy around me, taking the carriages with them.

The remaining members of our group waded through the shallow river that, at this time of the year, was already covered by a thin layer of ice. Leizer Zilber, Israel Goldblatt, and Misha Rubinsonas all managed to cross the river, avoiding the bridge, and returned feeble fire with their pistols. Trushin slipped and fell into the river but Boruch Lopjanski managed to pull him out. Meanwhile, the sub-machine gun cartridge was lost in the river. Returning fire, we retreated into the woods where we halted briefly, hoping Masha Endlin would catch up. Enemy fire continued as branches and pieces of bark, clipped by bullets, fell all around us. Then everything went quiet.

A few months after this mission, in April 1944, members of the Rudninkai Forest Partisans command, Marijonas Miceika (deputy to Zimanas) and Intelligence head, Antanas Barauskas, met with the leader of the AK Vilnius region, Colonial A Kszyzanowski (code name: General Wilk), in the forest not far from the Vilnius-Grodno highway. They discussed coordinating military activity against the Germans. It was agreed that members of the AK and the pro-Soviet partisans would cease to attack each other and spheres of influence were decided upon, especially who controlled which part of the Rudninkai Forest.

But, on that particular night, we were mercilessly attacked by them. Our group returned to base camp disconsolate and dispirited. We had lost three of our comrades and all the food, though I still gripped the small bag of salt in my hand. The commanders of our detachment were livid and sought out scapegoats for the disaster. They blamed the submachine gunners, the scouts, the informers and us, the fighters. The commissar repeated his favourite expression: "What kind of people are these? What kind of nation?"

Upon our return from this unsuccessful sortie, another group of escapees from Kaunas was waiting for us. Among them was Sara Gordon, the wife of Peisach Gordon, who had just perished on this mission. With her were two of our ghetto military instructors, Dovid Teper and Liova Sher, and my friend, Monik Holzberg. At first, as with the arrival of the other group of resisters, Kostas Radionovas refused to allow them to join. He reproached them for having arrived without enough weapons and for having brought too many women, saying that there would be nothing for them to do. After his tirade and his threats, Kostas again relented and allowed our friends from Kaunas Ghetto into the camp.

It was the evening of December 31, 1943 and we prepared to celebrate the arrival of the New Year. We all sat around the campfire. The campfire was not a place of entertainment and did not exist as a romantic symbol. It was an integral part of daily life that was, at once, difficult, hazardous, and heroic. A partisan could light a fire in the most inclement weather using the soggiest kindling and the wettest brush. A partisan could light a fire so well concealed that no passerby would ever notice it. It was at the crackling flame of the campfire that partisans dried their waterlogged clothing. It was the campfire that provided heartwarming heat whenever the evening cold penetrated down into the marrow of the partisan's bones. It was the campfire that provided indescribable inner warmth, opening up a person's soul. In the light of the fire, partisans could look at each other differently than they would in the foulness of their bunkers or caught in the icy grip of a skirmish. It was by the campfire that partisans would talk casually, clean their weapons and quietly sing songs of battle and freedom. Many songs, poems, and stories were created around partisan campfires.

BACK TO THE GHETTO AND
RETURN TO THE FOREST

THE TEACHER AND HIS STUDENT

The situation in our detachment had become quite appalling. We were painfully short of weapons: guns, ammunition, and explosives and, without weapons, it was difficult to seize new ones. Due to poor weather conditions and a shortage of fuel, Moscow had been unable to re-supply us. Throughout November and December, not a single aircraft had made it to Rudninkai Forest from Moscow.

As far as the AFO was concerned, we had only had one way communications. I did not even know if my letter had reached the AFO Committee. Misha and I talked about the situation and we agreed to approach Kostas with the idea of sending us back to the Ghetto to brief the AFO about our critical situation. We spent a long time formulating the idea into a mature, concrete plan, with weighty and convincing arguments and then I waited for the perfect moment to approach Kostas Radionovas. Such an opportunity presented itself at the beginning of January. Nearly all the detachment's fighters were out on routine missions and I was left to clean up the paperwork at headquarters. Once I was alone with Kostas, I began to lay out my argument.

"A partisan without a gun," I began, "is like a farmer without a horse." I told him that the AFO Committee probably had no idea about our situation and we needed to inform them so that they would send people with more arms. At this point, I suggested that Misha and I go to Kaunas along with a small group of partisans, to re-establish a two way contact and inform the Committee of our problems. Kostas heard me out, but he did not ask a single question nor offer any comment. He only nodded his head and said he would have to think about it. That was the end of our discussion. The next day, Kostas ordered Misha and me to make the six kilometer trek to the Mickevichius Detachment and lay out our plan for Jurgis (Zimanas).

In the midst of winter, Rudninkai Forest was abnormally still, buried in snowdrifts. The sun shone brightly as Misha and I walked, the light reflecting off the snow with a rainbow-like beauty. From time to time, our paths crossed groups of partisans from various detachments.

Suddenly, we would hear someone utter, "Stop. Who's there? What's the password?"

We would answer, "A strong gale," and, in turn, wait for the response.

"It has calmed down," would come the reply. Satisfied, we would embrace our comrades, exchange news, and wish each other good luck and success.

As we walked, Misha and I talked about Jurgis. We knew that Jurgis was the code name used by Genrichas Zimanas. In the prewar years, he had been the Lithuanian language teacher at the Sholom Aleichem High School and had been Misha's instructor and even his home form teacher for a time. I personally did not know him, but his family were close friends of my cousin's family, Dr. Isaac and Fruma Glikman.

Jurgis was already waiting for us when we arrived. He hadn't known exactly which Kaunas Ghetto fighters would be coming, but a visit from the two of us was the last thing he expected. A teacher meeting his former student under such unusual circumstances! Misha was also taken aback when he saw Jurgis as he bore no resemblance to his former teacher. He had grown a moustache, had put on weight, gone a little gray. He had a huge carbine slung over his shoulder. But his tinny voice still had the tone of a melodic tenor and his manner of speech had not changed. The teacher still had an instructing and questioning way. Since partisans did not stick to the formality of the regular military, we exchanged friendly greetings and Jurgis invited us to take a seat.

Misha presented him with our plan. He laid out convincing arguments as to the necessity of informing the AFO of our activities and reestablishing a channel of communication. He told Jurgis that we wanted also to establish a secure route between Kaunas and Rudninkai with appropriately trained guides from our ranks. Finally, Misha told Jurgis that we were both fully prepared to assume the roles of guides. He concluded by saying that we were married. Jurgis pretended not to take notice of our married status and said nothing about it.

Jurgis looked into Misha's eyes with a fatherly tenderness. It was obvious that he was taken with Misha's cool head, his convincing tone of voice and his arguments. Once or twice, he asked Misha a question of clarification, as if the teacher in him were giving his student a quiz be sure he had understood the lesson. As Misha explained the importance of the plan, Jurgis suggested that I offer my opinion. I did not get off on the right foot with him. As I began to list all the problems in our detachment and stressed the anti-Semitic atmosphere that had developed and how painful it was, I could see that Jurgis was not enthralled with my oration. He angrily ripped into me with his thin voice, stressing that the majority of the "Death to the Occupiers" Detachment was made up of Kaunas Ghetto escapees. He made it clear that this was not the time or the place to air our internal difficulties. He felt we should solve those on our own.

Shortly afterwards, Jurgis began to ask concerned questions about the Kaunas Ghetto situation. He asked us about the fate of several families, particularly the fate of the Shevelovich family. Misha had been a classmate of Paja Shevelovich and had known her well. Jurgis wanted to know the fate of her parents and siblings who had remained in Kaunas while Paja and her sister Frida had sought safety in the USSR. In Jurgis' voice and comments, I could feel the concern he had for the fate of the Lithuanian Jews. He sympathized with our efforts to help those trapped in the ghetto and with the AFO's fear regarding the fate of the ghetto inmates. Being a Jew, Jurgis was, of course, also extremely worried about the genocide of Jews that was being carried out by the Nazis and their henchmen in Lithuania. At the end of the conversation, almost as an aside, Jurgis asked when we had had time to be formally married.

"Last year on November 7, the day of the celebration of the October Revolution," Misha proudly proclaimed.

Jurgis smiled and offered his congratulations. Then Jurgis asked whom we would include on this mission. We told him that Nechemija Endlin and Shmulik Mordkovski were essential to its success. Both had previously been sent to the Augustava Forest and had successfully reached their targets and returned to the ghetto.

"I support your proposal," he began, slowly. "It is essential that we renew communications with the AFO and solve some other problems. This should include the training of guides from within our rank, establishing a reliable route between Kaunas and Rudninkai as well as establishing more contacts with the local population in Kaunas and the surrounding area. "However," he added, "a husband and wife cannot work on such a missions together. Therefore, Zose (my code name) will go to Kaunas. You, Misha, will not. But don't lose heart. You will have more than your share of important and risky assignments."

After our meeting, Misha was really disheartened. I tried to calm him down, saying that the mission wasn't that dangerous and that both Endlin and Mordkovski were experienced fighters and scouts, both with excellent orientation skills and instincts. I promised Misha that I would take care of his father and return to the partisans with his sister Sonya.

The next day, at Kostas' request, Misha took Endlin to see Jurgis. It was the last meeting about this mission but it would not be the last meeting between the schoolmaster and his student, Misha. There would be many more meetings in the Rudninkai Forest as well as in Vilnius after the war. On their return trip to the camp, Endlin told Misha that he had been placed in command of our group. Jurgis had given him complete instructions, a map, and other essential items for the mission.

"Don't worry," Nechemija said to Misha before we left, "I promise to return with your wife. We'll be back in two weeks time."

To Kaunus

In the early morning hours of January 7, 1944, five partisans – Nechemija Endlin, Zunia Shtromas, Shmulik Mordkovski, Boruch Lopjanski and I – left base camp and headed for Kaunas. Our principal mission was to renew ties with the AFO in the ghetto. But we were also to relay Jurgis' information and instructions regarding ties with the Kaunas underground Communist Party committees to the AFO, and to bring instructions for the assignment of fighters to the Rudninkai Forest. In addition to all this, we had to blaze a safe path from Rudnikai to Kaunas and establish potential contacts along the way. Each of us was given a pistol, some bullets, a watch and a compass, and some spending money.

By early evening, we reached the village of Inklerishkes, still within the boundaries of Rudninkai Forest. We rested there and waited for dusk before we crossed the Vilnius-Lyda railroad and headed into dangerous and hostile territory. Following only the footpaths that were at some distance from the Vilnius-Kaunas highway and other main roads, we set off. It was dark and eerily quiet in the forest at night. The only sounds we heard were those of our own breathing and footfalls on the snow. We walked without talking, each of us absorbed in our own thoughts. Each was thinking about how best to complete the mission, how to reach Kaunas and enter the ghetto. We wondered what was waiting for us there. What it would take to tear as many of our comrades as possible away from the jaws of the Nazi beasts and how we could help family members who had remained in the ghetto. We wondered in what condition we would find our loved ones. I thought about my mother, my sister, and close relatives as well as Misha's remaining family. The five of us trudged onward without resting, thinking, our feet sinking into the deep snow. It seemed as if the night and our march would never end.

Occasionally, we stopped for Nechemija and Shmulik to study the map and confer. Shmulik would bend his ear to the ground, listening for any reverberations. When he had determined that it was quiet enough to proceed, that we were far enough away from any roads or highways, we would continue on. By watching the swaying of the trees and listening to their rustling, Shmulik would define our bearing. This young Jewish religious seminary student was a child of the earth. Only to him would Mother Nature lay open her secrets. He was our guide and scout and he found his way without a compass. He only needed a map to navigate around villages.

The winter night was endless. Soon, my short fur jacket became too warm. I wanted to take it off and get rid of it but Endlin would not allow it. He was worried that I would become ill. I was parched and ate snow and ice with relish, rubbing it on my face in an attempt to keep myself going, the ice providing me with an extra burst of energy. The wind rang in our ears and the snow whipped our faces relentlessly. Finally, dawn began to break. As a cold drizzling rain began to fall, we spotted houses in the distance. It was the village we had chosen to rest for the day. We estimated that we had traveled about forty kilometers during that first night. The plan was to spend the entire next day resting at a peasant's home and continue the march that evening.

We chose a small house by the edge of the forest and knocked on the door and windows. After a few moments, we heard a frightened voice and a man appeared at the entrance with a tentative look on his face. He asked us many questions about who we were and what it was we wanted from him before he finally agreed to let us in. We told him that we simply wanted to rest in his house for the day and that we would leave the same evening. Endlin did tell him, however, that no one would be allowed to leave the house while we were there. The man told us that he was a shoemaker and said that he usually had frequent visitors. He added that for us to spend an entire day at his home without being noticed would be quite difficult.

At that moment, an elderly woman appeared at the door. The shoemaker's mother pressed us not to leave her home and offered for us to stay in the bathhouse, just at the edge of the woods. She and her son proposed to light the stove in the little outbuilding and to bring us some warm blankets and food. We decided to accept her offer. We warned them that we were armed and that should they make any attempt to tell anyone of our presence, they would be the first to suffer. The shoemaker left to light the stove in the bathhouse while his mother began preparing a meal for us. Owing to my state of exhaustion and because I had eaten so much snow, I began to have stomach pains. I was nervous about eating bacon, fresh baked bread, and the rich soup she put on the table. Offering my excuses, I asked if she might boil some eggs and heat some milk in exchange for a payment. She looked at me kindly, noticed my tired face and agreed to boil some eggs. She even offered me some crackers and stewed fruit.

My comrades were not pleased with me. They reminded me that we were not in a restaurant and how inappropriate my requests for special food were. My nerves were raw and I was complete exhausted. Hearing their reprimands, I broke into tears. Now, the men began apologizing and tried to calm me down. We began to eat our meal and then went to the bathhouse to rest. During the day, Endlin and the shoemaker discussed the prevailing mood among the local inhabitants, as well as German military movements in the area. When we left, we gave the shoemaker a few of our bulletins and pamphlets, and thanked our hosts for their hospitality. After exchanging warm farewells, we left their hospitable home behind.

It had snowed all day and the paths in the forest was completely obliterated. The five of us felt as if we were enfolded by the snow, wrapped in the darkness of the winter evening, and guarded by the trees. We spent the second night marching with almost no relief, just as we had the first night. After about thirty kilometers, we came across a village but Nechemija decided it was too populated and did not offer enough safety. We did not stop and carried on for another three or four kilometers until we found a more suited place.

We chose a tidy looking house and knocked at the door. It was early in the morning but the farmer's family was already up and about. The farmer peered at us warily through the window and refused to let us in. However, when he noticed that there was a woman with the group, he opened the door. Having brushed the snow off our boots in the entryway, we sat on a bench. Meanwhile Endlin explained that we only wished lodging for the day, that we would leave by evening and pay him for his services. In the house was the farmer, a recently widowed Pole of noble origins, and his young housekeeper. Endlin again warned the homeowner that no one would be allowed to leave while we were present and that he should not report our presence to anyone.

The day passed calmly and no one came to the door of the house. The young woman prepared lunch and dinner for us. During a conversation with Endlin, the farmer explained that, not far away, there was a village where half the population was Lithuanian and the other half was Russian. The village was not far from a side road and he offered to drive us there. We readily accepted his offer. So, in the evening, after some rest, we were ready to go. The farmer prepared his sleigh, and without waiting for nightfall, we all got in. He covered me with a warm fur blanket and told me to rest peacefully.

We crossed the Vilnius-Kaunas highway at a side road and were very soon near the village. About ten or fifteen kilometers before we reached it, Nechemija suddenly asked the farmer to stop. We said our good-byes and thanked him for his assistance. Wanting to be on the safe side, Endlin had decided not to disclose our exact strategy to the farmer. Once again we were hiking under cover of a cold winter night, on this, the third night of our trip. We headed into the woods and trudged through the knee-deep snow. I was so exhausted I could not even force myself to eat snow. All I could think of was a warm room, a clean bed, and a chance to wash up and shed my heavy boots. To keep myself going, I imagined meeting my mother and loved ones.

As the farmer had told us, our next stop was a village inhabited by Russians and Lithuanians. Without a moment's hesitation, Nechemija chose the Russian side of the village. The owner of one humble dwelling let us in. He began heating some water and preparing food. For the first time, I was able to wash and remove my shoes. My entire body and, especially my poor feet, began to rest.

We immediately made friends with our host. He told us that Lithuanian youths were being massively recruited and shipped off to Germany against their will. For this reason, it was very difficult and dangerous to set foot in Kaunas without having the right papers. We had planned to enter Kaunas by evening and slip into the ghetto by join up with a Jewish brigade at the Vilijampole Bridge. We now realized that this plan was not feasible. We knew, however, that in the Kaunas suburb of Petrashunai there was a Jewish brigade whose foreman was an acquaintance of Endlin's.

It suddenly occurred to me that we must arrive at that workshop wearing yellow Star of David patches. I could tell the German guard that I was a nurse who was arriving with four ailing Jews from the Kaishadoris Camp. I would then tell him that he must allow us into the brigade so that they could be sent to the ghetto hospital later on. My comrades liked the plan.

Our host found a strip of yellow cloth and we cut yellow, six-pointed stars. I sewed them onto the men's jackets, one over the left chest and one on the back.

Late that afternoon, the farmer, who eventually become a partisan supporter, drove us to a small village just outside Kaunas. We would spend the fourth night there and then proceed to Petrashiunai by horse-drawn carriage the next morning. For the first time on our journey, we did not spend the night hiking. We stayed in a small village hut near Rumshishkes.

The next morning, our host cautiously prepared the carriage and drove us to Petrashiunai. We stopped near the Jewish workshop and, while the men remained in the carriage, I went up to the German guard. I told him in German that I was from Shanchiai, a suburb of Kaunas that had been inhabited by Germans before the war. I added that I was a nurse from the Kaishiadoris Labour Camp and had just arrived with four Jews needing hospitalization. He told me to hand them over immediately to the foreman of the labour brigade. I had managed to get the guard to trust me and suggested that I get rid of the Jews as quickly as I could so that I could spend some time with him. He told me he was surprised that such a young, attractive woman had been forced to work with Jews. I promised to invite him over, but that meanwhile I had to lead the Jews to the workshop. Without hesitating, he allowed me to do my duty. The four men, dragging their feet and feigning illness, approached the guard where the pale and frightened brigade foreman was waiting for us. Immediately recognizing Endlin, he realized who we were and hid us in a large boiler until evening. Soon the German guard began to wonder where I had gotten to. The brigade foreman explained that I had needed to leave in a hurry as the carriage driver was waiting impatiently to take me back to Kaishiadoris.

To The Ghetto

That evening, when it was time to go into the ghetto, I had to change my appearance so that the guard would not be able to recognize me. One of the women in the workshop lent me her coat, a long scarf, and a pair of glasses. When we got into the truck with all the other labourers, I had transformed myself from a German nurse to a wizened Jewish intern. The brigade foreman asked the guard permission to drive into the ghetto through the less guarded Varniu gate, instead of the usual Krischiukaichiu route, because it was closer to the hospital. No one there checked us or held us up and we easily entered the ghetto. By this time, the ghetto had already been turned into a virtual concentration camp.

We, the five partisans, immediately dispersed in different directions.

I stood on Varniu Street, beside our family's little house. Suddenly, I was overcome with horror. I had come from a life of freedom, even though it was a dangerous and difficult one, and now found myself once again on death row. In the blink of an eye, the purpose of my trip had left me and the long-awaited meeting with my mother and sister seemed not so urgent. I wanted only to abandon the ghetto and walk by myself back into our Rudninkai Forest. I didn't care if it meant four nights of walking to be next to Misha and among my "Death to the Occupiers" Detachment comrades. Fortunately, these thoughts faded quickly and I regained control of my emotions. I began to shake off these fearful feelings and began repeating to myself, over and over, that I was not a slave, not an inmate of the concentration camp, but a partisan, a fighter against the kingdom of predators.

Suddenly, a distant relative opened the door to our apartment. We were both dumbstruck on seeing each other. Speaking first, she began explaining, almost apologetically, that the ghetto had been transformed into a concentration camp. She told me that recently, there had been one of the frequent purges and the ghetto territory had been reduced in size once again. It was then that she and her teenage daughter had moved into our room with my mother. She told me that my mother had gone, a short while ago, to visit my sister and she was expecting her to return shortly. I sat down on the corner of a stranger's bed, still wearing my fur trimmed jacket and filthy boots, a pistol stuck in my pocket. I was hungry and worn out. I just sat there and waited.

I must have fallen asleep and didn't hear my mother's footsteps. I awoke to my mother's embrace. We stood together, hugging and embracing, both crying, both feeling intense joy and fear. Mother spoke first.

"Why? Why did you come? We received your letter and were overjoyed that you had escaped the gates of hell. Why have you returned?" By now I was holding my mother in my arms, kissing her. "Everything is all right," I murmured quietly in her ear, "Don't worry."

I promised to recount all that had happened to me the next day. But all I wanted now was to wash, to remove my lousy clothing and lie down in clean sheets. Mother soon turned the kitchen into a small bathhouse. She rinsed my head with kerosene to kill the lice, combed my hair, and then washed my hair and body. The family 'council' decided to put me up at my sister's parents-in-law, in their daughter's room. Rita had gotten married and had gone to live with her husband

Itzik Dembo. I lay down on her clean bed and, before I could thank everyone and wish them a good night, I drifted off to sleep.

When I awoke, I was unable to recognize my surroundings. My joints ached, my head was splitting, and I was feverish. I had come down with pneumonia. My comrades-in-arms were immediately informed about my illness and my mother and sister remained by my bedside for days on end. I took medicines, drank warm milk, slept. Gradually, I began regaining my strength. I was still reveling in the white bedding, the cleanliness, and the presence of my mother's smile, when the Benjaminovich family, Aunt Fanya, Misha's sister Sonya and her father, Lipe, came to see me. When they saw me, they cried tears of joy just as my mother had. I calmed down as much as I was able and began telling them about our life in the partisans, about the skirmishes, and our circle of comrades.

I discussed with Sonya and Rita Dembo the possibility of smuggling them out of the ghetto to join our detachment. Rita was an uncommonly brave and tenacious woman with a strong fighting spirit, but she was unwilling to leave her husband, Itzik Dembo, behind. As a ghetto policeman, he was under constant Nazi surveillance and should he have disappeared, his entire unit would have been summarily shot. Beyond that, he was an only child. His father had perished during the first days of the war and he was unwilling to leave his mother behind. Rita was intransigent.

Sonya was also in no hurry to join the partisans. She was still working in the German hospital, had taken over Misha's former connection with the German pharmacist, and was supplying the AKO and the partisans with medicines. My mother, Alice, and Aunt Fanya all discussed their plans for escape from the ghetto. They all had forged documents testifying that they were Polish refugees. Our family's former housekeeper, Frania Grunskaite, was searching for a Lithuanian family where they could hide temporarily. In any case, Frania had a friend who lived in a village at the outskirts of Kaunas who had promised to take Fanya's toddler, Tanya. Frania's sister, Liuda Buziene, would probably find a hiding place for my mother. Dr. Elena Kutorgiene had agreed to help Alice. A place in the hideout inside the ghetto had been secured for Misha's father, Lipe, my aunts and other close relatives.

Even though I was still weak, when I had sufficiently recovered from my illness, I went to meet with the AFO Committee members. The ghetto had changed drastically. It was much smaller and there were hardly any inmates to be seen. The German SS patrolled the streets and the SS men were rude, self-satisfied. They were absolutely confident in their power and their own veracity. How badly I wished I could meet them in the Rudninkai Forest. There I could show them, with a rifle in my hand, who they really were and explain to them what we, the Jews of Kaunas, were made of. Here in the ghetto, though, we had to play by their rules.

From AFO Committee member, Chaim-Dovid Ratner, I learned that Chaim Jellin was not in the ghetto. Having received the message from Endlin about the shortage of weapons and the other problems we faced, he had immediately left for Rudininkai Forest. Shmulik Mordkovski had managed to guide Albina and, later on, Chaim to the Rudninkai Forest. A large group of resisters, led by Endlin, Shtromas, and Lopjanski, had also already escaped the ghetto and joined the partisans. The AFO was preparing another large group of resisters for me to lead into the forest as soon as I was physically able.

It was during my conversation with Ratner that I learned that Dima Gelpernas had been brutally beaten by the Germans. Although he was weak, he wanted to see me. I went to see him the next day. Dima was in bed, his head was bruised and wrapped in bandages. He was eager to hear first hand information about our life with our partisans. He wanted to know what I thought about the possibility of sending more resisters, especially women. He knew they were not welcomed by the leadership of our detachment. I explained our situation, glossing over our actual circumstances and our relationship with the commanders. The most important request we have, I stressed to Dima, was for more rifles and arms. Men and women who arrived armed would be accepted into any detachment. We already had enough skilled guides within our ranks. We had blazed a reliable trail from Kaunas to Rudninkai, so that ghetto resisters could now reach the partisans on foot. I added that I knew it would be safer and easier to reach Rudninkai by truck, but it was not easy to obtain vehicles and arrange for drivers. There was no point in delaying any longer. What we needed, I told him, was armed resisters who were instructed in how to reach the Rudninkai Forest on foot. At the present time, I told him, taking into account the situation in the ghetto – Concentration Camp-Kauen, – the AFO needed to encourage and help the young people to obtain weapons, to escape from the ghetto, and join the partisans as soon as they could. They had to do it, any possible way they could. I asked Dima when he and Chaim would be ready to leave the ghetto and join the partisans but he didn't answer my question directly. The leader of the AFO, Chaim Jellin, and his deputy, Dima Gelpernas, had committed themselves to staying in the ghetto for the meantime. They would only leave with the last group of ghetto resisters. Unfortunately, neither of them succeeded in escaping the ghetto. Chaim Jellin was murdered by the Gestapo and Dima Gelpernas was deported to the Dachau Concentration Camp, Germany.

After our conversation with Dima, Ratner informed me that the AFO Committee had changed my departure date and I was to leave immediately. Now, the time for the heart-wrenching farewell with my mother, sister, and loved ones had arrived. I tried to convince myself that I could not help them by staying in the ghetto. I suppose I was looking for a justification to leave my family behind to the vagaries of fate. I begged my sister to look after our mother as best she could. She promised never to leave mother's side. My sister Alice kept her word. She never left our mother's side, protecting her in every way possible. Clinging to her until our mother's last breath, in the end, Alice did not have the strength to save her and the other relatives.

Our entire family, as well as Misha's father Lipe and sister Sonya, came to say goodbye. Lipe Rubinsonas held my hand firmly and, with tears in his eyes, asked that I look after Misha. We all cried. There was a common feeling, even though we did not wish to believe it, that we might never have the fortune to be together again. At that moment, I truly wanted to believe that the retreating Germans would not kill the remaining Kaunas Jews. Perhaps, I prayed, they would be unable, or even unwilling, to murder or deport the remaining ghetto inmates. The Front was approaching Lithuania and it seemed that freedom was not far off. Nobody wanted to die. Everybody hoped to survive. Naturally, hope and the will to live are essential traits of human existence. Unfortunately, our hope and will to live was not fulfilled. The Holocaust does not have a happy ending. Up until the final moments of their defeat, the Nazis used all possible means to continue the murder of Jews. They were determined to deport them and move them around from camp to camp even during their own march to death.

We hugged one more time, exchanged some brave words and I left. It was the last time I had the opportunity to say farewell to my Mother, to my sister Alice and her husband Philip, to the Benjaminovichi family, to Misha's father Lipe and his sister Sonya Rubinsonaite, and to my aunts.

Back to the Forest

That day, I fled the ghetto for our partisan detachment with two ghetto inmates. Chone Kaganas had to flee immediately because the Gestapo was looking for him and Aba Diskant, who had recently come to the ghetto from our detachment for a special assignment. Israel Goldblatt, one of our partisans, was also in the ghetto on a mission. He was guiding a larger group of ghetto resisters out to the partisans.

On February 8, 1944, Chone, Aba and I met at the ghetto fence where Peisach Shateris was waiting for us. He helped us climb the fence and we walked through the graveyard of the Christian Cemetery, crossed the Vilijampole Bridge, and, in the old part of Kaunas, met the car and the driver that was waiting for us. The car drove rapidly through the streets of Kaunas, left the city, and drove through the Trakai Forest in the direction of Vilnius. In my thoughts, I was already far from the ghetto, with Misha, whom I missed terribly. Soon we turned onto an unpaved road and drove slowly towards partisan territory. We passed the railroad crossing and could now see our forest. A few more kilometers and we reached the densest part of the forest. The car stopped briefly to let us out and turned quickly back in the direction of Kaunas. From here, the three of us knew our way blindfolded and we reached our base by nightfall.

The first glimpse we had of the partisans from our detachment was of those guarding the second outpost. There we were greeted by our comrades. They told us that Chaim Jellin had been there briefly and that he had already left for his return to Kaunas Ghetto. Misha had just returned from a mission and his unit had killed several Germans and captured their bicycles. After a short chat, we went to the headquarters dugout to brief our superiors. We received an uncharacteristically warm reception, presented our short report. Then I ran to see Misha. He already knew of my return and a few moments later, I felt his strong arms around me. We were together again. The whole world, it seemed, belonged to us alone.

ESCAPE FROM THE NINTH FORT

At the beginning of 1944, a group of escapees from Kaunas Ghetto arrived at our detachment. But this was not a group of regular ghetto resisters. Eleven of them were escapees from the Ninth Fort.

Throughout the three years of German occupation, the Ninth Fort, which was located about ten kilometers from Kaunas and about seven kilometers from the ghetto, had been operating as a death factory. The Nazis cynically called the Ninth Forth, *Schlachtfeld*, which means both battlefield and massacre site. Thousands and thousands of people were murdered there. Most of those murdered were Jews. Among the Jews slaughtered were inmates of the Kaunas Ghetto, a group of Jewish police from the Kaunas Ghetto (1944), all victims of the 'Big' and 'Small' *Aktzions* (1941), and many distinguished Jewish individuals and their families from Kaunas and from other Lithuanian cities. One such family was that of Dr. Nachman Shapiro. He was the eldest son of the late Rabbi of the Jewish community in Kaunas, Avraham Dov Ber Shapiro. On December 2, 1943, the Gestapo came into the Kaunas Ghetto and arrested Dr. Nachman Shapiro, his wife, his only son, a fourteen-year-old boy, and his seventy-year-old mother. They were arrested because one of the Rabbi's relatives in the USA had asked the International Red Cross and the Catholic Church to find out if the Shapiro family was alive. The Gestapo received a request to send the family to Switzerland. Instead, the Gestapo murdered them all at the Ninth Fort.

Along with the Jews from Lithuania who were murdered at the Ninth Fort, Jews from Poland, the Soviet Union, Germany, Austria, Czechoslovakia, and France were also murdered. Among the murdered non-Jews were former political activists, members of the Lithuanian underground resistance organizations, members of the underground Young Communist League and others. The ranks of the 'Valley of Death' were swelled by the young and the elderly; men, women, and children of all ages; the sick and the weak; the healthy and the strong.

In August 1943, the Gestapo in Kaunas received an order from Berlin to destroy the evidence of the mass murders at the Ninth Fort. At the very moment when the 'operation' began, the Gestapo replaced the Lithuanian guards with Wiener Schutzpolice officers. Now there were almost as many guards as prisoners. By November 1943, a brigade of sixty-four prisoners was assembled. It was made up of inmates from the Kaunas Ghetto, with Soviet POWs, and several local Russian members of the resistance movement in Kaunas, and one Polish woman. The brigade was divided into four squads, each with its particular jobs. The prisoners were assigned the task of exhuming and burning the corpses. The commandant of the Fort, SS Captain Gratt, and the Gestapo men in charge of the operation appeared at the site every morning to supervise the prisoners. Supervision consisted of beating the prisoners while shouting at them, '*schneller, schneller*' (faster, faster).

Three of the squads wore leg shackles while working and were very limited in their movements. The first squad was required to shift the top layer of earth from fifteen pits and, using shovels, remove the first layer of corpses. Then the digger squad would lift the bodies out, layer by layer, with long poles that had hooks on the end. They would check for valuables and extract gold teeth which they would put in a box that was guarded by a German guard. Then the bodies would be put on stretchers and taken to the burning site. The burner squad would pile the corpses on special wooden pallets and tiered, a layer of bodies, a layer of logs, forming a large cube. Then fuel would be pour over the piles of the dead and the whole thing would be set on fire. The bodies would burn all night and then the ashes would be loaded onto trucks to be dumped over a wide area of the countryside. About four hundred bodies were reduced to ashes daily. The fourth squad was engaged in various other work at the Fort, some on kitchen duty, some in workshops, some in the garage, and others elsewhere.

The inmates did not have any illusions about their fate. They knew very well that their days were numbered. The Nazis would never permit witnesses of their crimes to live. So, it was inevitable that someone would consider escape. The first persons who believed he could organize and implement an escape plot was a Soviet prisoner of war, Alexander Podolski, whose real name was Sasha Khailovski. Part of the fourth squad, Sasha was one of those who could freely move around the territory of the Fort. Observing all the facilities and constructions inside and outside the building of the Ninth Fort, he discovered a route of underground tunnels and other areas that could be used to escape from the Fort. Sacha told his idea to Ivan Vasilenko, whose real name was Israel Veselnicki.. They both shared one cell and one plank. First, they decided to establish a resistance group consisting only of POWs. Then they shared their strategy with some ghetto resisters who were members of the AFO. A committee was formed consisting of the POWs Alexander Podolski, Ivan Vasilenko, and Roman Shachov; and Kaunas Ghetto inmates Tevje Friedman and Michke Zemelovitch (The Pock). Michke was one of the most active member of the underground group at the Ninth Fort and had the greatest authority, not only among the inmates from Kaunas Ghetto, but among the POWs as well. Later on, a few more inmates were included in the Committee.

After carefully studying all the possible escape routes, the Committee adopted a detailed plan of action. They needed to forge keys to their cell doors and drill a passage through metal doors leading to an underground tunnel. They also needed to remove the logs stored in the tunnel and to construct two ladders made of rope. The ladders would be used, among other things, to climb over the concrete wall surrounding the Fort. From the beginning, the escape strategy was kept secret from the other inmates, although it was decided that all sixty-four prisoners would have to escape together. Some twenty to twenty-five other inmates, whose help and participation in the escape was badly needed, were informed of the plot.

Pine Krakinovski, a brilliantly skilled locksmith, played the most important role in the escape operation. In accordance with the regulations imposed by the Germans in the Fort, Pine feigned illness and a Jewish doctor permitted him sick leave for a while. In his cell, Pine made lock-picking devises and other tools from pocket-knives that the prisoners found in the clothing of corpses. He had two model saws that could cut through the iron door leading to the escape tunnel. At the same time, Pine and two other locksmiths, using the most primitive tools, were secretly drilling through the metal door while the others continued burning corpses outside.

As far as the removal of the logs was concerned, the prisoners suggested to the Germans that they could improve their work efficiency by adding dry wood to the fire and permission was granted for the use of the logs. The tunnel was now free of obstacles. Knowing they risked the lives of all the other prisoners as well as their own, the committee members took the greatest care in working out every detail of the plan. Finally, the day they had been preparing for arrived.

The Committee had decided that Christmas Eve or Christmas Day would be the ideal time for this escape. On December 25, while their guards were merrily singing Christmas carols and drinking vodka, Shimon Eidelson with an earlier prepared forged key, opened the doors of the cells. Sixty-four prisoners of the death camp, the Ninth Fort, were set free. Moving in total silence, they left their cells exactly was planned. All prisoners reached the stairs near the opening to the tunnel, and holding hands in the complete darkness, the line of sixty-four people made its way along the long, winding passage until they reached the outer wall of the fort. When they came out the other end, they descended a steep slope and found themselves at the deep ditch along the six-meter-high wall. With the help of their ladder, they climbed the tall, smooth, concrete wall. It took about an hour for the heroic sixty-four prisoners to escape the territory of the Ninth Fort.

Relieved and free, these brave people faced a new dilemma. Where should they go? The prisoners had not formulated a plan on where to go when and if their escape was successful. Each one could go on their own or they could try to make it in groups. They decided to split into groups, each with a leader. Some groups of two or three went to the surrounding villages to hide for the time being. The largest group, mostly the POW, however, decided to go to the forest and try to reach the partisans. Unfortunately, they circled around in the dark and the next morning found themselves in a sparse forest not far from the Ninth Fort. Most of them were caught, one by one, by the Gestapo and murdered. Among those were the courageous heroes and organizers of the escape, Alexander Podolski and Michke Zemelovitch. Altogether thiry-seven escapee perrished in this forest and in some other places. twenty-seven escapee from the Ninth Fort survived.

One group of escapees, headed by Vasilenko, made their way into the ghetto. They climbed the ghetto fence and in the late night

hours, reached the home of AFO Committee member, Chaim-Dovid
Ratner. By chance, Moishe Musel and Chaim Jellin were there. Taking extraordinary precautions, Chaim Jellin had them hidden immediately in various hideouts in the ghetto. They were forbidden to leave
their hiding place or to inform even members of their families or their
closest friends. Only a few members of the Jewish Administrations
were told so that they could help hide the escapees in the ghetto and
aid their escape into the forest. The AFO undertook to prepare a
report explaining what 'jobs' these prisoners had been forced to perform at the Ninth Fort. An official record was written by a member
of the AFO and was signed by all eleven escapees. Today, a copy of
this report is kept at the Museum of the Ninth Fort in Kaunas. In
1957 another document regarding the details of the escape from th
Ninth Fort was signed by seven wittnesses. The document is kept in
the Lithuanian State Archive and in the Museum of the Ninth Fort in
Kaunas and the State Jewish Gaon Museum in Vilnius.

Meanwhile, in the ghetto, Chaim Jellin himself was in charge
of securing the escapees' safety and, and as soon as possible, organizing their escape and transportation from the ghetto to the partisans
in Rudninkai Forest. First he had to organize a public bath for the
escapees and a way to burn their clothing. This was the only way to
get rid of the smell of burned corpses on the escapee's bodies, their
hair and their clothing. In the same night, not waiting for the morning hours, Chaim appeared at the house of Rabbi Oshry, who was in
charge of the 'Delousing Institute', the bathhouse. He asked Oshry
to prepare a bath for the escapees at once, not to wait for morning.
Chaim explained that these people needed to be thoroughly bathed in
order to get the stink of the cadavers out of their skin and hair. Rabbi
Oshry immediately began heating the water himself so that no one
else would have to know about it. The escapees entered the bathhouse,
washed and donned clean clothes.

Three of the escapees, Aaron Vilenchiuk, Tevje Pilovnik and Shimon Eidelson, had decided to make their own way to the outskirt of
Kaunas when they had escaped from the Ninth Fort. They found an
empty barn in Lampedziai on the Nemunas River, about ten to twelve
kilometers from Kaunas, and stayed there without food for three days,
When a peasant discovered them there, he brought them food and

then told them to leave. In the evening, they had traveled back to Kaunas, safely crossed the Vilijampole Bridge and climbed over the ghetto fence. The first place they went was to see Misha Rubinsonas, Aaron's best friend,. Misha and I had already gone to the partisans by that time but they met with Misha's father, Lipe. He immediately contacted Chaim-Dovid Ratner and the three escapees, still in their clothes stinking of burnt corpses, were hidden with the others.

For the time being, all of the escapee were safely hidden in their bunkers, but Chaim felt no relief. He believed that the escapees were still in danger. One never knew, and could not assume, what measures the Gestapo would implement in their search for the escaped prisoners. In order to send the escapees to the partisans in Rudninkai Forest as quickly as possible, Chaim ordered Moishe Musel to acquire a covered truck. Musel promptly procured a truck and soon had it awaiting for the escapees at the ghetto gate on Varniu street. As was usual in the escape procedure, the waiting truck was supposedly there to take Jewish workers to a night shift. Chaim asked that the highest ranking, and most reliable, Jewish policemen and a representative of the labour department of the Jewish Administration be on duty at the gate that night. Everything fell into place and the operation went smoothly.

On January 6, 1944, Chaim Jellin, Moishe Musel, and twenty ghetto resisters, including the eleven escapees from the Ninth Fort, climbed into the truck waiting outside the ghetto. The truck made its way towards the forest. On the outskirts of Kaunas, Moishe was ordered to return to the ghetto. Another important assignment was waiting for him there.

NEW MISSIONS

By the spring of 1944, there were 300 partisans in our detachment, mostly Kaunas Ghetto fighters. By that time also, we had amassed a well stocked arsenal of weapons and explosive material. Altogther, our living conditions had improved considerably. The leadership decided to split the detachment and two additional military units were established: *Vladas Baronas* and *Pirmyn* (Further). Both new units had their own leaders, but Kostas Radionovas remained the chief commander of all three units.

Unfortunately, shortly after my return from Kaunas Ghetto and the arrival of the escapees from the Ninth Fort, our detachment suffered an irreplaceable loss. During a mission, our comrade, Borisas Lisauskas, the chief of intelligence, had to spent the night in Senoji Macele at the home of his liaison, Jurgelevich. Early the next morning, soldiers and police from the German garrison surrounded the house. It was obvious that somebody from Jurgelevich's family had betrayed him. Although he was wounded, Borisas returned fire and managed to escape through a window and disappear into the forest. Hearing the shooting, partisans from our detachment quickly arrived on the scene and found Borisas who was severely wounded. The Germans had already dispersed and the partisans carried Borisas back to camp. Despite valiant efforts, our nurses, Riva Epshteinaite-Kaganiene and Ania Borisova, were unable to save his life and Lisauskas died the following day.

Our partisans tried two members of the Jurgelevich family. We confiscated their horse along with some of their other possessions. The strong, beautiful horse was named "Jurgelevich", and our partisan Meyer Tainovich lovingly cared for him. I, myself, rode him on patrols of our territory. There was only one serious problem with Jurgelevich. That horse would not budge unless it heard a particular Russian swear word. So I was forced to learn the word and utter it directly into his ear. It was not an easy task but, little by little, my communication problem with Jurgelevich was solved. I fell in love with the horse and even got used to the swear word.

Now that our strengthened detachment was able to mount much more effective assaults against the enemy, all the men and women were involved in a large variety of military activity.

We carried out many acts of sabotage and participated in battles against the German garrisons, blew up sawmills, food processing and dairy plants, seized weapons and food warehouses. Those of our partisans in combat units, like Misha Karecki (Liberman), Leizer Tzodikov, Yudel Birger, Israel Goldblatt, Dovid Teper, Hirsh Smoliakov, Liova Sher and many other Kaunas Ghetto fighters, were often involved in military actions far from Rudninkai Forest. They derailed military trains and blew up the railway trucks that constantly moved from Vilnius, Kaunas, and Riga (Latvia) to the front line. We, the partisan fighters, regularly cut miles of telephone line and destroyed telegraph poles and underground cables. Our guide, Nechemija Endlin, managed to return three more times to Kaunas Ghetto and Israel Goldblatt went back twice more. They managed to bring five more groups of ghetto resisters to the forest.

I remember April 24, 1944 very well. On that day, a large number of partisans from all three detachments went out on a very important and dangerous mission. We had to destroy a crucial German garrison in the city of Rudninkai and to seize their weapons and ammunition. Misha and I were both assigned to the same combat group. Side by side, proud of our allegiance to the partisans and confident in our right to fight the enemy, we went together to carry out the assignment.

Perez Kliachko, Rocha Lifshitz, and Zunia Shtromas began the operation by blowing up a new bridge over the Merkys River. The explosion was a signal for our fighters to begin the attack on the garrison. Shmuel Pasternak, Liova Sher, and Perez Volbe fired on the enemy's positions with their sub-machine guns. Misha Rubinsonas, Aaron Vilenchiuk, and I were lying in a pit, positioned closer to the enemy barracks. At close range, we fired toward all the exits of the barracks. Meanwhile, one group of partisans destroyed the telephone center, while another laid mines on the roads that the Germans could use to send help to their soldiers. The entire military operation lasted four hours. The garrison, the barracks, the telephone line, and the other military facilities were completely destroyed. Without the loss of a single one of our fighters, or much of our ammunition, we all returned to our base together, happy at the successful completion of the operation and received deep appreciation from our commanders. The war against the German occupiers went on. We fully intended to fight the enemy until the last drop of our blood.

At the end of May 1944, we were informed that the Germans were planning to comb the forest and surround our base. It was decided that all the partisans of our detachment should leave the base and move to the eastern part of Rudninkai Forest. During the march, I received an order to stay on guard on the road and to observe the whole territory. After a while, I noticed a small German military unit approaching. They were moving very quickly along the road, their sub-machine guns turned towards both sides of the road. I lay down and turned my rifle in their direction. When they drove by, I ran to report what I had seen to our commanders, but, to my surprise, nobody was there. I returned to my post, waiting to be replaced, as was required by regulation.

After about an hour or so, I saw Misha approaching with another partisan. The command had forgotten all about me. The commanders were very pleased with my performance and, on May 24, I received official gratitude from our commander. I was very disappointed, however, that I did not receive an automatic rifle, as I had been promised. How, I wondered naively, could I enter the ghetto and liberate the inmates without a proper gun.

Also in the spring of 1944, the commanders of the "Death to the Occupiers" Detachment began planning the destruction of the German military garrison in the village of Vechiorishkes which was also a military training facility and an arsenal. Members of all three partisan units participated in this operation.

On the morning of the attack, only a few defenders remained behind at our base camp along with some medical personnel and supply staff. I was assigned to the unit of sub-machine gunner Liova Sher, while Misha served under the commander of the entire operation. Not long before his death, Misha described the battle that took place in Vechiorshkes village. It was published posthumously.

THE LAST GRENADE
by Misha Rubinsonas

'Our' Rudninkai Forest...that same pine grove, those same roads and footpaths...But at the same time not quite the same. In the past twenty years the pine and fir trees have grown. The undergrowth has been cleared away carefully and the forest is not quite as dense as it once was. The roads are wider now and better quality. Where peasant carts had great difficulty passing, now huge trucks thunder by. A few footpaths remain unmolested and lead to the underground bunkers or to the restored and protected complex of bunkers that were the headquarters of 'our' Rudninkai Forest partisans.

When the weather is pleasant, especially in the summer, you can hear the adult visitors talk quietly among themselves, and their voices are drummed out, at times, by the louder, younger generation and by youth groups. People come here to become acquainted with the war that was fought here with the worst of mankind – the Nazis.

For us, the survivors who fought against Hitler's occupying forces, this place in the Rudninkai Forest is more than a museum. The place reminds us of the reality of our past and it triggers many memories. This was our spiritual home. To this place came many fighters from the ghettos of Kaunas and Vilnius. Having undertaken risky, and dangerous, life-threatening missions, we would return to the shade of the pine and fir trees as if we had come home. Here we would breathe freely; here we were the masters of our fate; here we were the commanders; here our rules prevailed. The Germans and their collaborators never dared to set a foot here because they were too afraid of running into us. We were never afraid to attack them in the places where they believed themselves to be safest. But nowhere in the Rudninkai Forest were the Germans safe. The forest was under our control, not theirs.

Today, I am walking the paths and roads, the streets in towns and villages, the highways where deadly battles were fought with the occupiers. Here are the places that are holy to us. Here our best and bravest fighters spilled their blood.

Vechiorishkes is also the same and yet not quite the same. It is a village about 10 kilometers from what was our headquarters. It has now grown. There are new homes there, chemical plants and agricultural facilities that were not here before. Wherever you glance, you see electricity cables and the road to Vilnius and Grodno has been repaired. But the forest is there and at the boundaries of the forest there is Vechiorishkes. The Germans had established a large garrison there to secure the valuable wood they could use for building materials. Barbed wire and barricades surrounded their base. Our goal was to liquidate this hornet's nest.

That dark and cool April night, the partisans of all three units of our detachment went on a mission to destroy the garrison. We were split into groups, each with a specific assignment. Trushin, the commander of the fighters squad, began the operation. He took out the guard near one of the bunkers with a well-aimed shot and that was our signal to attack. We cut through the barbed wire and entered the army base. Our attack was so sudden that the Germans did not know what had hit them. They were not even dressed when they left their bunkers. Some sought hiding places for the luggage in which they had stored their booty. Three of our machine gunners, Pine Krakinovski, Aaron Gefen and Itzik Nemzer, and other fighters killed the enemy soldiers with great precision. Those who decided to defend themselves in their bunkers were forever silenced by our hand grenades, thrown by Hirsh Smoliakov and others. More and more grenades were thrown into the main building. After a while, a group of partisans went on a mission to destroy the factories assisting the Germans, the train station, and to take out the telegraph poles. Meanwhile, another group of partisans pursued those Germans who had managed to break through our lines and were trying to flee in the direction of the centre of the village. Only one small group of partisans were still attaching the main building of the military base.

After the first few minutes of shock, the Germans started to return fire. Somehow, they had been able to get word of our attack to their commanders. A column of trucks with reinforcements arrived from Vilnius. Our leader sounded the retreat since he realized the enemy forces had grown. We retreated in an organized way with as many captured weapons and prisoners we could lay our hands on. The small group of 16 partisans, the rear guard, fought the enemy until their bullets ran out. They were surrounded on all sides and were losing fighters quickly. The Nazis' shells ripped through our Kaunas Ghetto fighters, mortally wounding one after another. Only one partisan survived. It was Taibele Vinishski, our Tania, as we referred to her.

I remember Taibele as she was when she first joined our detachment. She had grown very beautifully with blond wavy hair that barely fit under her hat. She wore a thick belt and had a gun slung over her shoulder. The majority of our detachment was made up of young people who had fled the Kaunas Ghetto. We did not have very much battlefield experience, so we always had a couple of veterans among our ranks. Taibele had already spent much time fighting in Belarus as well as in the Rudninkai Forest with the Vilnius Jewish unit. She was never tired and never lost heart. She participated in many missions and operations and always wanted to be where the action was most intense and dangerous. This was how she sought revenge on those who had murdered her entire family, spilling their innocent blood into the rivers of her ancestral home.

Taibele was the last one to hold her ground. She had been shot in the shoulder during the gunfight and had no bullets left. She raised her hands to surrender. Just as the Germans were about to take Taibele into custody, she pulled the pin from the grenade she was holding and took several of Hitler's murderers with her to the grave.

Everything here in the village of Vechiorishkes is the same. Everything here in the surroundings reminds us of the courageous partisans who fought against those who wanted to enslave the world and push humanity into the abyss. We remember our 16 fallen comrades here in the Rudninkai Forest at the edge of the village of Vichiorishkes. We remember their deeds, their courageous lives, and their last battle.

THE YOUNGEST PARTISAN: SAMUELIS ROZINAS

Samuelis (Mulik) Rozinas was one of the youngest partisans in our detachment. In the ghetto, as a talented and promising artist, he was employed in the Paint and Sign Workshop. Draftsmen, fine artists, and designers worked in this graphics office to produce the official ghetto insignia, armbands for the ghetto administration staff, work passes, and many other requisite documents. Peter (Fritz) Gadiel, a German-Jewish graphic artist, established and led this workshop. Gadiel was born in Germany and happened to be residing in Kaunas when the Germans invaded Lithuania in June 1941. Along with the other Kaunas Jews, he was imprisoned in the Kaunas Ghetto.

In 1942, the Jewish Administration decided that the workshop should produce important official documentary artifacts to preserve the ghetto history and it was virtually turned into a record center. A sizable archive containing examples of nearly all of the ghetto's official drawings, certificates, forms, maps, posters, insignia, statistical reports, and stamp impressions were hidden in the ghetto.[89] Mulik was sometimes contacted by the AFO, with whom he had indirect connections, to design forged certificates or other documents.

In the early morning hours of April 9, 1944, we heard footsteps approaching our detachment and three escapees from Kaunas Ghetto appeared out of the forest. They were Samuelis (Mulik) Rozinas, Feige Zilberman and her future husband, Joshua Vershvovsky. They had come by themselves, on foot.

Mulik was the first to tell us the news about Chaim Jellin's tragic fate.[90] On April 5, Chaim was looking for a driver to transport a large group of ghetto resisters, including Mulik, to the forest. As soon as Chaim succeeded in finding a driver and a truck, a command was given for the group to be ready to escape from the ghetto. They assembled in a pre-arranged place in Vilijampole, outside the ghetto, and waited there for the truck. When the driver did not show up, Chaim ordered the people to disperse and hide in the neighbouring bunkers. Mulik and a few other ghetto resisters hide in a basement for the night. Very late that night, an exhausted Chaim Jellin walked into the bunker. He said that he had made arrangements with another driver, whom he was going to meet the next morning. He was confident, he said, that the truck would arrive the next day. Chaim advised the escapees not to return to the ghetto. These were to be Chaim's last words, spoken in the basement of an abandoned house to the last ghetto inmates who spoke to, or saw, Chaim Jellin alive. He left the bunker early in the morning and did not return.

Later that day, the ghetto resisters in the bunker found out that a fire fight had broken out between Gestapo agents and a young man on Daukanto Street where Chaim was supposed to meet the driver. After this news reached the ghetto resisters, the fighters, who stayed with Chaim in the same bunker, left the place. Some returned to the ghetto but Mulik, Feigale and Joshua were determined to go on foot to Rudninkai Forest. All of them safely crossed the Vilijampole and Aleksotas Bridges and began their 160 kilometers trek to the Rudninkai Forest and the partisans. In the suburb of Aleksotas, they got a ride with a passing truck to the southern city of Alytus. From there they walked, by themselves, the remaining seventy to eighty kilometers to the Rudninkai Forest.

Mulik had a map of the Rudninkai region and some guidelines about the forest. But they traveled without knowing the regular partisan routes, walking during the day through small cities and villages. It was a great help to them, though, in their pilgrimage to the forest, that all three hardly looked Jewish and were dressed like local peasants. It was already the spring of 1944. The Red Army had liberated a greater part of Belarus and was not far from the Lithuanian border. It was obvious that the days of the German occupation were numbered and not many people were still eager to assist the Nazis. Moreover, Mulik and Joshua were too young to be recruited into the Lithuanian or German Army, and Feigale, a beautiful blond girl, did not arouse any suspicious either. And so, all three of them safely reached the Rudninkai Forest and our detachment in the partisan controlled territory. Upon their arrival, they spoke briefly with our commander and commissar and were admitted to our detachment and assigned to the Forward unit.

Very soon after Mulik's arrival, he was sent on an important mission. Along with five other fighters commanded by an experienced military man, Peter Fediunin, their assignment was to blow up a military train about sixty kilometers from Kaunas. Not far from the city of Vievis, at the railway station of Kaugonis, the group came under attack and was surrounded by German military. Returning fire, the partisans retreated to a river. The Germans, following the partisans, wounded Mulik. The commander ordered Mulik to cross the small river and the others to cover him as they moved further along the river. He managed to swim across the river and the Germans lost sight on him. The rest of the group also crossed the river safely. From the other side of the river, the five partisans found a boat and attempted to cross a lake. The Germans spotted them and continued firing. Two of the partisans, Sasha Boldin and Moishe Garber, were killed in the boat. The three remaining fighters reached the shore. Since they could not find Mulik anywhere, they retreated to the safety of the dense forest. Meanwhile, after crossing the river, Mulik also made his way to the lake.

The only choice he had was to swim across the large lake to the other side. Despite his serious injuries, Mulik managed to reach shore. It turned out that the shore was not the other side of the lake but a small island. Hungry, thirsty and wet, with a bleeding wound, Mulik hid in the bushes by the shore, barely conscious. Later, a fisherman from a local village noticed him. He got Mulik out of the bushes, and bandaged his wound. The fisherman promised to bring him food and to get him across the lake. In the evening, as promised, the fisherman returned. He brought Mulik dry clothes, some bread and milk, and took him by boat to the other side of the lake. He was the first to tell Mulik that two of his colleagues were dead and that the rest had managed to retreat. The fisherman showed him the direction to the partisan territory and left.

Hardly able to walk, Mulik could only make it to the nearby village of Shairishkes. There, he knocked on the door of a peasant's hut. Mulik explained who he was to the lady of the house and asked for help. Agota Mikalauskiene and her family hid Samuelis Rozinas in the attic and nursed him back to health. Agota became like a second mother to him. Their decency and gentleness did more that just help him to recover from his wounds. This good family also strengthening Mulik's will and spirit. Their kindness restored his trust and confidence in other people.

He lived with the family until he was healed and could make it back to the partisans. Once Mulik was well enough, Agota's son, Kazys Mikalauskas, led him to the forest and, although he was still weak, he managed to reconnect with *Geny's* detachment. From there, Misha Rubinsonas, Leizer Zilber, Shloime Baron, and Aaron Vilenchiuk helped their young friend. Laughing, Misha would later tease him and say that they had to carry his emaciated, forty kilogram body for a distance of forty kilometers.

After the war, Mulik asked Agota if she had been afraid to provide sanctuary to a Jew. He wanted to know why she had risked her life. Agota calmly replied, "At that moment, and even later, I did not think about the risk. I simply took pity on a young boy and decided to help him out." Agota Mikalauskiene passed away in 1950.

The renowned graphic artist, Samuelis Rozinas, painted Agota's portrait in woodcut and water colours and wrote a poem dedicated to her. In memory of the partisans who helped him to return to our detachment, he dedicated a cut linoleum painting depicting a partisan carrying his wounded friend.

WOMEN OF OUR DETACHMENT

All the partisans of Rudninkai Forest lived according to the well-established rules and traditions of the Soviet Union. We observed Soviet holidays with great fanfare. At the beginning of March 1944, we began preparations for the celebration of International Women's Day. We invited Jurgis (Zimanas) and the women from his unit and also the women from other detachments. I was asked to deliver the official address.

I sat at a desk in the headquarters' dugout with a blank sheet of paper before me. I didn't know what to write or what I should say. I knew very little about the International Women's Movement or about how it was run in Lithuania or in the Soviet Union. I had no knowledge of war heroines or their achievements. Noticing my confusion, the commissar offered his help. I accepted without hesitation and he proceeded to prepare an appropriate introduction for me to read. First, I was to thank the Communist Party of the Soviet Union and its leaders for having freed women from their 'double yoke'. Although it was not very clear to me exactly what this equality and freedom from the 'double yoke' consisted of, I did not bother to argue. I simply did what was asked of me and then proceeded to write about the women of our detachment, about their responsibilities and their bravery.

Sitting at my desk, I did not think of the inequality of women partisans. At that time, I, personally, did not feel any gender discrimination. I also did not feel any dependence on my husband, or any male, because I was a female. But, looking back today, I ask myself if there were any problems for a woman in that man's world. Certainly, the life of the women in our, and in other, detachments in Rudninkai Forest was somewhat different from the lives of their counterparts, the men.

The main issue for the girls who wanted to join the partisans was to find a way to be enrolled in the ranks of escapees from the Kaunas Ghetto. The most important requirement was to be an active member of the AFO. Women who were members were the first to join the partisans. Those women who were less active or did not belong to the underground organization had to acquire a gun or pay the equivalent black market price of a weapon. Only then would they be included in a group escaping from the ghetto to the forest.

Most of the men – ghetto resisters – had girlfriends or were already married. At the beginning of 1944, many of those men were already in the forest or were soon to leave with an upcoming group. Their wives and girlfriends would later be enrolled on the list of escapees and many of them came with guns. I would say that seventy to eighty percent of all Jewish women in our detachment were themselves members of AFO and (or) married to ghetto resisters. It is important to note, however, that all the marriages in the ghetto were about true love, not a means to escape. We were all married at a very young age. We all felt there was no point in waiting any longer for a better time to come. Young couples wanted to be together, to fight together, and to survive or die together.

All the women who came to the forest did not come to save their own lives or avoid death. As soon as a new group from the ghetto was admitted to our detachment, the Jewish women were treated as equals to the Jewish men. Upon entry to the detachments, the same basic rules applied to men and women. All the Jewish partisan men and women were equally motivated to fight the enemy by any and all possible means.

Of course, there were the centuries old male-female divisions in responsibilities and duties. The women were regarded as weak, frail, and unfit to play a part in difficult and dangerous missions. Their participation in combat was often not appreciated. Even the Jewish partisans were not eager to take women along on dangerous missions far from our base. They felt that girls would only make a difficult situation worse, that they might require shielding during a retreat or a battle, that they might be a burden. Since the Soviet government rejected such distinctions, our women were not discouraged from carrying arms and they did participate in military endeavors.

Most of our girls were perfectly suited to the demands of forest life. They were young, physically strong, fearless and courageous. But, I must emphasize, they were not super-women. None of us were unique. We were ordinary women with all the shortcomings of any average person. Altogether, then, the lives of the women in our detachment were not that different form the lives of the men aside from the fact that duties and responsibilities were divided along gender lines.

There were only four women in the "Death To The Occupiers" Detachment when the eleven of us joined the partisans. They were Jekaterina Radionova, Liza Orlova, our nurse, Ania Borisova, and, lastly, Taibele Vinishski, who had fled the Vilnius Ghetto. Later on, women would make up about fifteen percent of our detachment. Our daily life was complicated and unusual. We trekked the winding, snow-blown paths alongside the men, usually with only brief periods of rest. Nobody taught us how to fight or to perform our duties. We learned by ourselves, not only how to clean and use a gun, but how to conduct ourselves in combat and battle, how to blow up a bridge or a train, how to cut communication lines, and how to stand on guard. And all of us, young but fully self-reliant adults, managed to do all that was required of us.

For a long time, we had neither a bathhouse nor an outhouse. We had to go far into the woods through deep snow in order simply to wash. The female partisans were often plagued by lice. They sucked our blood mercilessly and our attempts to eradicate them always proved fruitless. Our menstrual periods were as torturous as the assault of the parasites, particularly when we were on missions or on guard duty. Because we had no female hygiene products, we resorted to shredding sheets or buying rags from the local peasants which we washed in cold water in the woods. Very often they would not dry thoroughly and we had no choice but to use them anyway.

In addition, the women had to bear the brunt of the daily chores around camp. When we were not out on sorties or on guard duty, we were peeling potatoes or doing kitchen chores. We washed 'our' men's clothes and also the clothes of those men that were not 'ours'. The diminutive Beile Ganelina, with hands raw and swollen from the cold, voluntarily washed, rinsed, and dried almost all the men's clothing. Our record-setting potato peeler, Leja Sher, was first at everything. Following a successful mission, she helped her husband, Liova Sher, clean and polish his gun. Other women, such as Ania Borisova and Zoja Tintate-Sherman, attended to the ill and wounded around the clock. An experienced head nurse, Riva Epshteinaite-Kaganiene, performed operations that should have been done by a surgeon.

Sara Gordon arrived from the Kaunas Ghetto the day after her husband, Peisach Gordon-Stein, was killed in action. She had the fortitude to continue on after his loss and avenged herself as best she could for his needless death. At sixteen, Sulamita Lermanaite-Gelperniene was the youngest girl in our unit, but she worked and fought the enemy alongside the rest. Alte Boruchovich-Teper was not only a fighting partisan but, just as she had been in the ghetto, she was a second mother to the girls. In our unit, she served as our confidante and supporter and we continued to call her our *Mamele* (little mother). One could safely say that she was both a fearless warrior and an affectionate, devoted friend.

During my time with the partisans, I became close friends with Riva Bloch. We looked somewhat alike and shared similar tastes. We were both tall and blonde and preferred similar trousers and knee-high boots. We were both poor singers and shared a dislike for women's work. For a time, we were assigned to work in reconnaissance and would go together to Senoji Macele where the local people thought we were sisters. Janchevski, our liaison in Inklerishkes, often mistook Riva Bloch for me. Once, when we went to Inklerishkes together, Janchevski asked which one I was, Riva or Zose. Laughingly, I simply told him that I was Riva when I wanted to be, and Zose when I needed to be.

In the spring, our daily life and food supply improved. We saw the construction of the bathhouse, baking oven, field hospital, and a workshop at our base. We also had a number of cows that needed grazing, feeding, and milking. These chores, once again, became the responsibility of the women. There were no meadows in the forest so we tried to find relatively flat and less densely wooded areas for the cows to graze on. I was never able to manage this task easily. The cows would never listen to me. They would trip over themselves or get caught on large branches and tree trunks that had fallen on the ground. I would no sooner finish helping one get itself out of a mess when another would find itself in a similar situation. After consistent failures, my eyes swollen from crying, our commanders agreed to free me from the burden of taking the cows to graze.

Our partisan women experienced all of the severity of partisan life, fought bravely against the enemy and never complained. At the same time, we were able to maintain our feminine sensitivity and softness, which was a comfort to our companions, our male friends and our husbands, both in combat and in the daily life at our base. We did everything in our power to temper the difficulties we all experienced as warriors, friends, wives, and partisans in Rudninkai Forest.

So, on March 8, to celebrate International Women's Day, all the women in the unit were given a day of rest. We were not required to do work or be on guard duty, and even the most 'womanly' work was done by the men. Early in the morning, the men, wanting to be particularly attentive and respectful to the women, lit the stove in the recently built bathhouse. All the women took showers with what was, under the circumstances, the greatest level of luxury. We put up our hair and helped each other to dress as attractively as we could. Some of us wished to appear especially feminine and we wore skirts and blouses, and put on lipstick. Others wished to dress so as to underline their equality with men and wore trousers, jackets, and belts.

I put on a new pair of pants that had been made for me by Tevje Friedman, one of our partisans, and a warm brown shirt. I wore two belts, one for my pants and the second belt for my pistol. As Misha was helping me put it on, we heard Jurgis' tinny voice.

"Hey Misha, dressing your wife? Good man! But she's fine just as she is!" Even though this remark delighted me and I was in an excellent mood, I was becoming extremely nervous at the thought of standing on the podium to deliver an address. As I stood in front of almost 300 people, my voice wavered and all I wanted to do was disappear into the dugout. It was only when I came to speak about the women of our unit that I managed to calm down.

On that special celebration on March 8, I spoke not only of the women of our detachment but also of the women in the Kaunas Ghetto and the city's underground movement. I told the story of Janina Czizinauskaite who was a member of the underground resistance movement in Kaunas and was shot at the Ninth Fort. She shared a death row cell with AFO member Polia (Pesha) Karnauskaite-Musel. Later on, Polia, after being miraculously released from the Ninth Fort, continued to be an active member of the AFO. Among other assignments, Polia risked her life when she smuggled a Jewish child to safety. I also mentioned our ghetto resisters, Ida Shater, who participated in smuggling Jewish children from the ghetto, but who did not manage to join the partisans. Sonya Rubinsonaite also did not succeed in joining the partisans. I spoke of our courages women: Malke Sinjor, Sheina Levi, Esya Shtrom, Ida Pilovnik-Vilenchiuk and others. All of them were fearless fighters; dutiful and conscientious workers.

On the occasion of International Women's Day, many women of our detachment were honoured by our commanders and officially thanked for their bravery and valour in combat. My happiest surprise was the receipt of a rifle from Kostas, our commander. It was so unexpected and I was so joyful that I forgot to thank him and just kissed my prize. I was one of the first women of the detachment to receive her own personal rifle.

Part Five

Destinies

THE MARCH TO VILNIUS

Usually June in Lithuania is a warm and pleasant spring month, but, in 1944, June was very hot. The temperature hovered from 25 to 30 degree and the forest was full of berries, sorrel, and many of nature's gifts. In our swampy home, though, the mosquitoes also arrived in June. They sucked our blood mercilessly, continuously following us around the base and the forest. The only way to save ourselves from their torment was to stay in the bunker or at the campfire. Because mosquitoes cannot stand smoke, we kept our bunkers filled with smoke, day and night. Even though we could hardly breathe, not a single blood sucker was able to enter our 'bedroom'. But that June, the hot days and the struggle with the mosquitoes were not the only things on our mind. The Red Army was advancing and there was a perception of liberation.

Two branches of our "Death to the Occupiers" Detachment, Forward and Vladas Baronas, had already received a command to move to the forests of southwestern Lithuania as reinforcements for the partisans operating there. In the meantime, the partisans of our branch remained in Rudninkai Forest and began preparations to take part in the battle to liberate Vilnius from the German occupiers. Vilnius was a particularly important position in the German military command's system of defense. As a strategic location for defending routes to eastern Germany, they kept a large division of German troops stationed in the city. Incredibly difficult battles were taking place at the approaches to the city.

During our final days in the forest, we hurriedly prepared to leave our camp. It was my duty to pack the documents in our headquarters. The quartermaster and the cooks prepared food for the march to Vilnius, boiling and smoking meat, and baking bread. Whatever food supplies and livestock were left, we distributed among the peasants of Senoji Macele and Zagarine. Our detachment's cargo fit easily into one horse-drawn carriage.

Minsk, the capital of Belorus, was less than 300 kilometers from Rudninkai. On July 3, 1944, it was liberated. On July 5, an exceptionally hot day, we left our camp behind. We bade farewell to our bunkers, our bathhouse, our baking oven and kitchen. Most difficult to leave was our unforgettable campfire. It was a bittersweet departure. This small spot in Rudninkai Forest had been our home, the one place that had offered us solace and security. Here, after three years of slave labour and humiliation, we had found freedom, and stood, weapons in hand, ready to fight our enemy to the death. Here we tasted the joy of victory and the sorrowful loss of our comrades. Offering each of our fallen comrades a final salute, we walked one last time through the graveyard of our base camp.

We passed through Senoji Macele, Zagarine, Inklerishkes, and other villages. From them, we could see Rudishkes in the distance. Because it was the stronghold of the German military garrison and where its fortification were located, it was a place we had always been forced to avoid. Now the fortifications were dismantled and the town abandoned.

On our march to Vilnius, we noticed a Soviet tank and troops resting by a small river. Overjoyed to see our liberators, all of us, women and men, cried at this sight. We greeted our liberators with firm handshakes, with kisses and adoration. The tank troopers themselves were emotional at this greeting. They had thought that they were in enemy territory, already somewhere in East Prussia, but we told them that they were in Lithuania and that we were partisans who had been fighting the Germans.

On July 7, the first Soviet Army troopers reached the city boundaries of Vilnius and the siege of the city began on July 8, 1944. On July 10, some the partisans were seconded to a small army unit as support. We were stationed at the old Rasu cemetery, about four to five kilometers away from Vilnius. This area was still under the control of the Germans who were entrenched there. During the previous night, the Germans had launched an attack in the hopes of breaking our ranks and forcing us to flee, but all of their attempts had been repelled.

How well I remember July 11, 1944. That morning, our military unit was preparing to launch an attack against the Germans. It was an attack in which I was hoping to participate. But the commander refused to take me and I was deeply offended. I decided not to give in and began to explain to the commander about women's rights, equality, and my experience as a combatant. He listened and argued with me, but, in the end, he lost patience and cut me off by saying that guarding was also an important military mission. He told me to obey orders and made it clear that he would have no more arguments or discussions.

"You are not a partisan any more," he said with a stern gaze. "You are on the front lines now and here there are military rules." With that, he disappeared into the denseness of the cemetery to lead the attack.

I was left alone on lookout duty, where there was not another one living soul around. Even the birds had vanished. All I could hear was shooting coming from the direction of the cemetery. I was very hot, deeply upset and disturbed, but I had no choice but to obey orders. I was in the army now and on the front lines, with the Germans only a few steps away. I took out my field glasses, my rifle, grenades, and pistols. Now I was fully equipped and I was beginning to calm down a little. Suddenly, an American-made jeep drove up and stopped right beside me. I pulled out my gun and shouted, in my typical partisan manner, "Stop! Who are you? What is the password ?" A Soviet officer, with cameras dangling from his neck, got out of the vehicle and looked at me in amazement. When he asked me who I was and what I was doing there, I was taken aback. I hadn't expected such a curt response. I told him this was the front line and asked him what he wanted. "I want to take your photo," he replied seriously. Major Jacob Riumkin explained to me, that he was a military journalist and, on hearing that, I agreed to his request. He looked me up and down, but seemed somewhat displeased.

"Strap the gun across your chest," he said, smiling. Not amused, I remembered the pain I had experienced when I had been denied an automatic weapon.

"It's strange," I said, refusing to move the rifle, "that you can't tell the difference between an automatic weapon and a rifle. No one straps a rifle across their chest."

At that, he changed tactics. Very politely, he asked if I would do it for the sake of the photograph. With that, he won me over and I took the rifle from my shoulder and strapped it across my chest, both of us laughing out loud.

"Don't laugh," he said. "just smile." The camera shutter snapped and we were both still laughing when our fighters returned from the attack, all still alive, happily leading captured German soldiers behind them. Riumkin took a photo of the Germans and left. Not long afterwards, the photo he took of me appeared in the pages of the Moscow journal, *Ogoniok*.

On July 13 1944, all the partisans were ordered to leave the army units and to gather together. All eleven partisan detachments of Rudninkai Forest, along with the Vilnius and Trakai partisan brigades of more than 2,000 partisan fighters, were called on to participate in the final liberation of the city of Vilnius. Didzioji Street had already been liberated, but the worst fighting was still taking place on Vokieciu (German) Street and at the foot of Gediminas Hill near Cathedral Square.

I was part of a small group of seven partisans, under the command of Misha Rubinsonas, who were asked to comb the burning buildings on Vokieciu Street and take any surrendering German soldiers prisoner. We, of the "Death to the Occupiers" Detachment, marched into the city through the ancient Gates of Dawn. Stopping at an apartment building on Didzioji Street where a daycare centre had previously been located, we stowed our belongings and the cargo from our horse-drawn carriage. From there, we turned onto Vilniaus Street, where an intense firefight was raging. The Germans had barricaded themselves in a department store and were firing machine guns at Soviet soldiers. We joined the military unit and began firing at the German snipers while I tossed a few grenades through the windows. When we ran into the building, we found nobody on the first floor, but the Germans continued shooting down at us from the second and third floors. I followed our group as they began to climb the stairs but was abruptly stopped by a Soviet officer who barred my way to the second floor. He asked me to stay and guard the first floor. Then everything went quiet.

Before long, all our fighters returned. They had found no one alive. When we left the building, the Soviet officer in charge of the operation approached me, handing me an automatic rifle and some flowers that he had found somewhere. It seemed that my dream had finally come true. I had an automatic rifle. But at that moment, the flowers meant more to me than the rifle ever could. After so much misery, living in the balance between life an death, it was difficult to believe in the possibility of such a peaceful gift. The simple wildflowers brought out feelings in me that I had completely forgotten existed. They reminded me of a different world, a world without brutal killings, deportations and humiliation. At that moment, I had only one dream and one desire, to enter what had been the Kaunas Ghetto with flowers, not with an automatic rifle.

I dreamed of meeting there the liberated Jewish survivors from Kaunas. But the war was not yet over. Kaunas was still under German occupation and the fate of the Jews in the Kaunas Ghetto was unknown to us. The reality of those sweet words 'freedom and liberty' had not yet been achieved for our loved ones.

The same day, July 13, 1944, at 5:00 pm, the Soviet Information Bureau, TASS, announced the liberation of Vilnius from under Hitler's yoke. Exhausted, starving, but deliriously happy, we, the seven members of the "Death to the Occupiers" Detachment, returned to our station at Didzioji Street. We ate some sweet porridge from the former daycare centre's storage and, in true partisan style, fell asleep on the floor.

A few days later, we were released from military service. We were required to return our rifles, automatic weapons, and grenades, but allowed to hold on to our pistols. Misha and I found lodgings in a residence and waited patiently, yet fearfully, for the liberation of Kaunas. We thought it would only take a few days.

IN MEMORIAM

OUR LEGENDARY LEADER, CHAIM JELLIN

In many chapters of this book, I have made reference to the founder and leader of the Anti-fascist Fighting Organization, Chaim Jellin Here, I only wish to offer a few illustration, not only of the battle he waged against the Nazis from behind the barbed-wire fence of Kaunas Ghetto, but of his humanity, his genuine kindness, his faithfulness to our common purpose, his respect for life, and his tragic fate.

Chaim was not only the charismatic leader of AFO. He was a constant and fearless participant in the most crucial and dangerous operations against the Nazis and carried out acts of sabotage to disrupt the German war efforts. At great personal risk, Chaim repeatedly traveled outside the ghetto, disguised as a railway worker, to find partisan bases in the forest around Kaunas. Refusing to acknowledge any danger, he maintained close contacts with the underground Pro-Communist and Communist Resistance Movement in Kaunas. It is because of his courage and persistence that the success of the resistance movement in the Kaunas Ghetto is indivisible from the man who began it. When we speak of resistance in the Kaunas Ghetto, we nust see Chaim Jellin in our minds. When we speak of Chaim, we speak of the ghetto resistance. It is true that he was one of many, but at the same time, his courage, his sense of mission, his integrity, and his steadfastness to the cause were unique.

In transporting about 300 young people from Kaunas Ghetto to the forest where they joined the Soviet partisans fighting the German troops, Chaim Jellin succeeded in achieving the primary, and most important, goal of the AFO. But, for Chaim, this was not enough and he continued, cautiously but ceaselessly, in his constant efforts to send the resisters of Kaunas Ghetto to the partisans. Until the last day of his life, he tried to find ways to transport more and more young ghetto resisters to the forest.

He commanded authority, not only among his comrades and supporters, but among the Ghetto administrators as well, particularly the Chairman, Elchanan Elkes. The success of his underground organization and, more importantly, the success of the mission to send people to the forest, required cooperation with others, outside our organization. Ghetto resisters included, not only the members of AFO, but youth from other organizations, particularly, from the Zionist underground, as well. Chaim knew this and was able to reach agreements with the Jewish ghetto authorities, who supplied money and protection, and with the Zionist underground. The workshops outfitted resisters with clothing, the ghetto police at the gates aided them in safe passage for escape.

Chaim Jellin was a remarkable, extraordinary personality. He was not only a writer, a fighter, and a leader, but also a friend. As an intellectual, Chaim was convinced that, despite the frightful conditions and terrible situation in the ghetto, children must learn. He was determined that they should read, play, and sing. Chaim Jellin made an enormous effort to establish an illegal school for the children of the members and supporters of the AFO.

In the ghetto, Chaim continued to write stories in the form of a diary. Part of this diary was saved by Chaim's comrade and close collaborator, Dr. Elena Kutorgiene. The rest of his writing went up in flames and was burned along with everything else in the Kaunas Ghetto.

In 1941, Chaim wrote in his diary:

So this is the ghetto for Kovno's Jews. Pious Slobodka with its yeshivas and study houses, with its scrupulously observed Sabbaths and holidays. Slobodka with its crooked, interconnected tangle of alleys. Old Slabodka: half-ruined cottages, hunchbacked little houses with roofs of moss-greened shingles, half caved-in rafters, and walls split by the wind... Jewish Slobodka with the sparkle of a small town, with the unique dialect; the poverty of Kovno, and workers' families, revolutionary fighters... New Slobodka, 'Christian Slobodka', with airy and sunny houses, with gardens and orchards, and new apartment blocks, was originally supposed to be part of the ghetto. Someone, however, was not pleased with

183

the Jews and soon cut out whole streets, took them out of the ghetto area, violently ripped the Jews in two parts... Now we encircle the small ghetto, a part of the left side of Paneriu Street, which extends a "How do you do" to the large ghetto by way of a bridge. The bridge is six meters high, wooden, like an arch bent over the street. It leads upstairs, downstairs, connecting one part of Dvaro Street to the other, and with Paneriu Street beneath, on which horse-driven carriages and cars travel. Under the bridge Christian life goes on. Over the bridge walk the 'criminal' Jews...[91]

Chaim Jellin was offered sanctuary by his comrades outside the ghetto many time. Genrikas Zimanas, the commander of the partisan brigade in Rudninkai Forest and secretary of the underground Communist Party Central Committee of Southern Lithuania, warned Chaim that he should not wait until the last minute, but that he should join the partisans in good time. He told Jellin that he was always welcome. Chaim, however, rejected all proposals saying that the captain is always the last to leave the ship. He, and his closest friend and deputy, Dima Gelpernas, committed themselves to staying in the ghetto. They would escape only with the last group of ghetto resisters. Neither of them protected themselves and Chaim did not live to see the liberation.

In 1944, the Kaunas Ghetto was turned into a de-facto concentration camp. It became obvious that the days of its inhabitants were numbered. Chaim himself tried continuously to find more drivers and more trucks, to prepare more ghetto resisters to escape to the forest. In March and April, the Gestapo arrested a few members of the Kaunas underground Communist Party Committee. After their imprisonment, the Gestapo began looking for Chaim. They knew what he looked like and knew of his relationship with the underground Communist Party in Kaunas. Chaim also knew that the Gestapo was searching for him. But, despite personal danger, he decided to organize the escape and transport of a large group of ghetto youth to the forest.

On April 5, 1944, he made arrangements for a driver to pick up the ghetto resisters. The driver never showed up. The next day, Chaim left the bunker where he had spent the night with a few ghetto inmates and went to meet another driver. He went to Daukanto Street in downtown Kaunas, not far from Laisves Aleja. While he was waiting, Chaim was approached by Gestapo agents who asked for his documents. With a smile, Chaim placed his hand in his pocket as if he was going to take out the documents. Instead, he pulled out two pistols and began to shoot, slightly injuring one agent. Continuing to fire at his pursuers, he managed to disappear into a backyard on Maironio Street and hide in a basement where fuel was being stored.

The police and the Gestapo searched everywhere in the yard for Chaim but could not find him. Then, they brought in the dogs. When Chaim was discovered, he had no bullets left. With a small razor blade, Chaim cut his vein. Covered in blood, he was lying unconscious on the ground when the police found him. They took Chaim Jellin to the Gestapo headquarters and then to a hospital.

The Nazis interrogated him day after day, night after night. Fearing reprisals against Kaunas Ghetto's remaining Jews, Chaim hid his identity and gave a false name, Chaim German. Even though the Nazis tortured him and he was in great pain, he insisted that he was a Soviet paratrooper who had been staying in Vilnius. He told them he had made contact with the partisans in Rudinikai Forest and was looking for a truck to drive him back in Vilnius. Chaim knew that Vilnius Ghetto had already been liquidated, but he was trying to divert the Nazis' attention from the Kaunas Ghetto. He hoped that the Nazis might bring him into the forest where he could either try to escape or perish with them at the hands of the partisans. But the Nazis did not dare go to the forest. In early May 1944, Chaim Jellin was executed. His final resting place was never found.

Like every human being, Chaim Jellin wanted to live. He wanted to see liberation, the defeat of Germany, and the collapse of the Nazi regime. But the commitment he had made to save lives and to fight the enemy, in whatever means possible, became his life and it was his main priority. In the end, his commitment was stronger than his instinct to survive. Although Chaim Jellin lost his life when he was barely thirty-two years old, his life has become a legend.

The United States Holocaust Memorial Museum in Washington is preserving the memory of the ghetto resisters and is building a remarkable monument to their actions. Every year it pays tribute to the outstanding leaders and heroes of the resistance during the Holocaust. On June 15, 1999, Chaim Jellin was awarded a posthumous medal by the United States Holocaust Memorial Museum for heroism and resistance in the Kaunas Ghetto. The medal was accepted by his niece, Esther Jellin. In December of 2001 a Street in the city of Rechovet (Israel) was named in ChaimYellin (Jellin) name. Nothing can be forgotten. No one is forgotten.

FALLEN FRIENDS

Many of our friends and comrades did not survive the war. They were killed in action by the Germans and their collaborators or were murdered by the Nazis. We established a small cemetery next to our detachment, but not all of those killed found their resting place there. After the liberation, all of those buried in this cemetery, as well as those who were buried in other places, were transferred to the military cemeteries in Vilnius and other cities. But some of those killed were never found and their final resting place has never been discovered. But we have never forgotten our fallen friends and their brave deeds. We remember them in the depths of our hearts.

Altogether, over fifty-five of our comrades perished outside the Kaunas Ghetto while on missions. Some of them were killed during their search for partisan bases, others during the march to Augustova Forest. Elijahu Olkin was killed on his way to Rudninkai Forest, when he was already in partisan territory. Sixteen partisans from our three detachments, all of them ghetto resisters, were killed during the battle with a German garrison in the city of Vechiorishkes. In all, forty-six Jewish partisans from the "Death to the Occupiers" Detachment and both its branches were killed in action. Among them were Taibele (Tania) Vinishski, the young girl from the Vilnius Ghetto and Mejer Liberman (Misha Karecki), a Soviet paratrooper originally from Kaunas. Another forty-four of our fallen comrades were from Kaunas Ghetto. Among them were three escapees from the Ninth Fort: Tevje Pilovnik, Shimon Eidelson, and Aba Diskant. Chaim-Dovid Ratner, a member of the AFO Committee, was killed in action. Two of my close comrades-in-arms, Shmulik Mordkovski and Boruch Lopjanski, with whom I trekked from the Rudninkai Forest to the Kaunas Ghetto, were killed when they were outgunned in a firefight near the Kaishadorys train station. Three other fighters: Leizer Tzodikov, Meishe

Goldberg, and Shmuel Abramovich perished with them. In the spring of 1944, the commander of our fighting unit, Michail Trushin, along with our young comrade-in-arms, Jekaterina Radionova, were killed by a sniper not far from the village of Zagarine, Bronius Olishauskas in Senoji Macele.

Death took these comrades in the full bloom of their youth. Most of them were hardly twenty years old. Fighting the most monstrous enemy of all mankind, our fallen comrades paid with their lives so that others could survive and live to see liberation and freedom.

It is always difficult to accept the death of a colleague, of a friend, of a comrade, of a loved one. Time has eased the pain of these losses, but the memory of these fallen friends is still with me and with those of us who survived the Holocaust and the war. We have not forgotten them and their heroic deeds.

It is probably impossible to live entirely through one's memories, but yet one cannot live without them. Without memories and knowledge of the past, there can be no future. And so we feel a responsibility to preserve the history of our cities and villages, of Lithuanian and Eastern European Jewry. We feel that responsibility so that our children and grandchildren will know how those who proceeded them fought against the enemy and struggled to maintain the sanctity of life. Many of us who survived will continue to tell the tales of heroism, daring, and courage to our readers and listeners. We will retell the stories of our lost comrades, our brothers and sisters, as memorials to these fallen friends and the loved ones.

Elsewhere in this book, I have already recounted the story, written by Misha Rubinsonas, of our young heroine, Taibele Vinishski, and the other comrades who fell in the battle in Vechiorishkes. I will tell the story of a Soviet paratrooper, Meyer Liberman, who was also a young man from Kaunas and partisan from our Detachment.

MEYER LIBERMAN

Misha and I became close friends with Meyer Liberman (code name Misha Karecki), on New Year's Eve, while sitting around the campfire. Searching for consolation from his turmoil and spiritual pain, he told us the story of his life.

Meyer was a student at the Jewish technical school in Kaunas. His father worked at a candy factory and his mother stayed at home, caring for two younger siblings. The day the war started, Meyer was able to board a train heading for Latvia in the east. On the same day, his father, working the night shift at the factory, called home. His wife told him that she was going to dress the children and that he should meet her at the train station right after work. But Meyer's father got on a train bound for the Soviet Union before his wife arrived at the station. Meyer's mother and her two young children arrived too late, the train had already left. Determined to get away, she was able to join some strangers and leave Kaunas by horse-drawn carriage.

"Without warning," Meyer told us, "my train stopped at the Latvian border. I stepped onto the platform and saw my mother and my brother and sister. They were on the platform waiting for the next train. We were overjoyed at this unexpected meeting."

But, Meyer's train had already begun rolling out of the station and he barely managed to get back on as his mother shouted, "We'll meet in Russia!" In a few seconds, they disappeared from view and Meyer never saw them again. Later, during the evacuation, when Meyer met up with his father, he learned that someone had told his father that his wife had returned to Kaunas because the train she had wanted to catch never appeared.

Meyer served in the Red Army and fought against the Germans in the ranks of the Sixteenth Lithuanian Division. In 1943, he was sent to complete his airborne training and that same year, he was air-dropped into the forests of Belarus. With Kostas Radionovas and others, he had formed the "Death to the Occupiers" Detachment in Rudninkai Forest. Meyer was a calm, brave nineteen year-old with much fighting experience. He was assigned to a team of sappers whose job it was to blow up the railway lines to Kaunas, Vilnius, and Shiauliai.

He had a fondness for dressing in a neat, almost elegant manner, despite the conditions under which we lived. Slim and of average height, he always wore a stylish pair of brown *galife* (calf-length) pants and a jacket of a similar colour that suited him very well. He was good-hearted and always smiling. This is the way he appears in my memory to this day. He stands before my eyes in all his physical and spiritual beauty.

At the end of February, Dima Parfionov, our commissar, gave Meyer Liberman and three other partisans an assignment to blow up a railway junction in the Kaishiadoriai region. Somehow, the make-up of this unit seemed suspect. It consisted, not of partisans who normally served under Meyer, but of POWs who were the commissar's close associates, his 'yes men'.

All of Meyer's close friends from the ghetto resisters asked Meyer to resign from the mission, not because of the target, but because of its unusual and suspicious make-up. With a broad smile, Meyer was able to convince us that he faced no danger. He told us we were all partisans from the same detachment and we all had the same goal: to make war on the Germans.

So, on February 22, 1944, Meyer left camp never to return. According to intelligence reports, the mission was successfully completed and there were no engagements with the enemy noted. But, on February 27, the three POWs returned without Meyer. They gave a cursory explanation that Meyer had been killed in the line of duty by German fire. However, they provided strangely contradicting intelligence reports and date of death. Their reports did not coincide with the date on which the junction was blown up. Even stranger was the fact that they had Meyer's watch and personal pistol. The commanders of the "Death to the Occupiers" Detachment did nothing to investigate Meyer's death. We, on the other hand, had no doubts that the commissar, who wished to be rid of him, had ordered his death.

Meyer's death shocked his friends. We wanted the circumstances and the time and place of his death to be investigated and made public. But neither Kostas nor Dima Parfionov took any heed of our request. During one meeting of the Young Communist League, I once again brought up the question of Meyer's death. I was told by the commissar to be quiet or that I would face a similar fate. Upon hearing him utter these words, Misha and I left the meeting and resigned from the organization. We took this step even though, according to the regulations, membership could only be terminated by expulsion of a person from the organization. Both of us were expelled from the Young Communist League, even though, after the war, this action was not recognized and Misha rejoined the League in 1945. I no longer had any desire to be a member of this organization. Much later, after pressure from the Communist Party leadership at Vilnius University and personal conversations with Zimanas, I agreed to be reinstated.

Meyer Liberman perished at the hands of his enemies even though those who murdered him were fighting on the same side he was. He lived and died fearlessly, another victim of the Jewish genocide. Meyer's father, Abraham Liberman, survived the war but did not find his wife or children when he returned to Lithuania. All three had perished in the Kaunas Ghetto.

THE FINAL DAYS OF THE KAUNAS GHETTO

The delay of Kaunas' liberation dragged on. It was obvious that the Nazis were defeated and the liberation of the three Baltic States was imminent. The remaining Jews in the Kaunas Ghetto, as well as those of us who were in Vilnius, hoped that a breakthrough toward Kaunas was within reach. Even more, we hoped that the Germans would be routed before they would have a chance to liquidate the ghetto. Besides, we felt sure that the Germans would be concentrating all their possible efforts on evacuating their troops and people in order to defend their own soil. But the Germans were not yet done with their bloody deeds. Their plan was to carry out the Final Solution and to liquidate and deport the remaining ghetto inmates. In the meantime, the Third Byelorussian and First Baltic Front Divisions had decided to bypass Kaunas and, from Vilnius, the Soviet Army moved to the north and to the southwestern regions of Lithuania. Alytus, Prienai, Panevezys, and Marijampole were not liberated until July and it would be August 1 before Kaunas was freed.

Kaunas was the city in which I was born, where I grew up, went to school, studied, and dreamed. It was there I had had a home, a past, and hopes for a future. But Kaunas was also the city in which I was incarcerated, forced into slave labour, and condemned to death. For what crimes had I, and the rest of Kaunas' Jews, been convicted and punished? Of course, I thought about Kaunas the first time I walked into Rudninkai Forest. When I came back into the ghetto as a partisan and returned to our detachment in the forest, I also thought about Kaunas. Kaunas was in our minds when we greeted new ghetto resisters who came to join the partisans. Whenever I thought of Kaunas, I imagined participating in the recapture of the city. I saw myself with a new automatic rifle, liberating the surviving Jews and, especially, my own loved one. Indeed, Kaunas was in my thoughts and in my dreams when all of the Rudninkai Forest partisans marched into the center of Vilnius through the Gates of Dawn.

However, none of these dreams were fulfilled. I did not participate in the liberation of Kaunas. I entered the boundaries of the city without a gun or an automatic rifle, or even a pistol. I came back to Kaunas by truck with the permission of the Ministry of Education where I was already working. I went to Kaunas on August 3 or 4, a few days after the Soviet troops had entered Kaunas and the German Army had retreated without a struggle.

My journey from Vilnius to Kaunas took two hours. The truck brought me to Vilijampole but the shocking sight of the former ghetto was already visible from a distance. What had been the ghetto was enveloped in a cloud of smoke through which only the stone fence and the chimneys of the charred houses were barely visible. The houses of the former ghetto had burned for almost three weeks, until even the earth was scorched and the people who had been hiding in them had become sacrificial offerings. All I saw, as I looked around, was one vast ruin, shrouded in the smell of burnt flesh and charred wood, and strewn with corpses lying in front of their houses along with piles of bricks and other rubble. It was apparent that the Germans had been very thorough in their unrelenting search to unearth people in their hideouts and bunkers. The former ghetto had become one gigantic cemetery. The district of Vilijampole had died with its Jewish population.

In front of the burned houses lay personal belongings such as glasses, photographs, identity cards and certificates, shoes, and clothing that had been scattered everywhere by the wind. Although every building in the former ghetto had been burned to its foundations, I recognized at once what had once been our small house on Vigriu Street. Outside the burned-out house lay our partly burned kettle, the bed, some loose photographs, and my father's business cards. On the other side of the house, where the neighbour's bunker had been, I spotted five, or perhaps more, completely unrecognizable bodies. I froze in my tracks at this horrifying sight. Numb, I didn't faint, or scream. I didn't even cry. I felt as if I had gone instantly insane. This could not be reality but only some horrifying dream, some incredible figment of my imagination.

I can remember perfectly how I just stood for a long time beside our house and stared at the charred kettle and looming chimney. When I recovered a tiny bit, I gathered the photographs and picked up the kettle, only to drop it after walking a few steps. I moved, like in a dream, among the corpses of people who had been shot and lay on both sides of the fence until I came to the ghetto cemetery. Since the Germans had not bombed the graveyards, the little bench beside my father's tombstone was still intact. I sat down for a while and then left the district of Vilijampole and the Kaunas Ghetto. Standing there, I had witnessed the tragic end of the Kaunas Ghetto. The following events describe the last days of Kaunas Ghetto.

THE KINDER AKTZION

In all my life, I have never forgotten the German notion of collective murder which they called in German, *Aktzion*. The liquidation of the Kaunas Ghetto had begun at the end of 1943 with what was called the 'Estonian Aktzion', the deportation of Kaunas Jews to the concentration camp in Estonia and the displacement of many other ghetto inmates to different camps around Kaunas. The liquidation of the ghetto ended in July 1944, when the Germans implemented the Final Solution to the "Jewish problem" in Kaunas. But, the severest event took place during the *Kinder Aktzion* (Children's Action) by which the Germans meant the murder of the children and the elderly. On March 27 and 28, 1944, the Germans went after the little ones and the old people in the ghetto.

When I met Frania Grunskaite later on the day I returned to the smoking ghetto, I learned from her that little Tanya was safe. She had been hidden in a village on the outskirt of Kaunas and Frania visited her there every week. Frania told me that during the *Kinder Aktzion*, three-year-old Tanya had been hidden in a basement where, along with the neighbours' children, the little girl had remained for two entire days. None of the children had betrayed themselves with the slightest twitter or twitch. All the children's clothing in our apartment had been hidden to make it look as though only adults, working the night shift, lived in the room. A few days after the *Kinder Aktzion*, my sister, Alice, managed to let Frania know that she would bring the child to her at a prearranged hour so that Tanya could be taken to the neighbouring village. Tanya was injected with a sedative. The sleeping girl was wrapped in a sack and placed in a large basket which Alice carried through the ghetto and safely through the gates with a Jewish workers brigade. As the brigade approached its workplace, Alice put on a jacket without a yellow star and escaped unnoticed into the city. Risking her life, Alice walked through the center of Kaunas carrying the large basket which contained the greatest treasure imaginable, a three-year old child. Frania Grunskaite, a committed humanist and tremendously good-hearted woman, took Tanya and thus saved the little girl's life. She even had a photograph of the child taken to reassure her mother, which my sister delivered to Aunt Fanya.

In their book, *Kaunas Ghetto and its Fighters*, Meyer Jellin (Elinas) and Dimitry Gelpernas, both of whom were witnesses to that tragic event, described the ghastly Nazi *Kinder Aktzion*.

> March 27, 1944 began like any other spring day in the Kaunas Ghetto. The sun rose, the workers gathered at the gates to be grouped into brigades and, at the usual time, with guards shouting, kicking, and swearing at them, they were led into the city to work in the various workshops and other facilities. The Jewish ghetto police assembled in the square to listen to safety instructions regarding 'aerial bombardment' as they had been ordered to do the previous evening. Even though this was the first time they had been asked to gather for such instructions, no one suspected that anything was amiss because Soviet planes seemed lately to be passing overhead with greater frequency.
>
> Most of those who still remained in the ghetto at that time were children, the elderly, invalids, people working overnight shifts and those who worked in the workshops within the ghetto. All was calm and quiet when, suddenly, the inmates became alarmed. A German police battalion was marching by on the other side of the barbed wire fence. The battalion quickly formed a chain around the ghetto as a reinforcement to the regular guards and buses, covered trucks, and cars full of heavily armed Nazis drove into the ghetto. A car equipped with a loudspeaker began making the rounds of the narrow, unpaved streets of Vilijampole, broadcasting the same tinny message over and over in German: '*Achtung! Achtung!* (Attention! Attention!) Everyone

remain in your houses. Anyone leaving their house will be shot on sight.'

Even though it was unclear what all this was about, the inmates' blood began to run cold. A 'visit' from Hitler's troops never signaled anything good. The Gestapo men, their Ukrainian henchmen, and the *Vlasovians*,[92] most of whom were already drunk, began combing the wooden ghetto houses for their new round of victims – the small children.

All those under thirteen were taken from their parents or relatives and those adults unwilling to give up the children were also arrested. All of them were being crowded into trucks to be sent away. For what? It is difficult for someone with a sane mind to answer this question. But the Gestapo had formulated a 'legal' justification for their blind malice. The ghetto was being converted into a concentration camp and no children were allowed.

It was fairly simple for them to seize children in the first houses they stormed. No one yet recognized what they wanted and the children had not been hidden. But as soon as word began to get around that the Germans are taking the children, the news spread through the ghetto with lightning speed. Parents feverishly sought places to hide their young ones: in basements, cellars, closets, and under beds. In some cases, hiding places had been prepared long before and the children, instinctively sensing imminent danger, now lay silently in the dark, small spaces. But many others had not prepared for this eventuality and some children were alone in their homes while their parents were away at work.

One woman on Liutauras Street, acting in despair, yanked the tablecloth off a table, wrapped her child in it, tied off the corners and hung this living, breathing bundle on a nail in the wall. 'When the Germans come, I won't breathe a word,' said her four year-old son. And he did remain silent, even when a soldier poked at the bundle. His life was saved on that day. In another courtyard, a mother hid her child under a stack of firewood. The Gestapo men did not find the child, but when she went to retrieve her little one, he had suffocated to death. Many other children were hidden in cellars, attics, and behind sacks and boxes in the ghetto workshops. In one laundry facility, a woman hid her six-year-old under a pile of dirty clothes. When the Ukrainian nationalists forced their way in, the pile raised their suspicion. They poked at it with their bayonets but when no noise or movement emanated from it, they left. The mortified mother pulled her daughter out from under the pile to find her severely injured and bleeding. The child had stoically borne the stabbings without even a whimper.

One could observe terrifying scenes at every step. Holding a rifle in one hand, a drunken *Vlasovian* led a tiny girl with frightened eyes with the other hand. The seven-year-old begged for help in a barely audible voice as her mother followed, wringing her hands and begging for the release of her child. The mother received a rifle butt to her solar plexus as the fascist carried the girl under one arm, like some kind of inanimate object, to the waiting truck.

Understandably, women attempted hopelessly to safeguard their children by lying on top of them or holding on to them with all of their might. The Gestapo men simply ripped the children from their mothers' grip, injuring both in the process. In some cases, to make their job easier, the Nazis used trained dogs to hold the women down. And some mothers were simply shot when the Nazis were unable to wrest their children away.

The lawyer, E. Bruch, grappled with the Fascists to the bitter end. They beat him until he was mortally wounded and carried him out with the others. Another ghetto prisoner, Mrs. Rankachiski, unwilling to be separated from her children, climbed onto the bed of the truck to accompany them. Many mothers, fathers and grandparents did the same...

The entire day, as the Nazis stormed the ghetto, meticulously searching each house and probing every alcove or crevice, the ghetto loudspeakers blared German marches and dance music that mingled with the muffled cries of mothers and the children being stuffed into the outgoing trucks. Near the hospital, there was an orphanage for those children who had previously been left without parents. Even though the staff tried every means possible to hide and defend these children, the Gestapo simply took to throwing the children from a second-story window into a truck waiting below. Yet, in spite of the obvious, the Nazis, as usual, lied about the fate of the children. They tried to maintain calm by telling the inmates that the children would be taken to special camps where they would be supervised by educators.

Toward the end of the day, the work brigades began returning to the ghetto from the city. Once they were through the gates and began to realize what had been happening in the ghetto, they scattered in every direction, each running home as quickly as possible to see if his or her children had been saved. But it was a only a small few who had been spared and a new wave of sorrow reverberated through the ghetto. The heartbreaking cries combined with the Nazi polkas blaring on the loudspeakers to create an unspeakable cacophony. And it was not until the sun began to set that the Gestapo departed, their day's work complete. The women of the ghetto, however, continued their howling and wailing throughout the night.

Everyone, especially those who had somehow managed to hide their children and elderly relatives, waited in dread for the following morning. It was still unclear whether the Gestapo would return or not, whether the inmates would have to go through all the horror one more time. But once the work brigades left for the city the next morning, it started all over again. According to the Nazis' registration cards, they were short about 1,000 children and elderly people. So, on March 28, the *Aktzion* continued; this time with even greater brutality. Places that the Gestapo suspected might be used as hideouts were blown up, in some cases with hand grenades. When the *Aktzion* had begun, the AFO had made all of its hideouts available, which helped save a few hundred of those who faced capture. Not a single one of these hideouts were found by the Fascists. At the end of the day, after a second thorough combing of the ghetto, another few hundred victims were found and driven off.

This two-day horror, the *Kinder Aktzion*, was organized and commanded by the head of the Kaunas Ghetto (at this point the Concentration Camp-Kauen), SS Obershturmbanfuerer, Captain Wilhelm Goecke, and his assistants: SS Sharfuerer Auer and SS Untersharfuerers Pligrem and Fiveger. The capture of ghetto children and old people was supervised and directed by the man who was then Head of the Gestapo in Lithuania, SS Oberfuerer Dr. Wilhelm Fux, with much heartfelt assistance from his well-known Gestapo henchman, Helmut Rauka.

Aside from the Children's Action, another tragedy occurred that day. The Jewish ghetto police who had been summoned for bombing raid instructions were suddenly surrounded by the Gestapo. With great pleasure, SS Scharfuerer Bruno Kittel, Head of the Gestapo, told the surrounded policemen to relax and announced, 'Enough is enough. You will no longer lead us Germans around by the nose!' All the policemen were then forced into three buses that had arrived to take them away. When (the Jewish police) Officer Levner resisted, he was shot right there on the spot.

The heavily guarded buses left the ghetto and headed for the Ninth Fort. Anyone who resisted or tried to escape was killed. Kittel himself led the convoy in his car. He had become obsessed with the 'Fine Case' and was determined to liquidate the entire resistance movement in the ghetto. Ghetto inmate, Fine, was a Gestapo stool pigeon who had promised to reveal the underground command to Kittel. However, our partisan comrade, Chone Kaganas, had terminated Fine and the body was hidden and never found.[93]

At the Fort, Kittel immediately began interrogating the Jewish policemen. First, he called Meishe Levin, the ghetto police chief, who Kittel believed to be one of the principal ghetto commanders. Of course, Levin knew the answers to many of Kittel's questions but bravely refused to comply. Finally, the crazed Gestapo officer shot him in front of the entire group and ordered his body to be thrown into a waiting fire. Then Kittel ordered the other policemen to line up and, threatening them with an automatic rifle, began shouting:

'Now you will finally answer my questions. Where are the weapons hidden in the ghetto? Who commands the terrorists? Where are your secret bunkers and hiding places? Who killed my man, Fine? Anyone who refuses to answer will burn there, where your beloved Levin is burning!'

Kittel threatened and tortured the policemen for three days, trying to get information about the ghetto underground out of them. Thirty-six men, including all the Gate Police, were shot. Those who had been wholeheartedly assisting the resistance organization, Yudel Zupovich and Yehuda (Ika) Grinberg, heroically died taking their secrets with them to the grave.[94]

THE TRAGIC OUTCOME

All the children and elderly were murdered at an unknown site. The Jewish policemen were killed at the Ninth Fort. This inconceivable crime and unimaginable tragedy was the beginning of the end of Kaunas Ghetto. In a few months, by July, 1944, the leading villain of the Kaunas Ghetto, SS Captain Wilhehn Goecke, initiated and executed the stunning and bewildering liquidation of Kaunas Ghetto, all in only a few days. On July 6, he informed the Chairman of the Jewish Committee, Dr. Elchanan Elkes, that Concentration Camp-Kauen would be completely liquidated and that all the inmates were to be taken to Danzig (then part of Germany and now Gdansk, Poland) for forced labour. Since he was unable to organize trains, the evacuation, he said, was set to begin on July 8, and was to be carried out by boat. The inmates would be transported by barge down the Nemunas river to the coast and then would go by sea to Danzig. Goecke ordered that a notice be posted ordering everyone to gather in the square between Varniu and Paneriu Streets. He warned Elkes that every home would be searched and anyone found hiding would be shot on the spot.

The news spread instantly and exacerbated the panic that already gripped the inmates. Most decided not to obey the order. Some of the people ran to the fence in an attempt to escape but were immediately shot dead. Many had already prepared hiding places within the ghetto and those families climbed into their bunkers, ready to hold out there for days or even weeks.

My mother and my sister's family went down into the bunker that had been built under the Benjaminovitch's family home. My aunts and relatives, as well as Misha's father and his sister, also went into their hiding places. Aunt Fanya hid in the neighbour's bunker.

On July 8, very few people appeared at the square where the deportees were expected to gather. Accompanied by German SS soldiers, a furious Goecke ran from house to house but only managed to root out some of the hidden inmates. The next day, the German SS and a Security Police squad arrived with axes and crowbars. They ransacked every house, ripping open floors, walls, and ceilings as they went. On Monday, July 10 and Tuesday, July 11, the Nazis brought in dogs and threatened the inhabitants over loudspeakers. Anyone discovered would not only be summarily shot, but the house would be blown up as well. Goecke informed the inmates that they would be deported, not by boat, but by train, since the boxcars were arriving and would be waiting for the deportees. The people hiding in their bunkers could hear the voices of the Germans, the explosions and gunfire, the barking dogs, and the music playing over the loudspeakers. Still, few were ready to leave the safety of their hiding places.

In the early morning of July 12 1944, the ghetto was very quiet. My mother felt ill. She could barely breathe and wanted to leave the bunker. Alice and her husband, Philip, went with her. They climbed out, let some fresh air in, and very quickly closed the door to the concealed bunker behind them. At that moment, an SS man broke into the house, and after discovering the three of them, ordered them to run to the square, where they found terrified people, surrounded by police, seemingly going out of their minds. Heart-wrenching cries came from all sides, blood-thirsty dogs barked incessantly, children cried, women wailed, men prayed. Shocking warnings blared repeatedly over the loudspeakers and explosions and shooting could be heard all around. The smell of smoke fumes and gunpowder filled the air.

At about 3 pm, Goecke's menacing voice announced that the 'evacuation' was ending. Every house would be blown up and every individual discovered would be shot dead. Then, the loudspeaker went silent as sounds of explosions and gunshots became louder and more frequent. On that day, my mother Rebecca Giniene, my sister Alice and her husband Philip Benjaminovichius, my aunts and cousins, and Misha's sister, Sonya Rubinsonaite, walked through the streets of Kaunas for the last time on their way to the train station.

From July 13 to 15, the Nazis blew up and burned all the homes in the former Kaunas Ghetto, along with all the people hiding in their basements and attics. The sealed cattle cars arrived at the train station on July 14 and 15 and the train carrying the remnants of the prisoners of Kaunas Ghetto(Concentration Camp-Kauen) left Lithuania. The women were taken to the concentration camp in Stutthof, a small town in Eastern Germany. The men were taken to the concentration camp Dachau at Landsberg-on-Lech, not far from Danzig.

In August 1941, there were over 30,000 Jews imprisoned in the Kaunas Ghetto. More than two-third of them perished during the first months of German occupation, when Lithuania still regarded itself as an independent country and its Provisional Government was in place. About 8000 to 10000 Jews held on until July 1944. During the liquidation of the ghetto, 2000 to 2500 were killed on the spot or burned alive, while another 7000 to 7500 inmates were deported to concentration camps in Germany. Only a small number of those have survived and most of them never returned to Lithuania. Some ghetto prisoners managed to escape while on their way to the trains or from the trains themselves, at the last minute. One group of thirty four people survived in a bunker in the ghetto. During the liquidation of the ghetto, a certain number of Jews were saved by Gentiles in Vilijampole. Many of the ghetto fighters, who had escaped to the partisans, returned from the forest and some of them participated in the liberation of Kaunas. Many Kaunas Jews who had managed to flee to the Soviet Union and had survived military combat there, returned to Lithuania. Also some of those who were deported to Siberia returned. According to a census in 1959, about 5000 Jews were living in Kaunas at that time. Most of them were newcomers from other parts of the Soviet Union.

In the year of 2000, there were about 1000 Jews in Kaunas. There is a very modest Jewish cultural life and the Jewish community is trying to revive some of its religious and educational traditions. There is one operating synagogue and a Jewish school. The Ninth Fort in Kaunas has been turned into a Genocide Memorial – a powerful symbol of painful memories. Monuments have been erected along the 15 ditches dug along the length of the hill where thousands of lives, mostly Jewish lives, came to a brutal end. In the museum's display of objects found in the clothing and pockets of dead people, I saw a boy's drawings found in a woman's pocket. The boy had drawn a colourful Menorah and had written his mother a poem in German. Most likely, the mother and son were from Germany. Obviously, this mother had held on to that drawing until she drew her final breath.

As a result of the efforts of the local Jewish community, a monument has been erected at the Gates to the Kaunas Ghetto, on Krischiu-kaichiu Street. It commemorates the end of the once populous Kaunas Jewish community. Internationally renown and socially active, it had once been a great and important force in the lives of Eastern Europe's Jews. Now, it lives only as a memory to the past.

THE FATE OF OUR FAMILY

The fate of our closest relatives differed little from the fate of the other Jews from Kaunas. The day the Germans entered Lithuania, our four families: the Ginas, Virovichius, the Benjaminovichius, and the Rubinsonas, consisted of thirty two persons. Most members of our immediate families did not flee to the Soviet Union but remained in Lithuania. During the short period of Lithuania's independence and the reign of its Provisional Government, from June 23 to August 5, 1941, three of my mother's brothers, Abrasha, Solomon and Isaac Virovichius, were killed at 28 Vytauto Prospect in Kaunas by the Lithuanian partisans, the White Armbanders. Their mother (my grandmother) Malka, died a few days later. My aunt, Mina Giniene, and one of her sons, Joske, most likely were killed during their attempt to flee Lithuania. Her other son, Leibe was murdered in Vilnius at the Paneriai killing site in July 1941. There was also murdered my cousin, Zlata Ginaite. On August 25, 1941, my father, Josif Ginas, passed away. Altogether, during the first months of the occupation, our families lost nine of its members. The rest of us were incarcerated in the ghetto. My sister's husband, Philip Benjaminovichius, lost three members of his family: his mother Roza, his father Leiba, and his sister Rita. All were killed in 1944 during the liquidation of the ghetto. Rita's husband, Ytzic Dembo, was murdered at the Ninth Fort along with the other thirty-six Jewish policemen. Misha's father, Lipe Rubinsonas, also perished during the liquidation of the ghetto.

All the other members of our families were deported to the Stutthof and Dachau concentration camps in Germany. During the Death March from Stutthof, yet another concentration camp, my aunts, Berta Jurovitski and Zina Virovich, and Zina's daughter, Nadya, were all shot by German guards because they were exhausted and hungry and unable to continue walking. My father's brother Samuel and his wife Berta, as well as my uncle, Lazar Jurovitski, perished somewhere in Germany. Another aunt, Anya Virovich, and her children, Miriam and Ilja, were transported from Stutthof to another camp and were murdered there. My husband's sister, Sonya Rubinsonaite, died of exhaustion after her liberation in Germany. On March 21, 1945, my mother, Rebecca Giniene, died in Stutthof of starvation, cold and overwork. She had not yet reached fifty years of age. My sister, Alice, was there during her dying moments, sharing her last crumbs of bread with her.

Out of thirty two family members who had stayed in Lithuania during the German occupation, six had survived: Alice and Philip, Tanya, Bronia Ginaite, Misha and I. Twenty-six members of our immediate families perished in the Holocaust. According to my analysis, over 90% of Lithuanian Jews, who were under the German occupation, did not survive. In my own family, this figure translates as almost 83%.

My father sister's family, the Ginzbergs, had managed to get to the Soviet Union. All of them returned to Lithuania. Today, Shaja Ginzberg's granddaughter, (Masha and Moishe Ginzberg's daughter) Eva, is a music teacher and her daughter, Eshter, is a biologist. Both live in Lithuania. Basya Ginzberg-Schvartz lives in Israel with her daughter Bella and her children, Rita, Boris, and Zana. Doctor Isaac and Fanya Glikman's son, Liova, is also a doctor and lives in Israel with his wife Ruth, a survivor of Kaunas Ghetto, and their two sons, Daniel and Elija. Asya Ginzberg's children, Eva and Leiba, live with their families in the United States.

My mother's brother, Liova Virovichius and his wife Basya, who had immigrated to Palestine in 1936, raised two daughters and a son there. Basya became one of the best-known physical education instructors in Israel and her students revered her just as we had in Kaunas. All three of their children, Esther, Malka and Joshua, completed their education and served in the Israeli army. My uncle Liova has nine grandchildren and four great-grandchildren.

Alice was liberated by the Soviets and her husband Philip was freed by the Americans. After the liberation my sister, with much difficulties, managed to reach a Jewish Gathering Camp in Lodz (Poland). Philip found her there and after some time, they moved to Belgium. There they continued their studies and, in 1952, they immigrated to Canada. Alice and Philip Benn's daughter, Rita Benn-Lapedis, and her husband, Steven, have three children, David, Jeremy, and Marissa. They live in the USA. Alice and Philip Benn's son, Daniel and his wife Elaine have two children, Michael and Ceitlin. In 1969, Philip Benn passed away. He was only 51 year old. His death can be considered a result of the of slave labour and persecution he suffered in the concentration camps.

As for Misha and me, both barely twenty in 1944, the tragic fate of our closest family members prompted us to decide never to live in Kaunas again and to stay in Vilnius. Misha and I had to put the past behind us and find new challenges in life. After the war, Misha and I both graduated from Vilnius University. Misha went on to become a journalist while I taught political economy at Vilnius University. Our older daughter, Tanya Rubinsonaite, received her doctorate degree in economics at Moscow university. Our younger daughter, Anya Rubinsonaite, received her degree in physics from Vilnius University. In 1975, Anya and her husband, Fima (Efim) Sorkin, a doctor of mathematics, emigrated to Canada where their daughter, Riva, was born. Riva Sorkin was graduated from Queens University (Canada) and received her Master's degree from Tufts University in Boston. In 1983, I also immigrated to Canada, along with my daughter, Tanya, her husband, Tilis Vasiliauskas, and their son, Daniel, who has recently defended his doctoral thesis in genetics.

At the end of 1977, my husband, Misha Rubinsonas, died in Vilnius at the age of 53. His premature death was, for all intents and purposes, a result of the Holocaust. His death was unexpected, painful, and difficult to overcome.

Should Misha have lived to see 1993, he would then have been seventy years old. In December of that year, a large group of people gathered at the Jewish Cultural Center in Vilnius to commemorate his seventieth birthday. It was an event organized by the State Jewish Museum to illustrate and present the story of his brief, yet eventful, life. Recollections of Misha's life were offered by the Kaunas Ghetto AFO leader, Dima Gelpernas; Professor Elvyra Uzhkurelyte-Baltiniene, a classmate Fira Bramson; a colleague Hirsch Smoliakov; journalist Igor Kashnicki; and editor of *The Evening News*, Simonas Grigoraitis. The young vocalist, Liora Grodnikaite, sang partisan songs at the event. Here, I will reprint excerpts of the talks given at the Museum and a summary of a letter written by Moishe Musel.

Simonas Grigoraitis:
I will never forget my good, selfless, sincere, and close friend, Misha Rubinsonas. It was difficult to believe that he would no longer be there in his office, that we would no longer hear his voice and would no longer be graced by his smile. Our good friend left this life early and unexpectedly.

Veterans of the newspaper simply called him Misha, newcomers addressed him by his last name or sometimes, more formally, as Comrade Secretary. But everyone loved and respected Misha Rubinsonas. And he returned their respect in kind. As a sports reporter, he had the chance to see most of the world and represented Lithuania during the Olympic Games and other sporting events.

A person does not leave this life without leaving behind a few footprints. Rubinsonas left us with many fond memories. But not only memories. He worked at *The Evening News* for nineteen years. As far as journalism is concerned, he worked in one of the most difficult possible positions as a Secretary. All in all, his nineteen years represent almost 6000 issues of our newspaper and he had much input into every one of these. The work of a journalist involves giving part of one's heart, health, and life to other people.

Misha started working at the newspaper from its very inception in 1958. He was known for his good humour, his principles, his support of young journalists, as well as his ability to get along with both the young and the old. It is, therefore, not surprising that after so many years, so many of us have gathered here to commemorate his seventieth birthday.

Hirsh Smoliakov:
Today he would be seventy years of age. Unfortunately, it has already been sixteen years since he was laid to rest beneath the tombstone, in Vilnius' Antakalnis Cemetery, that marks his eternal resting place…I remember his funeral. A huge crowd had gathered to see him off on his final journey. For me, this was quite unexpected. A funeral is not a party nor a performance. People do not attend out of mere curiosity. People come with their heads bowed in order to show their respect for a man they valued in life. He was not a great writer, nor a renowned musician, neither a well-known actor nor a high official. Misha Rubisnonas was a journalist. I wouldn't say an average one, for one way or another, he was a Secretary for the daily, *The Evening News*.

I knew him from childhood. Fate decided that we, even though we were not particularly close friends, would work side by side. We were students together at the Sholom Aleichem High School. We played on the same basketball team. He was captain, I mainly a benchwarmer. Together we were incarcerated in the Kaunas Ghetto and belonged to the same underground organization. He as a leader, I as a humble member. After the war, we lived for many years in the same city, Vilnius, and both worked as Secretaries. He for a daily newspaper, I for a weekly. I have searched my memory to explain this incredible phenomenon: a simple, average man and also a Jew. And yet so many are here at his memorial.

He was tall, slim, and handsome. An exemplary family man who did everything he could for his two daughters. And he had a good wife, Professor Sara Ginaite, who understood him well, his ideals and his weaknesses. He was friendly, polite, and gentlemanly with all – his friends and with… No, he did not seem to have enemies, and if he did they were very few in number. If we add up all of his acquaintances, his friends, associates, and admirers, they cover a broad spectrum. Misha Rubinsonas lived for barely fifty-three years. Today he would be seventy. Much time has passed, but even today his friends, colleagues, and family speak highly of him. Many have gathered here to commemorate his seventieth birthday on December 23. His colleagues and friends have placed flowers on his grave…

Moishe Musel:

October 1 is a day that is always remembered in our family. On that day in 1977, we were shocked to learn of the sudden death of Misha Rubinsonas. It has been almost two decades since our beloved childhood friend passed away but that unfortunate day always takes us back in time; it was a long time ago but for us it is still the recent past. On that day, my wife and I look through photo albums that have yellowed with age. They contain the photos that bound us all during our youth and young adulthood. We turn a page and there in a photo we see Misha and his radiant smile. His entire appearance reflects his elegance and intelligence.

I met Misha for the first time in the Kaunas Ghetto at the beginning of 1942. At that time, I was close friends with Elyezar (Leizer) Zilber. Leizer and I were discussing organizing an anti-Nazi resistance movement and searching for like-minded individuals toward that effort. During one conversation, Leizer offered to introduce me to a friend who could help us in discussing these crucial issues. That friend was Misha Rubinsonas, who introduced himself to me by using his alias, *Langman*. That evening, we talked honestly and at length. It felt as if we had known each other for years. The conversation I had with him was not only open and interesting but also very sincere, and Misha invited me to join the resistance movement immediately. I was assigned to be secretary for one of the threesomes that was then running that movement. That fateful meeting with Misha played a role of such great importance that it changed the rest of my life. You see, the secretary of one of the other threesomes was a young attractive woman, Polia (Peshe) Karnauskaite, who like myself, was also undergoing military training under Dovid Teper. I fell in love with her at first sight, the very first day I met her. Polia and Misha had been in the same high school class and she was on the women's basketball team that he coached. It was thanks to Misha that I not only joined the underground resistance, but also met the woman with whom I fell in love and started a family in the Ghetto in 1942.

Misha was in charge of the youth wing of the Ghetto underground movement. He was successful in recruiting many youths of differing political persuasions to our cause. "The enemy is one," he was fond of saying, "and we need to fight him together in order to harm him. We need to prepare together for the armed struggle." The young people in the organization all liked and trusted him. In 1943, Misha was one of the first to go by truck to the Rudninkai Forest to join the partisans. Chaim Jellin and I escorted this truck to the forest. Then we said our farewells, wished each other success, and agreed to meet in Kaunas after the war.

Just after the liberation of Kaunas, we met the Rubinsons in Vilnius. We could hardly believe that we were free. We spent the entire night catching up on each other's lives, listening to what had happened to everyone's family members and making plans for the future. Our friendship became stronger even though we lived in Kaunas and the Rubinsons lived in Vilnius. Their apartment became our second home. It was there that we always stayed when we came to Vilnius; there that we had our long discussions and where we shared our own personal problems and those problems we had in common. We were always present at each other's family celebrations.

The Rubinsons extended an open door not only to us but also to all their friends and former partisan comrades. In the first years following the war, we called their home 'partisan headquarters'. It was there that we discussed the necessity of rebuilding the Jewish museum in Vilnius, wrote letters to the government requesting the preservation and restoration of Jewish cultural artifacts, as well as letters of protest when the government decided to shut down the Jewish schools and orphanages. Those returning from concentration camps to Vilnius also stayed with them. Misha always did his best to help his friends. During the darkest years of Stalinist anti-Semitism, Misha, as an editor, took huge personal risks by printing articles by Jewish writers. He himself wrote about the Jewish *Stachanovtzi* (blue collar workers whose factory performances were exceptional), their victories and the fruits of their work.

Misha was an avid sportsman from the time he attended high school. This love of athletics was with him his entire life. After the war, Misha went on to finish a journalism degree at Vilnius University and became a sports commentator. We would always read his reports whether he was covering sports in Lithuania, the Soviet Union or abroad. We especially relished his objective descriptions of life abroad when reporting on different sporting events. Often, he punctuated these descriptions with healthy doses of humour. It seemed as if Misha had it all: an interesting job, a great family, and good friends. Unfortunately, a difficult youth, the ghetto, and life in the woods had all taken their toll on his health. We all knew that Misha was ill, that he often felt unwell and that he took medication thinking no one noticed. We had never thought, though, that his illness was as serious as it was; that his heart would fail him even though he hadn't yet turned fifty-four.

It was very painful to see Misha leave this world so prematurely at the peak period of his life and creativity. He was still so young. Handsome, honest and humble. This is how he is remembered by our family and this is how he looks back at us from the photos in our album.

Misha is no longer with us, many other friends are also no longer with us. They were all comrades with whom we suffered the atrocities of the German occupation, who stood with us in the line of battle, and who crawled out from under the rubble to begin a new life. This is the reality of life. We, the last generation of Holocaust survivors and witnesses, are all gradually departing this world. Paying tribute to the memory of the direct and indirect victims of the Holocaust in Lithuania, we, the survivors, continue to share our experiences with the younger ones and continue to emphasize that nothing is forgotten and no one is forgotten.

THE FATE OF LITHUANIAN JEWRY

There is no precedent in Lithuanian history that comes close to matching the catastrophic destruction of the Jewish civilization in Lithuania under the German occupation. During those three years (1941-1944) more than 90 percent of Lithuania's Jews were murdered. This was the end of 600 years of Jewish life there. All that is left in Lithuania is one gigantic tombstone that towers over ditches where the mass murder of innocent people took place.

How many Lithuanian Jews were killed and how many remained? At this point in time, it is impossible to calculate an exact figure. Accurate statistical data for the number of Jews in Lithuania during the German occupation, or for the number that survived the war, does not exist. Different researchers have come up with different data, using different statistical methods in their work. Some hypothesize that before the war there were between 220,000 and 240,000 Jews and that 200,000 were killed. This number might only roughly correspond to reality. According to my understanding, this number is somewhat inflated.

The official statistics shows that, in 1940, there were 210,000 Jews in Lithuania.[95] That year, and in the first half of 1941, a fairly large number of Jews, especially refugees and Jews from the Vilnius area, managed to leave Soviet Lithuania. The Japanese Consul-General in Lithuania, Chiune Sugihara, oficially issued over 2000 transit visas in July and August 1940 that saved 4000 to 6000 (even possible more) Jews who were then able to flee Lithuania.[96] They were able to find asylum in Japan and later in China. All of them survived the war.

In addition, in spring of 1941, the Soviets deported several thousand Jews to Siberia, Altaj, and Kazakhstan. During the first days of the war (June 1941), around 8500 Jews managed to retreat to the Soviet Union.[97] Accordingly, it could be estimated that not more than 190,000 to 195,000 Jews remained in Lithuania during the German occupation.

It is very difficult to estimate how many of these Jews survived the Holocaust in Lithuania and how many of them perished. The number can only be calculated approximately and would, therefore, be incomplete.

The analysis of the documents of the Jewish deportations by the Germans shows that 14,000 to 16,000 Jews from the Vilnius, Kaunas, and Shauliai Ghettos were displaced to concentration camps in Latvia, Estonia, and Germany. Of those deported, about 2000 to 2500 survived the concentration camps. In Dachau Concentration Camp, for instance, about 1000 Lithuanian Jews lived to see freedom. Some 1500 Jews found their way to the partisans or to small family units in the forests of Lithuania and Belorus. Altogether about 2,000 Lithuanian Jews survived by living and fighting in the forest and by hiding in bunkers.

Also, a certain number of Lithuanian Jews were saved by Gentiles. One has to admit, though, that most Lithuanians tried to distance themselves from the catastrophic disaster that befell their long time neighbours. Fortunately, some Lithuanians found the orders not to shelter Jews immoral and inhumane and did not comply. The saving of individual Jews gained momentum towards the end of 1943 and was especially evident in 1944. Local inhabitants hid Jews in their homes, drove them to the countryside to stay with relatives, helped them to obtain forged documents, and accepted Jewish children into Gentile daycare centres and orphanages. They disobeyed German orders and, regardless of the grave danger to themselves and their families, helped, not only to save the lives of individuals, but to reaffirm the Jewish belief in goodness. These people embodied the ultimate difference between themselves and the active collaborators and silent bystanders of Lithuania.

Information about the rescuers has been collected at Yad Vashem, The Holocaust Museum in Jerusalem and Jewish Gaon State Museum in Vilnius. According to their lists, some 3000 rescuers have been identified. The list of Lithuanians and other Gentiles who helped to save the lives of the Jews in Lithuania include the writer, Sofija Czurlioniene and her daughter Danute Zubov's family; actors Ona Kuzmina-Dauguvietiene and E. Zalinkevichaite-Petrauskiene; Professor Pranas. Mazilys; Dr. A. Ragaishiene-Biliuniene; Ona Landsbergiene; and the Jackus-Sondeckis Family from Shauliai. Many children were saved by

J. Nemeiksha and Dr. Petras Baublys, director of the daycare centre in Vilijampole and by their nurses, E. Uborevichiene and P. Vitonyte. They, working with the Director, Dr. Baublys, saved the lives of dozens of children despite the mortal danger to themselves.

Twenty-five people were saved by the Kazys Binkis family. Jews were saved by Vladas Varchikas, Prane Shpokaite-Juodvalkiene, Jonas Zeruolis, Andrius Bulota, Elena Kutorgiene and her son Viktoras, D. Dubnikova, M. Orlova, Natalija Jegorova,Frania Grunskaite, M. Shimelis, the Jonas Vasiliauskas family from the village of Karklishkiai. The priests Juozas Stakauskas, J. Jankauskas, Bronius Paukshtys, Teofilius Matulionis and Polikardas Macijauskas, nuns, Agota Misiunaite (Angele), Marija Mikulska, and many others saved their Jewish neighbours.

Some of the rescuers, many priests among them, were imprisoned and a few even lost their lives along with those they were trying to save. Ona Shimaite from Vilnius was arrested and deported to a concentration camp because she gave aid to Jews. The courageous German soldier, Anton Schmit, saved 250 Jews from Vilnius Ghetto by helping to hide them. He also supplied the underground organization of Vilnius Ghetto with forged papers and weapons. In January 1942, Anton Schmit was arrested and tried before a Nazi military court in Germany. He was executed on April 13, 1942.

The humanitarian acts of most of these saviors and well known to the public. Their heroism has been documented in many articles and books. In her collection, *Warriors Without Weapons*, about those who saved the Jews from death, Sofija Binkiene, a writer and rescuer of Jews herself, has written much about the righteous Lithuanian humanitarians. Almost all the righteous have been honoured for protecting, giving shelter, and saving the lives of persecuted Jews. Their remarkable efforts prove that, even in the worst years of state terror, there was a choice and some people chose to take the chance. These brave people have been honoured at Yad Vashem, The Holocaust Memorial Museum in Jerusalem, and trees have been planted in Israel in their names. The Jewish Foundation for Christian Rescuers in the United States was created to offer assistance to those who rescued Jews.

The exact number of people who, directly or indirectly, risked their lives to help save the Jews in Lithuania is not known. It might be slightly higher than the 3000 identified by the Jewish Museum in Vilnius. The search for rescuers continues, new names are still being added to the list. Some investigators are suggesting that 12,000 Lithuanians, or more, were involved in rescuing Jews.[98] I believe this figure is greatly exaggerated and is not realistic. Many of the figures presented are not reliable, often based on pure speculation. There is no confirmation as to how many Jews were actually saved and survived. If their numbers are correct then a logical question arises: Who and where are these "thousands" of rescued Jews?

It is safe to say that, after all the massacres, deportations to concentration camps, natural and deliberate deaths, no more than 6000 to 7000 Lithuanian Jews survived to see liberation. The gruesome reality then is that about 185,000, or over 90 percent, of Lithuanian Jews were killed during the German occupation. Most of them were murdered in Lithuania; the rest were killed in Germany, Latvia, and Estonia, or died of starvation, cold, unbearably hard work or infectious diseases rampant in the concentration camps. In addition, about 10,000 Jews from Germany, Austria, Czechoslovakia, and France were murdered in Lithuania, most at the Ninth Fort in Kaunas. More significant, then, is the fact that the essence of the catastrophe of Lithuania's Jews cannot be found in precise figures. The shocking demographic statistics simply reveal that there are almost no indigenous Jews left in Lithuania. There are virtually no Jews left at all.

The process of destroying the Lithuanian Jewish culture began as early as during the first years of the Soviet occupation. In 1940 to 1941, countless Jewish cultural institutions were closed, including most of the synagogues, Jewish libraries, religious academies, Hebrew schools, as well as numerous Yiddish language newspapers and journals. The Lithuanian Jews, who proudly called themselves *Litvaks,* are extinct. There are no children or grandchildren remaining to follow in the footsteps of those who created the religious academies in Slabodka (Vilijampole), Telshiai, Panavezys, and Kelme. There are no successors to learn from those who built schools and other educational and cultural institution, who printed books and newspapers in Yiddish and Lithuanian. There are no more children and grandchildren to take leadership roles from those who defended the interests of independent Lithuania to international bodies, or to those who built houses, hospitals, and enterprises. There are no successors to those who sang in the Kaunas Opera, played violin in the Lithuanian Symphony, performed in theatres, created artistic masterpieces, wrote musical scores, books, and poems. There are no children and grandchildren to take the place of those whose hard work, creativity, and intellect made a major contribution to the economic and cultural life of Lithuania. The longstanding culture and traditions of Jewish Lithuania died with the Lithuanian Jews in the Holocaust.

There is no doubt that immediately following the war, it would have been possible to revive Jewish cultural life to some extent. However, the Soviet 'nationalist' policies of the Stalin era, especially those directed against ethnic Jews, was successful in eliminating what was left of Jewish culture in Lithuania. Between 1945 and 1948, Jewish schools, daycare centers, orphanages in Kaunas and Vilnius, and the Jewish museum in Vilnius, which had been re-established in 1944, were all shut down. It was forbidden to publish Jewish newspapers, put on Jewish theatre productions, or re-open any religious institutions.

During the post-Stalin years, no real changes in the cultural life of the Jewish Community occurred, despite the fact that in the 60's and 70's in Lithuania there were over 26,000 Jews who included, some Holocaust survivors but mostly those who returned to Lithuania from different parts of the Soviet Union.[99] From 1970 to 2000, most of these people emigrated to Israel, USA, Canada, and Western Europe. The Soviet government, during those years, continued the same policies of oppression and destruction of Jewish cultural, education, and religious inheritance. In *The Book Of Sorrow*, Levinson writes, " The Jewish genocide did not end in the mass graves. During the following years of Soviet occupation, the victims of the Holocaust were doomed to spiritual annihilation through oblivion."[100]

When Lithuania regained its independence in 1990, the Jewish community began to re-established itself. In Vilnius, a Jewish State Museum, several Jewish schools, a Yiddish language study course, a newspaper and a daycare centre were opened. Today, the Jewish community maintains ties with Israel and the World Jewish Congress. Traditional Jewish cultural and religious life, as well as educational traditions, are developing. Two synagogues are functioning in Lithuania. The Jewish community has erected monuments honouring the victims of the Holocaust. Commemorative granite plaques have been

215

hung on houses here and there. Efforts are being made to restore the ancient, abandoned Jewish cemeteries which, over the long years of German and Soviet occupation, had become sadly deteriorated and overgrown. Some had even been turned into parks, entertainment venues, and even garbage dumps. There are nicely maintained new cemeteries in Vilnius and Kaunas. These few, tiny steps at reconstruction are all that remain of Lithuania's Jews.

We, the survivors, usually raise the question, " Did I, as a survivor, fulfill the legacy of my loved ones who did not survive?" Shimon Dubnov, the famous historian, just before being deported to his death from the Riga Ghetto, asked those Jews who remained to write down and tell of their experiences. He felt that the world had to know what the Nazis did to us. The same request came from our own loved ones. "Yes," I must answer. We have fulfilled their dying wishes. Many survivors have brought to light their own horrifying stories. Through their testimonies, these survivor-witnesses are participating in the construction of the Holocaust history of every shtetl, town, city, and country. Our grandparents, mothers, and fathers who perished prayed that we, the young ones, would be able to survive and rebuild our life. Their dreams have come true. We have built families, we have brought children into the world and raised them, and now our children are raising their own children and grandchildren.

The memory of the Jewish catastrophy does not belong only to the generation that lived through the Holocaust. Any tragic event is owned by the people of this community only temporary. And the memories of the Holocaust are not going to die with that generations. This is also the story of the country and it has to be told.

Endnotes

[1] Landsbergis, Vytautas. Kas palaiko zydu kulturos buvima, tas daro gero Lietuvai [Who Supports the Jewish Culture Favours Lithuania]. In *Lietuvos aidas*, December 5, 1995.

[2] Laudman, Isaac, ed. *The Universal Jewish Encyclopedia*, vol. 7:135-136. New York, 1985.

[3] Merkys, Vytautas., ed. *Vilniaus universiteto istorija* 1803-1940 [*The History of Vilnius University 1803-1940*]. Vilnius: Mokslas: 1977:244.

[4] Atamukas, Solomonas. *Lietuvos zydu kelias* [*The Road of Lithuanian Jews*]. Vilnius: Alma Litera, 1998:124.

[5] Ruzgas, Vytautas, ed. *Lietuvos gyventojai. 1923 m. rugsejo 17d. Surasymo duomenys* [*The Lithuanian Population. The Census performed on September17, 1923*]. Kaunas:37. *Visa Lietuva. Informacine knyga* [*The Entire Lithuania. Information Book*]. Kaunas: XXXVII

[6] *Encyclopedia Judaica*, vol. 11:374-376.Jerusalem: The Macmillan Company, 1971; Landman, Isaac, ed.
The Universal Jewish Encyclopedia, vol. 7:847-848. New York:1985

[7] Truska, Liudas. Ar 1940 m. zydai nusikalto Lietuvai? [Did the Jews in 1940 Commit a Crime Against Lithuania?]. In *Akiraciai*, July, 1997:4

[8] Ibid.

[9] Suziedelis, Saulius. Lietuva 1918-1940: Valdzia, visuomene ir politika [Lithuania in 1918-1940: Power, Society, and Politics]. In *Akiraciai*, 1995:4:5.

[10] Bluvsteinas, Jury. Dar karta apie lietuviu ir zydu santykius [Once More About Lithuanian and Jewish Relations]. In *Lietuvos aidas*, October 13,1994.

[11] Truska, Liudas. Lietuvos valdzios istaigu rusifikavimas 1940-1941[Russification of Lithuanian State Institutions in 1940-1941]. In *Lietuvos gyventoju genocido ir rezistencijos tyrimo instituto darbai*, 1996 1:7.

[12] *Lietuvos komunistu partija skaiciais* [Lithuanian Communist Party in Numbers. Statistical Abstract). Vilnius: Mintis: 1976:55.

[13] Truska L. Lietuvos valdzios istaigu rusifikavimas: 1996:1:7

[14] *Lietuvos komunistu partija skaiciais:.55*

[15] Truska, Liudas. Lietuvos valdzios istaigu rusifikavimas : 1996:1: 6-7

[16] Rudis, Gediminas, ed. *Lietuvos kovu ir kanciu istorija: Lietuvos gyventoju treminai 1941, 1945-1952. Dokumentu rinkinys* [*The History of Lithuanian Uprising and Suffering: The Exile of the Population in 1941, 1945-1952 Collection of Documents*]. Vilnius: Mokslo ir enciklopediju leidykla: 1994:21-23.

[17] Ibid.

[18] Atlantas, Vytautas. Aktualieji papludimo klausimai [The Urgent Problems of the Beach]. In *Lietuvos aidas*, August 26, 1938.

[19] *Vilnius Ghetto: List of Prisoners*. Supplement to the Jewish Gaon Museum Almanac. Vilnius: The Vilnius Gaon Jewish State Museum, vol. 1, 1996:8.

[20] After the war, a Soviet court sentenced Mykolas Kaminskis, the janitor at my grandmother's house who participated in the killings of 5 people in the yard of Vytauto 28, to 25 years in prison. Although he is probably no longer alive, in the wake of the mass rehabilitation of all Soviet political prisoners by the independant Lithuanian authorities, he might have been rehabilitated as the result of efforts on his behalf of his children or grandchildren.

[21] *Masines zudynes Lietuvoje,1941-1944.Dokumentu rinkinys. [The Mass Murder in Lithuania, 1941-1944.Collectiom of Documents, Vilnius:Mintis;Part I,1965;112*

[22] Survivors of the Shoa Visual History Foundation interview with Alice Benn (Alica Ginaite-Benjaminovich). Montral,1995

[23] Mishell,William W.Kaddish for Kovno :Life and Death in a Lithuanian Ghetto. Chicgo, Chicago Review Press:1988:39-40

[24] Istrauka is LV Ministru kabineto 1941 m.birzelio 30 d.rytinio posedzio pritokolo[Excerpt from the Protocol of the Cabinet meeting –Lithuanian government session on June 30,1941].LCVA [Central Lithuanian State Archive].FR-969,A2, B.39;25

[25] Knezys, Stasys.Kauno Karo komendanto Tautinio darbo batalionas 1941 m.[The National Labour Battalion of the Commenant of Kaunas in 1941].In *Genocidas ir rezistencija:2000;7;125-168*

[26] CBLMA. Rankrasciu skyrius :F. 264-1329 (The Archive of

the Central Library of the Lithuanian Academy of Science. Department of Manuscripts); LCVA: FR. 496. A. 1, B. 4, L12 (The Lithuanian Central State Archive).

27.Ibid.

28 Rozauskas, Evsiejus, Baranauskas, Bronislavas, Rukshenas, Kazys, eds. *Documents Accuse*. Vilnius: Gintaras, 1970:65-79; Lietuviu aktyvistu fronto (LAF) pedsakais. Dokumentai [In the Trace of the Lithuanian Activist *Front (LAF)*. Documents). In *Gaires:* June 1988.

29 Bubnys, Arunas. Vokieciu okupuota Lietuva 1941-1944 [Lithuania Occupied by the Germans in 1941-1944]. In *Lietuvos gyventoju genocido ir rezistencijos tyrimo centras*: 1998:31.

30 Brandishauskas, Valentinas. Lietuviu ir zydu santykiai 1940-1941 metais [The Relations Between Lithuanian's and the Jews in 1941-1944]. In *Darbai ir dienos*: Kaunas: Vytautas Magnus University, 1996:52.

31 *Masines zudynes Lietuvoje*, Part I:50-57.

32 Lietuviu tauta apsisprendusi [The Lithuanian Nation is Determined]. In *I laisve*, a newspaper published by the LAF, August 3, 1941.

33 Ibid, July 5, 1941.

34 Eidintas, Alfonsas. 1946 metu dokumentas VLIK'ui apie lietuviu-zydu santykius [A document of 1946 to VLIK (Lithuanian Liberating Committee) about Lithuanian-Jewish Relations]. In *Kulturos barai*, September 2000:9

35 Articles in the Lithuanian émigré press by Gurevichius Antanas. (pseudonym Kalnius), and Prakapas Stasys – both in Canada; Musteikis Antanas, Narutis Pilypas, Volertas Vytautas and Zygas Juozas – in USA, and others.

36 Slaveniene, Grazina. Zydu zudynes ir dialogas [The Massacre of Jews and a Dialogue]. In *Teviskes Ziburiai*. Toronto, June 19, 1990.

37 Lithuanian Telegraph Agency (ELTA). March 6, 1995.

38 Lithuanian Telegraph Agency (ELTA). March 6, 1995.

39 Truska, Liudas. *The Holocaust in Lithuania: Its Interpretation*. Paper presented at a Seminar at the Lithuanian Academy of Science. October 5, 2000.

40 Suziedelis, Saulius. 1941 m. sukilimo baltosios demes [White

Spots in the Uprising of 1941]. In *Akiraciai*, 1992 :1; Brandishauskas, Valentinas. Nacionalizmas rezistenciniu organizaciju valstybes modelyje [Nationalism in the Model State and of the Resistance Organizations]. In *Akiraciai*, 1995:5.

[41] Headland, Ronald. *Messages of Murder. A Study of the Reports of the Einsatzgruppen of the Security Police and the Security Service, 1941-1943*. London and Toronto: Associated University Press, 1992:37-43.

[42] Kweit, Konrad. Rehearsing for Murder. The Beginning of the Final Solution in June 1941. In *Holocaust and Genocide Studies*, Vol. 12, Spring 1998:3-26; Stahlecker, Franz Walter. *Operational Situation Report* (OSR-Eisatzgruppe A), March 1942, Washington National Archives. Microfilm Publication T125, Document L-180,
    PS-2273. Nuremberg Trial file numbers 3241, 3233, 3234.

[43] *Masines zudynes Lietuvoje,*Part II:25-28; 395-397

[44] Ibid

[45] Rabbi Oshry, Ephraim. *The Annihilation of Lithuanian Jewry*. Brooklyn, New York: The Judaic Press Inc.:2-3.

[46] Zemelis, Henrikas.Nesuvaldomo kersto padariniai.Juodasis Lietuvos istorijos puslapis [The Consequences of Ungovernable Revenge. The Black Page of ithuanian History]. In *Akiraciai*, 1998:5

[47] *Masines zudynes Lietuvoje*, Part I:231-232.

[48] Archives of the City of Ludwigsburg, Germany. Quoted from Slavinas, Alexander. *Gibel Pompeji[Destruction of the City of Pompei]*. Tel-Aviv: Ivrus, 1997:274. United States Holocaust Memorial Museum.(Washington, D.C.); The Ninth Fort Museum, Kaunas; The Vilniuss Gaon Jewish State Museum.(Vilnius); Yad Vashem Holocaust Museum.(Jerusalem).

[49] Sudetingas Premjero Slezeviciaus Adolfo vizitas Israelyje [The complicated Visit of Prime Minister   Slezevicius Adolfas to Israel]. In *Diena*, Vilnius, October 6, 1994.

[50] *Masines zudynes Lietuvoje*, Part I:335.

[51] Stang, Konrad. *Kollaboration und Massenmord: die Litauische Hilfspolizei, das Rollkommando Hamann und die Ermordung der Litauanischen Juden [Collaboration and Mass Murder: The Lithuanian Hilfspolizie, the Roll Commando Hamann and the Murder of Lithuanian Jews]*. Frankfurt: Peter Langa, 1996:170; Anushauskas, Arvydas. Kolaboravimas ir masines zudynes [Collaboration and Mass Murder]. In

Voruta (Lithuania), January 1998 and in *Lietuvos rytas*, January 15, 1998.

[52] Suziedelis Saulius. Kas iszude Lietuvos zydus [Who Murdered the Lithuanian Jews]. In *Akiraciai, 1998:4*

[53] Washington National Archives. Stahlecker, Franz, Walter. *Operational Situation Report (OSR-Einsatzgruppe A)*

Nuerenberg Trial file numbers:3241;3233;3234.Microfilm Publication T125, Document L-180,PS-2273, March 1942

[54] Ibid

[55] Ibid

[56] Report, Special Archive of the Highest Committee in Moscow.Secret State-Level Document.*Security Police and SD Head Strategic Unit 3 Kaunas, Dcember1, 1941.*Combined reports about strategic Unit 3, which operated in the territory up until the executions od December 1, 1941. F 500, A.1, B. 25, L.119 (PS-2076\41). Strategic Unit 3 took over security police functions in Lithuania on July 1, 1941. Lithuanian partisans following Jaeger's order and instructions carried out the executions. The text of the report is given in the Appendix

[57] Ibid

[58] Ibid

[59] Stahlecker, Walter, Franz.. *Operational Strategic Reports-* (OSR). L-180. PS-2273.

[60] Ibid

[61] Ibid

[62] Report, Special Archive of the Highest Committee in Moscow. F. 500. A. 1. B. 25. L. 119 (PS-2076/41).

[63] Reitlinger, Gerald. *The Final Solution. The Attempt to Exterminate the Jews of Europe 1939-1945.* New York: A.S. Barnes & Company Inc.; Hilberg, R. *The Destruction of the European Jews.* New York: Holmes and Meier; 1985

[64] Bauer, Yehuda. *Rethinking the Holocaust.* New Haven and London. Yale University Press, 2002:86-87

[65] Mendelsohn, Gerald, ed. *The Holocaust: Selected Documents in Eighteen Volumes,* vol.11. The Wannsee Protocol.New York:Garland:1982:1832

[66] Ignatieff, Michael. The New Republic. In *The New York Re-*

view of Books, November 21, 1991

[67] Pleckaitis, Vytautas. Birzelio sukilimo minejimas aklos politicos tesinys [The Celebration of the June Uprising Continuation of the Blind Policy]. In *Akiraciai,* 1998:5.

[68] Mackevicius, Mecislovas. Atsiminimai [Memories]. In *Akiraciai,* 1985:5

[69] Bubnys, Arunas. Vokieciu okupuota Lietuva:206-207

[70] Tory, Abraham. *The Holocaust: The Kovno Ghetto Diary.*England: Harvard University Press: 1990:73

[71] Although Chatzkel Lemchenas and his wife survived the war, both of their children were murdered during the 1944 'Children's Aktzion' in the Kaunas Ghetto. They did not have any more children after the war. Before her death, Lemchenas' wife asked that photographs of their children be placed in her coffin. In 1994, Chatzkel Lemchenas, aged 90, was decorated for his contributions to Lithuanian culture by the President of independent Lithuania, Algirdas Brazauskas. During that same ceremony, my late husband, Misha Rubinsonas, was decorated for his great services in the fight against the German occupiers. After the ceremony, Lemchenas reminded me of our days working together at the Noreikishkes farm.

[72] One copy of the AFO Oath is preserved in the Lithuanian Central State Archive. The text of the Oath was written and signed in Yiddish. It was signed by the following members of the AFO (pseudonyms – proper names):

Kot – Chaim Jellin; Katiusha – Alte Boruchovich; Schwartz – Meri Lan; Grabski – Peisach Gordon (Shtein); Osip: – Dima Gelpern; Langer – Misha Rubinson; Pavka: – Chaim-Dovid Ratner. See: LCVA, FR-1390, A1, B111; L2,3; B.107; L1,2.

[73] Ravinskyte-Geleriene, Rivka. Manuscript: A Letter to Zvi, Hirsh Smoliakov, with permission to be published. Petach-Tikva, Israel, 1998.

[74] Elinas, Meyer, Gelpernas, Dimitry. *Kauno getas ir jo kovotojai (The Kaunas Ghetto and Its Fighters).*Vilnius: Mintis: 1969:54.

[75] Our comrades called AFO leaders 'the mustachioed' because Chaim Jellin and others had grown mustaches.

[76] Smoliakovas, Girsas. *Akistata [Remand].* Vilnius: Periodika: 1988:24-25.

[77] Gelpernas, Dimitry. *Kai kurie pasipriesinimo Kauno gete nusvietimo klausimai [The Description of the Resistance Problems in Kaunas Ghetto]*. In:Zingeris, Emanuelis, ed. Atminties dienos. Vilnius: Baltos lankos: 1995:326-327, 331.

Additional information about the Zionist resistance movement in Kaunas Ghetto can be found in the Bibliography.

[78] Endlin, Nechemija. *Oif Di Vegen Fun Partizaner Kampf [On the Roads of Partisan Combat]*. Tel-Aviv:
The Committee of the Former Kaunas Ghetto Fighters: 1980:102.

[79] Mockunas, Liutas. *Pavarges herojus [The Tired Hero]*.Vilnius: Baltos lankos: 1997:93.

[80] Tory, Abraham. *The Kovno Ghetto Diary*:311-312, 357.

[81] Endlin N., *Oif Di Vegen Fun Partizaner Kampf*:112

[82] Brazaitis, Jonas. *Vienu vieni [All Alone]*. Vilnius: I laisve fondas: 2001:129

[83] Musel, Moishe.*Mit oitos zu di partizaner (By Trucks to the Partisans)*. In: Smoliakov, Zvi, Hirsh and other eds.: *Nit vi shaf zu der schite (Not As Sheep to the Slaughter)*.Tel-Aviv:Peretz Publishing House: 2001:129

[84] Eliniene, Dveira. *Gelbstant dukrele [Saving the Daughter]*. In: Binkiene,Sofija, ed. *Ir be ginklo kariai [Warriors Without Weapons]*. Vilnius: Mintis: 1967:80

[85] *Lietuvos liaudis Didziajame Tevynes kare 1941-1945. Dokumentu ir medziagos rinkinys [Lithuanian People in the Great Patriotic War 1941-1945.Collection of. Documents and Information)*.Vilnius: Mintis: 1982:244

[86] Ibid:255

[87] Ibid:244

[88] Elinas, Meyer, Gelpernas, Dimitry. *Kauno getas ir jo kovotojai*:138

[89] *Hidden History of the Kovno Ghetto*. United States Holocaust Memorial Museum. Boston-New York-Toronto-London: A Bulfinch Press Book, Little, Brown and Company:111-113. Note: After the war, much of this archive was brought to Israel. Peter Gadiel survived the Holocaust and resided in Boston.

[90] Interview with Rozinas Samuelis. Tel Aviv: January, 2001.

[91] Personal Archive of the Jellin's Family. Tel Aviv,1998

[92] Vlasov was a Soviet General who had surrendered, with his troops, to the Germans and now fought on their side

[93] It was because of this case that I had been ordered to leave the ghetto earlier than planned when I came from the forest to meet with the AFO Committee and why I had not been allowed to lead a new group of fighters to the partisans. It had become imperative that I leave the ghetto as soon as possible with Chone Kaganas and Aba Diskant.

[94] Elinas, Meyer and Gelpernas, Dimitry. *Kauno getas ir jo kovotojai*:157-164

[95] LCVA (Lithuanian Central State Archive) FR-743, A.5, B.46, L.172.

[96] Speisman, Leila. Chabad Honours Sugihara. In *Canadian Jewish News*, June,2000; Aleksandravichius, Egidius. Vizos i Gyvenima: Chiune Sugiharos Namu atidarymas Kaune [The House of Chiune Sugiharo Opening in Kaunas]. *Akiraciai*: 2000:6

[97] Bubnys, Arunas. *Vokieciu okupuota Lietuva*:206.

[98] Gurevicius, Antanas. *The List of A. Gurevicius. Thousands of Lithuanians Who Rescued Thousands of Lithuanian Jews in the Second World War.* Vilnius: Protevu Kardas, 1999.

[99] *Lietuvos TSR Liaudies Ukis per 40 metu. Jubiliejinis Statistikos Metrastis [The Statistical Abstract of the Soviet Lithuania in 40 Years]*. Vilnius: Mintis: 1980:11

[100] Levinson, Josif. *The Book of Sorrow*. Vilnius: Vaga: 1997:15

Appendix
The Jaeger Report

Einsatzkommando 3   Kovno, December 1, 1941
Secret State Document

Summary of all executions carried out in the sphere of action of
Einsatzkommado 3 up to December 1, 1941.

Einsatzkommando 3 took over its duties as security police in Lithuania
on the 2nd of July 1941.
(The area of Vilna was taken over by EK 3 on Aug. 9, 1941, and the
area of Siauliai on Oct. 2, 1941; prior to the above dates Vilan was proc-
essed by EK 9 and Siauliai by EK 2.)
In compliance with my directives and on my order Lithuanian partisans have carried out the following executions:

July 4	*Kovno, 7th fort*	416 Jewish men, 47 Jewish women	463
July 6	*Kovno, 7th fort*	Jewish men	2,514

After organizing a mobile unit under SS-Obersturmführer Hamann and 8
to 10 tried men of EK 3 the following actions were carried out in co-operation with Lithuanian partisans:

July 7	*Marijampole*	Jewish men	32
July 8	*Marijampole*	14 Jewish men, 5 Communist officials	19
July 8	*Girkalnis*	Communist officials	6
July 9	*Vandziogala*	32 Jewish men, 2 Jewish women, 1 Lith. woman, 2 Lith. Comm., 1 Russian Communist	38

July 9	*Kovno, 7th fort* 21 Jewish men, 3 Jewish women	24
July 14	*Marijampole* 21 Jewish men, 1 Russ. & 9 Lith. Comm.	31
July 17	*Babiai* 8 Communist officials (6 Jews)	8
July 18	*Marijampole* 39 Jewish men, 14 Jewish women	53
July 19	*Kovno, 7th fort* 17 Jewish men, 2 Jewish women, 4 Lith. Comm., 2 Lith. women Comm., 1 German Comm.	26
July 21	*Panevezys* 59 Jewish men, 11 Jewish women, 1 Lith. woman, 1 Pole, 22 Lith. Comm., 9 Russ. Comm.	103
July 22	*Panevezys* 1 Jewish man	1
July 23	*Kedainai* 83 Jewish men, 12 Jewish women, 14 Russian Comm., 1 Lith. Comm., 1 Russ. political instructor	125
July 25	*Marijampole* 90 Jewish men, 13 Jewish women	103
July 28	*Panevezys* 234 Jewish men, 15 Jewish women, 19 Russian Comm., 20 Lithuanian Communists	288
July 29	*Raseiniai* 254 Jewish men, 3 Lithuanian Communists	257
July 30	*Ariogala* 27 Jewish men, 11 Lithuanian Communists	38
July 31	*Utena* 235 Jewish men, 16 Jewish women, 4 Lith. Comm., 1 double murderer/robber	256
July 11 to 31	*Vandziogala* 13 Jewish men, 2 murderes	15

In August

Aug. 1	*Ukmerge* 254 Jewish men, 42 Jewish women, 1 Polish Comm., 2 Lith. NKVD agents, 1 mayor of Jonava who ordered Jonava to be burnt down	300
Aug. 2	*Kovno, 4th fort* 170 Jewish men, 1 US Jewish man, 1 US Jewish woman, 33 Jewish women, 4 Lith. Communists	209
Aug. 4	*Panevezys* 362 Jewish men, 41 Jewish women, 5 Russian Comm., 14 Lith. Communists	422
Aug. 5	*Raseiniai* 213 Jewish men, 66 Jewish women	279
Aug. 7	*Utena* 483 Jewish men, 87 Jewish women, 1 Lithuanian who plundered the remains of German soldiers	571
Aug. 8	*Ukmerge* 620 Jewish men, 82 Jewish women	702
Aug. 9	*Kovno, 4th fort* 484 Jewish men, 50 Jewish women	534
Aug. 11	*Panevezys* 450 Jewish men, 48 Jewish women, 1 Lith. & 1 Russian Comm.	500
Aug. 13	*Alytus* 617 Jewish men, 100 Jewish women, 1 criminal	719
Aug. 14	*Jonava* 497 Jewish men, 55 Jewish women	552
Aug. 15 to 16	*Rokiskis* 3,200 Jewish men, Jewish women & Jewish children, 5 Lith. Comm., 1 Pole, 1 partisan	3,207
Aug. 19 to 16	*Raseiniai* 294 Jewish women, 4 Jewish children	298

| June 27 to Aug. 14 | *Rokiskis* 493 Jewish men,. 432 Russians, 56 Lithuanians (all active Communists) | 981 |

Aug. 18 *Kovno, 4th fort* 698 Jewish men, 402 Jewish women   1,812
1 Polish woman, 711 intellecutal Jews from the ghetto
as reprisal for an act of sabotage

Aug. 19 *Ukmerge* 298 Jewish men, 255 Jewish women,   645
1 political instructor, 88 Jewish children, 1 Russian
Communist

Aug. 22 *Dvinsk* 3 Russ. Comm., 5 Latvians (incl. 1 murderer),   21
1 Russ. guardsman, 3 Poles, 3 gipsies, 1 gipsy woman,
1 gipsy child, 1 Jewish man, 1 Jewish woman, 1 Armenian
2 political instructors (prison revision in Dvinsk)

Aug. 22 *Aglona* Lunatics: 269 men, 227 women, 48 children   544

Aug. 23 *Panevezys* 1,312 Jewish men, 4,602 Jewish women,   7,523
1,609 Jewish children

Aug. 18 to 22 *district of Raseiniai* 466 Jewish men, 440 Jewish women, 1,020 Jewish children   1,926

Aug. 25 *Obeliai* 112 Jewish men, 627 Jewish women,   1,160
421 Jewish children

Aug. 25 & 26 *Seduva* 230 Jewish men, 275 Jewish women, 159 Jewish children   664

Aug. 26 *Zarasai* 767 Jewish men, 1,113 Jewish women   2,569
1 Lithuanian Comm., 687 Jewish children, 1 Russian
woman Communist

Aug. 26 *Pasvalys* 402 Jewish men, 738 Jewish women,   1,349
209 Jewish children

Aug. 26 *Kaisiadorys* all Jews: men, women, & children   1,911

Aug. 27 *Prienai* all Jews: men, women, & children   1,078

Aug. 27 *Dagda & Kraslava* 212 Jewish men, 4 Russian POWs   216

Aug. 27 *Joniskis* 47 Jewish men, 165 Jewish women,   355
143 Jewish children

Aug. 28 *Vilkija* 76 Jewish men, 192 Jewish women,   402
134 Jewish children

Aug. 28 *Kedainiai* 710 Jewish men, 767 Jewish women,   2,076
599 Jewish children

Aug. 29 *Rumsiskis & Ziezmariai* 20 Jewish men,567 Jewish   784
women, 197 Jewish children

Aug. 29 *Utena & Moletai* 582 Jewish men, 1,731 Jewish   3,782
women, 1,469 Jewish children

Aug. 13 to 31 *Alytus and vicinities* 233 Jewish men   233

Sept. 11 & 12 *Uzusaliai*   43
Punitive expedition against the population which gave provisions to
Russian partisans and some of which possessed weapons.
Sept. 26 *Kovno,*

4th fort	412	615	581	1,608

These children were sick and epidemic.

In October

Oct. 2   *Zagare*   633 Jewish men, 1,107 Jewish women,   2,236
            496 Jewish children (the Jews rebelled but were
            crushed at once: 150 Jews were killed on the spot,
            7 partisans were wounded)

Oct. 4   *Kovno, 9th fort*   315 Jewish men, 712 Jewish women,   1,845
            818 Jewish children (punitive action because a German
            policeman was shot at in the ghetto)

Oct. 29   *Kovno, 9th fort*   2,007 Jewish men, 2,920 Jewish   9,200
            women, 4,273 Jewish children (removal from the
            ghetto of surplus Jews)

In November

Nov. 3   *Lazdijai*   485 Jewish men, 511 Jewish women,   1,535
            539 Jewish children

Nov. 15   *Vilkaviskis*   36 Jewish men, 48 Jewish women,   115
            31 Jewish children

Nov. 25   *Kovno, 9th fort*   1,159 Jewish men, 1,600 Jewish   2,934
            women, 175 Jewish children (displaced from Berlin,
            Munich and Frankfurt A.M.)

Nov. 29   *Kovno, 9th fort*   17 Jewish men, 1 Jewish women   34
            who had violated the ghetto regulations, 1 German
            who had embraced the Judaic religion and had
            attended a school for rabbins, and 15 terrorists of
            the Kalinin gang

A section of EK 3 in Dvinsk

July 13   *Dvinsk*   9,012 Jewish men, women and children,   9,585
to   573 active Communists
Aug. 21

A section of EK 3 in Vilna

Aug. 12   *Vilna*   425 Jewish men, 19 Jewish women,   461
to   8 Communists, 9 women Communists
Sept. 1

228

Sept. 2   *Vilna* 864 Jewish men, 2,019 Jewish women,   3,700
          817 Jewish children (punitive action because
          German soldiers had been shot at by Jews)

	Jewish Men	Jewish Women	Jewish Children	Total
Sept. 12 *Vilna*	993	1,670	771	3,334
Sept. 17 *Vilna*	337	687	247	
and 4 Lithuan. Comm.				1,271
Sept. 20 *Nemencine*	128	176	99	403
Sept. 22 *Naujoji Vilnia*	468	495	196	1,159
Sept. 24 *Riese*	512	744	511	1,767
Sept. 25 *Jasiunai*	215	229	131	575
Sept. 27 *Eisiskes*	909	1,636	821	3,446
Sept. 30 *Trakai*	366	483	597	1,446
Oct. 4 *Vilna*	432	1,115	436	1,983
Oct. 6 *Semeliskes*	213	359	390	962
Oct. 9 *Svencionys*	1,169	1,840	717	3,726
Oct. 16 *Vilna*	382	507	257	1,146
Oct. 21 *Vilna*	718	1,063	586	2,367
Oct. 25 *Vilna*	—	1,766	812	2,578
Oct. 27 *Vilna*	946	184	73	1,203
Oct. 30 *Vilna*	382	789	362	1,533
Nov. 6 *Vilna*	340	749	252	1,341
Nov. 19 *Vilna*	76	77	18	171
Nov. 19 *Vilna*	6 POWs, 8 Poles			14
Nov. 20 *Vilna*	3 POWs			3
Nov. 25 *Vilna*	9	46	8	

and 1 Pole for possession of arms and other war material   64

A section of EK 3 in Minsk
Sept. 28 to Oct. 17
Pleshtsbenitsa, Bicholin, Shatsk, Bober, Usda
          620 Jewish men, 1,285 Jewish women, 1,126 Jewish
          children, and 10 Communists   3,050
                                                                                    133,346

          Before the EK 3 assumed security duties, the
          partisans themselves killed Jews through pogroms
          and executions   4,000
                                                                                    137,346

I can state today that the goal of solving the Jewish problem in Lithuania has been reached by EK 3. There are no Jews in Lithuania anymore except the work-Jews and their families, which total

in Siauliai	some	4,500
in Kovno	some	15,000
in Vilna	some	15,000

I intended to kill off these work-Jews and their families too, but met with the strongest protest from the civil administration (Reich Commissar) and the Wehrmacht, which culminated in the prohibition: these Jews and their families may not be shot dead!

The goal to clear Lithuania of Jews could be achieved only thanks to the setting up of a flying squad of tried men under SS-Obersturmführer Hamann who adopted my goal without any reservations and managed to secure the co-operation of the Lithuanian partisans and the respective civil offices.

The carrying out of such actions is first of all a problem of adequate organization. The decision to systematically clear each district of Jews required a thorough preparation of each action and an excellent knowledge of the conditions prevailing in the district chosen. The Jews had to be collected at one or at several collecting points. Their number required us to select an adequate place for the trenches, which had also to be dug out. The road of approach from the collecting points to the trenches averaged from 4 to 5 kilometers. The Jews were driven to the place of execution in batches of 500, the distance between the batches being no less than 2 kilometers. The difficulties and the trying work met with during these actions is best illustrated by the following example chosen at random:

In Rokiskis one had to drive 3,208 people 4.5 kilometers before they could be executed. In order to complete the work in 24 hours one had to detach for driving or guarding more than 60 men from the 80 Lithuanian partisans available. The rest, which had to be relieved every now and then, did the work together with my men. One must bear in mind that lorries are available but seldom. Escapes, which happened now and then, were foiled exclusively by my men at the peril of their lives. For instance 3 men out of the commando have shot dead all 38 Jews and Communist officials who tried to escape on a woodpath near Marijampole. The distance we had to cover while approaching the place of execution and then returning from it in the course of each action totalled from 160 to 200 kilometers. Only clever timing helped us to carry out 5 actions a week, and to do at the same time the current job in Kovno without endangering the routine service.

The actions in Kovno itself, where a sufficient number of trained partisans was available, can be described as parade shooting, especially if compared with actions in the country where the greatest difficulties had to be overcome time and again.

All commanders and men of my commando in Kovno took part in the large-scale actions in Kovno most actively. Only one Habitual Criminals' Registry official was set free from taking part in the actions because of ill health.

I consider the Jewish actions to be finished for EK 3 in the main. The working Jewish men and Jewish women left alive for the time being are badly needed, and I presume that when winter is over this Jewish labor force will be still needed badly. I am of the opinion that it is imperative to start at once with the sterilization of the male work-Jews to prevent propagation. If in spite of the measures taken a Jewish woman happens to become pregnant she is to be liquidated.

Alongside with the Jewish actions one of the chief tasks of the EK 3 was the revision of mostly overcrowded prisons in the various localities and towns. In each district town the number of Lithuanians imprisoned without the slightest legal grounds averaged 600. They had been arrested by partisans only a simple denunciation or the like which served to square accounts. Nobody had ever taken the trouble to inquire into their cases. One ought to have visited the prisons and to have stayed for a moment in the overcrowded cells which beggar any description in sanitary respects. For instance at Jonava—which is typical of many—16 men were imprisoned for five weeks in a dark cellar 3 meters long, 3 meters wide and 1.65 meters high. And all these 16 men could be set free for one could not impute anything to them. Girls aged 13 to 16 have been imprisoned solely on the grounds that they had joined the Communist Youth organization to be able to get any work. In this matter one had to resort to drastic measures to drum a clear-cut direction into the heads of appropriate Lithuanian authorities. The prisoners were lined up in the prison yard and checked according to lists and documents in the case. Those who had been imprisoned for minor offenses without sufficient grounds were ordered to line up in a separate group. Those whom we sentenced to 1, to 3, and 6 months' imprisonment were lined up in another group. A third group was constituted of prisoners to be liquidated as criminals, Communist officials, political instructors and other rabble. In addition to the adjudged penalty some prisoners, first of all Communist officials, were lashed on the spot from 10 to 40 times according to the gravity of their offenses. After the check-up the prisoners were returned to the cells. Those who were to be set free marched in procession to the market square where after a short address they were set free in the presence of numerous local people. The address read as follows (it was translated on the spot into Lithuanian and Russian):

"Had we been Bolshevists we would have shot you dead but as we are Germans we set you at liberty."

Then followed an admonition to abstain from all political activity whatsoever, to report without any delay to German officers the least instance of a resistance movement they happened to get to know about, and to take an active part in the rehabilitation of the country, especially by working in agriculture. But if any one of them should commit another offense, he would be shot. Then they were set free.

It is well-nigh impossible to imagine the joy, gratitude, and enthusiasm which is this measure of ours caused each time among the prisoners set free and the population at large. One had to use sharp words more often than not to drive off the grateful women, children, and men who with tears of joy in their eyes tried to kiss our hands and feet.

(signed) *Jaeger*
SS-Standartenfuehrer

BIBLIOGRAPHY

Books

1.Aleisky, J., Jellin, M., and others, eds. *"Haim Yelin – Der geto kemfer un schreiber."* Tel Aviv: Association of Lithuanian Jews in Israel, 1975.

2.Almanac Lietuvos, Supplement. *Vilnius Ghetto: Lists of Prisoners.* Vilnius: Valstybinis Vilniaus Gaono zydu muziejus, 1996: Vol. 1.

3.Arad, Y. *Ghetto in Flames: Struggle and Destruction of the Jews in Vilna in the Holocaust.* Jerusalem: Yad Vashem, 1980.

4.Atamukas, S. *Lietuvos zydu kelias. Nuo XIV amzaus iki XX a. pabaigos.* Vilnius: Alma Littera, 1998.

5.Baranauskas, B., Razauskas, E., Ruksenas, K., eds. *Documents Accuse.* Vilnius: Gintaras, 1970.

6.Bauer, Y. *A History of the Holocaust.* New York: Franklin Watts, 1982

7._____*Rethinking the Holocaust.*Yale University Press, 2002

8.Binkiene, S., ed. *Ir be ginklo kariai.* Vilnius: Mintis, 1967.

9.Birger, J., Goldblatt, I., Musel, M., Smoliakov, H., Zilber, E. *Nit vi shaf zu der schite.* Tel Aviv: Peretz Publishing House, 2001.

10.Bluvstein, J. *Na puti k dialogu.* Vilnius: Litovskij Jeruzalim, 1967.

11.Brandisauskas, V. *Siekiai atkurti Lietuvos valstybinguma (1940.06-1941.09).* Vilnius: Valstybinis leidybos Centras, 1996.

12.___. *1941 m. Birzelio Sukilimas. Dokumentu rinkinys.* Vilnius: Lietuvos gyventoju Genocido ir resistencijos tyrimo Centras, 2000.

13.Brazaitis, J. (Suduvis). *Vienu vieni.* New York: I laisve fondas Lietuviskai kulturai ugdyti, 1964.

14.Bubnys, A. *Vokieciu okupuota Lietuva (1941-1944).* Vilnius: Lietuvos gyventoju Genocido ir resistencijos tyrimo Centras. 1998.

15.Damusis, A. *Lietuvos gyventoju aukos ir nuostoliai antrojo pasaulinio karo ir pokario 1940-1959 metais.* Chicago: I laisve fondas Lietuviskai kulturai ugdyti, 1988.

16. Dawidowicz, L. *The Holocaust and the Historians.* London; Harvard University Press, 1981.

17.___. *The War Against the Jews.* New York: Holt, Rinehart and Winston, 1975.

18. Eckman, L., Lazar, C. *The Jewish Resistance: The History of the Jewish Partisans in Lithuania and White Russia During the Nazi Occupation, 1940-1945.* New York: Shengold Publishers Inc., 1977.

19. Eglinis-Elinas, M. *Mirties fortuose.* Vilnius: Mintis, 1976.

20. Eidintas, A. *Jews Lithuanians and the Holocaust.* Vilnius: Versus Aureus, 2003.

21.___, ed. *Lietuvos Zydu Byla.* Vilnius: Vaga, 2001.

22. Elinas, M., Gelpernas, D. *Kauno getas ir jo kovotojai.* Vilnius: Mintis, 1969.

23. *Encyclopedia Judaica.* Jerusalem: The MacMillan Co., 1971.

24. Endlin, N. *Oif di wegen fun partizaner kamf.* Tel Aviv: The Committee of the Former Kaunas Ghetto Fighters, 1980.

25. Erenburgas, M. "Naciu auku gelbejimo Lietuvoje specifika" (1941-1944)". *Atminties dienos.* Vilnius: Valstybinis Vilniaus Gaono zydu muziejus, 1995.

26. Erenburg, M., Sakaite, V., eds. *Hands Bringing Life and Bread.* Vilnius: The Vilna Gaon Jewish State Museum, 1997, 1999.

27. Ezergailis, A. *The Holocaust in Latvia, 1941-1944: The Missing Center.* Riga and Washington: The Historical Institute of Latvia, 1997.

28. Gar, J. *Umkum vun der Jidisher Kovne.* Munich: 1948.

29. Gefen, A. *Hope in Darkness.* New York: Holocaust Library, 1989.

30. Gelpernas, D. "Kai kurie pasipriesinimo Kauno gete nusvietimo klausimai." *Atminties dienos.* Vilnius: Valstybinis Vilniaus Gaono zydu muziejus, 1995.

31. Ginaite-Rubinsoniene, S. *Atminimo knyga. Kauno Zydu*

bendruomene 1941-1944 metais. Vilnius: Margi rastai, 1999.

32.___. *Zydu tragedijos Lietuvoje pradzia.* Vilnius: Misa, 1994.

33.Ginsburg, W. *And Kovno Wept.* Laxton, Newark: Beth Shalom, 1998.

34.Gordon, H. *The Shadow of Death. The Holocaust in Lithuania.* New York: University of Kentucky Press, 2000.

35.Greenbaum, M. *The Jews of Lithuania. A History of a Remarkable Community, 1316-1945.* Jerusalem: Gefen Publishing House, 1995.

36.Gurevicius, A. *The List of A. Gurevicius.* Vilnius: Protevu kardas, 1999.

37.Gutman, I, ed. *Encyclopedia of the Holocaust.* New York and Jerusalem: The MacMillan Publishing Co., 1990: Vol. 2.

38.Headland, R. *Messages of Murder.* London and Toronto: Associated University Press, 1992.

39.Hilberg, R. *The Destruction of the European Jews.* New York: Holmes and Meier, 1985.

40.Kasperavicius, A., Jakimaitis, R. *Pasaulis ir Lietuva. Naujausiu laiku istorija.* Vilnius: Krantai, 1998.

41.Katz, N. *Teach Us to Count Our Days.* New Jersey: Cornwall Books, 1999.

42.Laqueur, W., ed. *The Holocaust Encyclopedia.* New Haven and London; Yale University Press, 2000.

43.Lazar, C. *Destruction and Resistance.* New York: Shengold Publishers, 1985.

44.Landman, I., ed. *The Universal Jewish Encyclopedia.* New York: The Universal Jewish Encyclopedia, 1985: Vol. 7.

45.Levin, D. *Fighting Back: Lithuanian Jewish Armed Resistance to the Nazis, 1941-1945.* New York: Holmes and Meier, 1985.

46.___. *The Lesser of Two Evils. Eastern European Jewry Under Soviet Rule, 1939-1941.* Jerusalem: The Jewish Publication Society, 1995.

47.Levinson, J. *The Book of Sorrow.* Vilnius: Vaga, 1997.

48.*Lietuvos komunistu partija skaiciais 1918-1975. [Abstract Statistics].* Vilnius: Mintis, 1976.

49.Littman, S. *The Rauca Case: War Criminal on Trial.* Toronto, Markham: Paperjacks, 1984.

50.*Masines zudynes Lietuvoje (1941-1944). Dokumentu rinkinys.* Vilnius: Mintis, 1965.

51.Mendelson, J., ed. The Wannsee Protocol. *The Holocaust: Selected Documents in Eighteen Volumes.* New York: Garland, 1982: Vol. 11.

52.Merkys, V., ed. *Vilniaus universiteto istorija 1803-1940.* Vilnius: Mintis, 1977.

53.Mishell, W. *Kaddish for Kovno.* Chicago: Chicago Revue Press, 1988.

54.Mockunas, L. *Pavarges herojus.* Vilnius: Baltos lankos, 1997.

55.Monciunskas, T. *Rudninku girios partizanai.* Vilnius: Valstybinis politines ir mokslines literaturos leidykla, 1959.

56.Neshamit, S. "Lietuviu ir zydu santykiai vokieciu okupacijo metais." *Atminties dienos.* Vilnius: Valstybinis Vilniaus Gaono zydu muziejus, 1995.

57.Oshry, E. *The Annihilation of Lithuanian Jewry.* New York: The Judaic Press, 1997.

58.Prunskis, J. *Lithuania's Jews and the Holocaust.* Chicago: Lithuanian American Council Inc., 1979.

59.Rastikis, S. *Kovose del Lietuvos.* Vilnius: 1990: Vol. 2.

60.Reitlinger, G. *The Final Solution: The Attempt to Exterminate the Jews of Europe 1939-1945.* New York: A.S. Barnes and Company Inc., 1992.

61.Rudis, G., ed. *Lietuvos kovu ir kanciu istorija. Lietuvos gyventoju tremimai 1941, 1945-1952 m.* Vilnius: Mokslu ir enciklopediju leidykla, 1994.

62.Slavinas, A. *Gibel Pompei.* Tel Aviv: Ivrus Publishing House Ltd., 1997.

63.Shneidman, N.N. *Jerusalem of Lithuania: The Rise and Fall of Jewish Vilnius.* Oakville-Toronto: Mosaic Press, 1998.

64.Smoliakovas, G. *Akistata.* Vilnius: Periodika, 1988.

65.___. *Kauno geto noveles.* Vilnius: Valstybinis Vilniaus Gaono zydu muziejus, 1994.

66.Stang, K. *Massenmord: die Litauische Hilfpolizei, das Rollkommando Hamann und die Ermordung der Litauischen Juden.*

Frankfurt: Peter Langa, 1996.
   67.Staras. P., ed. *Lietuvos partizanai*. Vilnius: Mintis, 1967.
   68.Strom, Z. *Churben un kamf.* Tel Aviv: Zachrunot, 1990.
   69.Tory, A. *Surviving the Holocaust: The Kovno Ghetto Diary*. Cambridge: Harvard University Press, 1990.
   70.Truska, L. *Antanas Smetona ir jo laikai*. Vilnius: Valstybinis leidybos Centras, 1996.
   71.United States Holocaust Memorial Museum. *Hidden History of the Kovno Ghetto*. New York: Little, Brown and Company, 1997.
   72.Yoffe, M., ed. *Hitlerine okupacija Lietuvoje*. Vilnius: Valstybinis politines ir mokslines literaturos leidykla, 1961.
   73.Zeimantas, V. *Teisingumas reikalauja*. Vilnius: Mintis, 1984.

   Journals
   1.Balsys, A. "Apie tautos garbe ir geda." *Gaires.* 1998: No. 6, 7.
   2.Brandisauskas, V. "Lietuviu ir zydu santykiai 1940-1941 metais." *Darbai ir dienos.* 1996.
   3.Documents: The Testimony of V.Kreve to the USA Commission in 1953. In *Akiraciai*, 2004:10
   4.Eidintas, A. "1946 metu dokumentas VLIK-ui apie lietuviu-zydu santykius." *Kulturos barai.* Sept., 2000.
   5.Ginaite, S. "Alfonsas Eidintas.Jews, Lithuanians and the Holocaust" (Book review) *Canadian Slavonic Papers.* March-June 2004.
   6."The Holocaust in Lithuania." Collection of Articles. *Holocaust and Genocide Studies.* Spring, 1998: Vol. 12, No. 1.
   7.Ignatieff, M. "The New Republics." *New York Review of Books.* Nov. 21, 1991.
   8.Knezys, S. "Kauno karo komendaturos Tautinio darbo batalionas 1941 m." *Genocidas ir resistencija.* 2000: No. 7.
   9.Kweit, K. "Rehearsing for Murder. The Beginning of the Final Solution in June 1941." *Holocaust and Genocide Studies.* Spring, 1998: Vol. 12, No. 1.
   10.Lane, N. "Estonia and Its Jews: An Ethical Dilemma."

East European Jewish Affairs. Summer, 1995: Vol. 25, No. 1.

11.Mackevicius, M. "Atsiminimai." *Akiraciai.* May, 1998.

12.Suziedelis, S. "Lietuva 1918-1941: Valdzia, visuomenne ir antisemitizmas." *Akiraciai.* April, 1995.

13.___. "1941 metu sukilimo baltosios demes." *Akiraciai.* January, 1992.

14.___. "Kas iszude Lietuvos zydus?" *Akiraciai.* April, 1998.

15.Truska, L. "Lietuvos valdzios istaigu rusifikavimas 1940-1941 m." *Lietuvos genocido ir rezistencijos tyrimo instituto darbai.* 1996.

16.___. "Ar 1940 m. zydai nusikalto Lietuvai?" *Akiraciai.* July, 1997.

17.Zemelis, H. "Juodasis Lietuvos istorijos lapas." *Akiraciai.* May, 1998.

Newspapers

1.Birziska, M. Zydai ir lietuviai. *Literatura ir menas.* April 14, 1993.

2.Bluvsteinas, J. "Dar karta apie lietuviu ir zydu santykius." *Lietuvos aidas.* Oct. 13, 1994.

3.Pirockinas, A. "Kur tikroji zydu tragedijos esme?" *Tiesa.* Sept. 23, 1992.

Manuscripts

1.Ruksenas, K. *Hitlerininku politika Lietuvoje 1941-1944 m.* Library of Academy of Sciences of Lithuania. Vilnius, 1970.

2.Truska, L. *Holocaust in Lithuania: Its Interpretation. Holocaust History in Lithuania.* Library of Academy of Sciences of Lithuania. Vilnius, 2000.

INDEX

A

Abramovich, Shleime 187
Albina. *See* Glezer, Gese
Alekna, Jonas 105
Ambrazaitis-Brazaitis, Juozas 22. *See also* Ambrazevichius, Juozas
Ambrazevichius, Juozas 22, 26, 27
Aramshtam, Tanchun 97
Auer 198

B

Baleniunas, Pranas 105
Balsys, Antanas 32, 221
Barauskas, Antanas 137
Baron, Shleime 169
Barzda, Juozas 22
Baublys, Petras 213
Bauer, Yehuda 40
Benjaminovichius, Leiba 16, 203
Benjaminovichius, Philip 12, 13, 16, 18, 117, 201, 203
Benn 204, 205
Benn, Philip. *See* Benjaminovichius, Philip
Benn-Lapedis, Rita 204
Binkiene, Sofija 213
Binkis, Kazys 213
Birger, Yudel 161
Bloch, Riva 173
Bobelis, Jurgis 19, 20, 22, 43
Boeme, Joachim 33
Boldin, Sasha 168
Boreikaite, Elizaveta 14, 111
Borisova, Ania 126, 160, 172
Boruchovich-Teper, Alte 86, 88, 94, 173
Brandishauskas, Valentinas 32
Brauns, Moses 18, 57
Brazauskas, Algirdas 31
Bruch, E. 196
Bubnys, Arunas 32, 43
Bulota, Andrius 213

Butkunas, Andrius 22
Butkus, Viktoras 14
Buziene, Liuda 102, 149

C

Ceiko, Michail 130
Codikovas, Leizer 121
Cramer, Hans 46
Czizinauskaite, Janina 174

D

Damushis, Adolfas 31
Davydov, Dimitry. *See* Parfionov, Dimitry
Dembo, Itzik 149, 203
Diskant, Aba 118, 152, 186
Dubnikova, D. 213
Dubnov, Shimon 216
Dush-Dushevski 103

E

Ehrlinger, E. 33
Eidelson, Shimon 157, 158, 186
Eidintas, Alfonsas 32
Elinas, Meyer 87, 135, 194
Elkes, Elchanan 45, 58, 59, 76, 90, 183, 199
Endlin, Masha 136, 137
Endlin, Naum (Nechemija) 98, 105, 110, 141, 142, 143, 144, 145, 146, 147, 150, 161
Epshteinaite-Kaganiene, Riva 160, 172

F

Fediunin, Peter 168
Fine 166, 174
Fiveger 198
Friedman, Tevje 156, 174
Fux, Wilhelm 198

G

Gadiel, Peter 166
Gafanovich, Aaron 121

Hitler, Adolf 10, 27, 39, 84, 85, 95, 163, 165, 181, 195
Hofmekleris, Misha 76
Holzberg, Zalman (Monik) 14, 65, 82, 88, 111, 112, 137

I

Ignatieff, Michael 41

J

Jaeger, Karl 33, 36, 37, 38, 39, 46, 64, 69
Janchevski 135, 173
Jankauskas, J. 213
Jegorova, Natalija 213
Jelinas, Meyer. *See* Elinas, Meyer
Jellin, Chaim 86, 87, 88, 89, 90, 92, 94, 98, 99, 106, 107, 108, 109, 116,
    120, 121, 122, 134, 135, 150, 151, 152, 158, 159, 166, 167, 182, 183,
    184, 185, 186, 208
Jellin, Dveira (Busia) 117
Jellin, Esther (Esya) 117, 186
Jordan, Fritz 46, 56, 57, 59, 62, 63, 64, 72
Jost, Horst 33
Jurgelevich 132, 160, 161
Jurovitski, Lazar 13, 49, 203

K

Kaganas, Chone 111, 116, 152, 198
Kaminskas, Mikas 56
Kaminskas, Vytautas 14, 111, 112, 113
Kaminskis, Mykolas 4, 13, 17, 18
Karnauskaite-Musel, Peshe (Polia) 89, 91, 174
Kashnicki, Igor 205
Kazimieras, Motiejus. *See* Shumauskas, Motiejus
Kerecki, Misha (Meyer). *See* Liberman, Meyer (Misha)
Kirkila, Bronius 22
Kittel, Bruno 198, 199
Kliachko, Perez 161
Klimaitis, Algirdas 34, 35
Klis, Hirsh 4, 13, 15
Krakinovski, Pine 156, 164
Krupavichius, Mykolas 105
Kszyzanowski, A. 137
Kupric, Moisej 91

Molotov, Vyachislav 11
Mordkovski, Shmulik 110, 121, 141, 142, 150, 186
Morkunas, Leonardas 42
Moskovich, Mendel 106
Musel, Moishe 89, 91, 99, 107, 108, 109, 110, 112, 113, 120, 121, 122, 158,
     159, 174, 205, 207

N

Nagevichius, V. 105
Nemeiksha, J. 213
Nemzer, Itzik 164
Norkus, Bronius 22, 36

O

Obelinis, Juozas 22
Olishauskas, Bronius (Borisas) 132, 187
Olkin, Elijahu 119, 186
Orlova, Liza 172
Orlova, M. 213
Oshry, Ephraim 35, 158
Osovsky, Yudel 35
Osovsky, Zalman 35

P

Paleckis, Justas 12
Parfionov, Dimitry 126, 127, 134, 189
Pasternak, Shmuel 161
Paukshtys, Bronius 213
Paulauskas, Stepas 22
Pilovnik, Teve 91, 98, 118, 158, 175, 186
Pilovnik-Vilenchiuk, Ida 98, 118, 175
Plechkaitis, Vytautas 41
Pligrem 198
Pohl 22
Prapuolenis, Leonas 26
Pundzevichius, Stasys 35
Pushakov, Fiodor 123

R

Radionova, Yekaterina 126, 172, 187
Radionovas, Kostas 126, 137, 139, 160, 188

V

Z